PRACTICAL JUDGMENTS

Essays in Culture, Politics, and Interpretation

PRACTICAL JUDGMENTS

ESSAYS IN CULTURE, POLITICS, AND INTERPRETATION

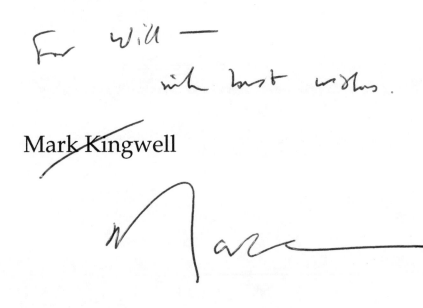

For Will —
with best wishes.

Mark Kingwell

UNIVERSITY OF TORONTO PRESS
Toronto Buffalo London

© University of Toronto Press Incorporated 2002
Toronto Buffalo London
Printed in Canada

ISBN 0-8020-3675-9

∞

Printed on acid-free paper

National Library of Canada Cataloguing in Publication

Kingwell, Mark Gerald
    Practical judgments : essays in culture, politics and
interpretation / Mark Kingwell.

    Includes bibliographical references and index.

    ISBN 0-8020-3675-9

    I. Title.

AC8.K55 2002   081   C2002-901514-6

The University of Toronto Press acknowledges the financial
assistance to its publishing program of the Canada Council for
the Arts and the Ontario Arts Council.

University of Toronto Press acknowledges the financial support
for its publishing activities of the Government of Canada through
the Book Publishing Industry Development Program (BPIDP).

For Brennan,
outside the door

Contents

Acknowledgments

This collection would not exist if not for the enthusiasm of Chris Bucci at University of Toronto Press, who gamely agreed that it might be worthwhile, then shepherded a sprawling manuscript through the necessary changes. On that score, my thanks also to two anonymous readers at the Press for their acute assessments of what should and shouldn't remain, and why. They helped me clarify my thoughts.

Other readers' work is implicit here, and I would like to thank again the editors who commissioned or handled (or just agreed to make room for) these pieces, especially those in Parts II and III. They are: Boris Castel at *Queen's Quarterly*, Danny Postel at the now-defunct *britannica.com*, Roger Hodge at *Harper's Magazine*, David Berlin at *Literary Review of Canada*, Stephen Bates at *Wilson Quarterly*, Peter Loptson at *Dialogue*, and Peter Euben at *Political Theory*.

The essays in this book have all been previously published with the exception of the Introduction, which was originally composed as the 2001 Munro Beattie Memorial Lecture at Carleton University in Ottawa. I thank the members of the English Department and the audience there for the opportunity to reflect on public intellectual engagement in such congenial company. Versions of that lecture were later delivered at the University of Toronto, the Power Plant Contemporary Art Gallery, and the Hot Docs Documentary Film Festival in

Toronto (all 2001), leading to further revisions. It was, in addition, the basis of my Marx Wartofsky Memorial Lecture, delivered at Baruch College, City University of New York, in May 2002. Many of the other essays also began as talks; the complete bibliographic details are listed below.

My thanks, finally, to Jennifer Heyns, who secured the permissions, and to Bill Douglas, who fashioned a perfect cover design for an eclectic (maybe eccentric) book.

Part I

'The Plain Truth about Common Sense: Scepticism, Metaphysics, and Irony' was a paper given to the Cambridge University Moral Sciences Club and the Edinburgh University Philosophy Colloquium (both 1992) and then at the Canadian Philosophical Association (1994); I thank all those who commented on it, especially Tom Baldwin, Peter Lewis, Chris Dustin, and Lynd Forguson. It first appeared in the *Journal of Speculative Philosophy* (Fall 1995); used by permission.

'Husserl's Sense of Wonder' was first published in *Philosophical Forum* (Spring 2000). It owes much to the inspirational example of the late Maurice Natanson of Yale and his seminar on Husserl in the late 1980s, where it was originally conceived.

'*Phronesis* and Political Dialogue,' an amplification of some arguments in my first book, *A Civil Tongue*, was a colloquium talk at York University and the University of Waterloo (both 1996) and then appeared in Stephen Esquith, ed., *Political Dialogue: Theories and Practices* (Vol. 46 of Poznan Studies in the Philosophy of the Sciences and the Humanities, 1996); used by permission.

'Keeping a Straight Bat: Cricket, Civility, and Post-Colonialism' was written for a conference on C.L.R. James at Wellesley College, which, in the event, I could not attend. It was nevertheless included in the resulting volume of papers, Selwyn Cudjoe and William Cain, eds., *C.L.R. James: His Intellectual Legacies* (Amherst, MA: University of Massachusetts Press, 1995); used by permission. I thank Jodi Mikalachki and John Loonam for conversations that prompted its beginning.

Part II

'Two Concepts of Pluralism' was commissioned as a critical notice and appeared in *Dialogue* (Spring 1998); used by permission.

'Critical Theory and Its Discontents' was also a commissioned critical notice, published in *Political Theory* (May 1996); used by permission.

'Nietzsche's Styles' originally appeared in slightly edited form on *britannica.com* (August 2000).

After a couple of false starts, 'Viral Culture' first appeared in *Harper's Magazine* (April 1999) and was later the basis for a talk to an audience at Trinity College, University of Toronto (1999), where Andrew Potter, among others, offered very helpful comments.

'Interior Decoration' likewise first appeared in *Harper's* (June 2001). I thank Naomi Klein for some useful discussion of its themes.

Part III

'Tables, Chairs, and Other Machines for Thinking' was the 2000 keynote address to the Furniture Society of America Annual Conference in Toronto and, later, delivered to audiences at the University of Regina and Trent University; I thank them all for their comments. It was published in *Queen's Quarterly* (Summer 2001); also, in abridged form with the title 'More Beauty and More Deep Wonder,' in Rick Mastelli, ed., *Furniture Studio Two: Tradition in Contemporary Furniture* (Free Union, VA: The Furniture Society, 2001); used by permission.

'Being Dandy: A Sort of Manifesto' first appeared in *Queen's Quarterly* (Fall 2000) and then, revised and expanded, in *Journal X* (Spring 2001); used by permission. The discussion of Cary Grant and *North By Northwest* was first published in the journal *Montage* (Winter 1999). I would like to thank Allan Hepburn and Russell Smith for their comments and for leading by example.

'Storage and Retrieval' began life as a speech deliverd at the University of Waterloo and University of Toronto; a version was later given as the Mary Donaldson Memorial Lecture for the Saskatchewan Library Association Annual Conference in Lake Waskiesu, Sask. (all 1999). It was published in edited form in the *Literary Review of Canada* (September 1999).

'Fear and Self-Loathing in Couchland: Eight Myths About Television,' a keynote address to the 1999 Banff International Television Festival, was published in *Queen's Quarterly* (Spring 2000) and later excerpted in the *National Post* (20 May 2000); used by permission. I thank Pat Ferns of the Festival for the original invitation.

'What Does It All Mean?' was written during a sabbatical leave at Clare Hall, Cambridge, in response to a half-serious request from a friend. I used various versions of it as a public talk for diverse audiences during 2000 and 2001; I thank them all for many illuminating comments. It was published simultaneously, in slightly different editions, in *Queen's Quarterly* (Spring 2001) and *Wilson Quart* (Spring 2001); used by permission.

PRACTICAL JUDGMENTS

Introduction: Representations of the Intellectual in Everyday Life

'It is the fate of almost all intellectuals to be forgotten, most of us sooner rather than later.'
– Randall Collins, *The Sociology of Philosophies*

I

The essays contained in this book were composed and published over a period of about ten years, roughly the first decade of my career as an academic philosopher. They are all concerned, in their various ways, with the related issues of culture, politics, and interpretation. They are, likewise, an attempt to illuminate some of the many complicated cross-fertilizations among those three subjects: the hermeneutic dimensions of political action; the ideological underpinnings of cultural experience; the need for nuanced stances of interpretation and criticism when one attempts to engage mass culture; and the role of wonder in both philosophy and everyday life.

This sort of convergence on a cluster of linked themes is the usual justification offered for books such as this, of course. We say: here is a longish time-slice of one's thought, depicted by the resulting works hovering around a central concern. But this is a principle of selection, indeed of sense, that can be applied only ex post facto and even then only somewhat tentatively. Sometimes one does not know one is in pursuit of a larger thesis until a chunk of work is examined in hindsight and certain common concerns seem to emerge. Even then, the stated themes may have a synthetic quality that does individual ideas a disservice, as if one's loose assemblage of half-thought instincts and personal proclivities were suddenly straightened into a rigid code of moral behaviour.

Sometimes, moreover, the announced larger thesis is actually, on examination, ephemeral or wispy or meandering; it seems to come apart in our hands. Or the collection simply does not really add up to what we usually think of as a thesis. The pieces pushed together are not quite reducible to a single intellectual project, and they fight for their individual identities. Maybe fortunately for us, the collection has loose threads and rough spots that do not fit into any tidy idea-package, but which nevertheless should not be snipped off or smoothed over, since they are part of what makes the ideas compelling in the first place.

All of that is certainly the case here, an admission I make with no particular sense of shame. These essays may – do – converge on certain more or less coherent ideas in the general area of hermeneutic political and cultural theory. But the arguments do not follow a straight line, and they do not contract to a simple set of linked propositions. There are also some tensions present, say, between the criticism of lifestyle pornography and the championing of the dandy as a challenge to mediocrity, which may seem to approach contradiction. I don't believe those two positions are in fact incompatible – on the contrary, viewed properly they reinforce one another – but I have not attempted to iron out that kind of wrinkle here, believing that the discrete pieces of one's mental activity should fend for themselves. Anyway, to eliminate all possible sources of discord would do a disservice to the kind of critical reader I hope to attract. So I have left all the articles as they first appeared, with the exception of correcting small errors of fact or grammar.

Why present them together at all? Because there is another important motive at work in selecting such a collection, and it is reflected not so much in any thematic equivalency as in the play of apparent disparity. I mean the range of tones, or styles, that are employed to pursue the task of thinking through the political and cultural implications of daily experience. So I have included work published in various scholarly journals, the sorts of articles that are peer-reviewed and then await eventual publication in those sadly little read forums of professional intellectual exchange. In addition, however, there are critical interventions made in, and concerning, what might be regarded as less-elevated quarters: articles in on-line magazines and general-interest publications; arguments about television or furniture or dandies.

The resulting collection is an illustration not just of a slightly idiosyncratic form of professional intellectual life, my own, but also of one (I think) important and often neglected intellectual mission for philosophy, which is to say, offering judgments that are, after a fashion, practical – that is, judgments beyond the sphere of purely scholarly debate, probes into the corners of daily life. The essays included here try to show an arc of intellectual movement, from more abstract and scholarly examinations of figures and ideas, through critical reactions, toward more or less practical interventions into the realm of the everyday.

I say 'more or less' and 'after a fashion' because even the most worldly of these efforts is not explicitly in the service of the political programs that I personally endorse, namely, those driven by commitment to social-democratic ideals, transnational citizenship, and the redistribution of wealth.[1] I have defended those programs elsewhere in the past and will again in the future, and they are present here by implication, but these essays are for the most part concerned with background philosophical issues: the workaday virtues of common sense, wonder, practical reason, and civility (in Part I); a range of critical engagements with existing bodies of literature or trends in

ideas (in Part II); and reflections on some particular forms of
material culture, such as chairs, clothes, and books, that illustrate the necessary, and too often neglected, embodiment of
ideas (in Part III).

These essays do not, in short, pose as direct policies for
change in the world around us. What is the practical upshot of
Husserlian wonder, after all? Of Waugh's views on dandies? It
is not clear what political action, if any, follows from the problem of Nietzsche's style or the dreaminess of furniture. But
they nevertheless argue for a form of critical engagement without which such change is impossible. In part I offer them as
an exercise in intellectual accounting: one person's thoughts
across a range of topics, loosely united in the belief that attention to everyday life is worthwhile, both in itself and as part of
a larger project of understanding ourselves, and our prospects.
To me, that is what philosophical reflection is all about. My
further hope is that the essays *illustrate* as well as *discuss* the
various virtues of practical judgment: attention to detail, useful distinction, a commitment to style's pleasures and dangers,
and so on. Here, *pace* most philosophical projects since Aristotle, *phronesis* is conceived as an end in itself, a kind of intellectual being-in-the-world, not as something subordinated to a
larger theoretical system.

From that point of view, then, the implied general theme of
the collection is the implied general theme of philosophy itself,
namely, the ongoing question of its own possibility. I do not set
up the collection as an explicit 'philosophy against philosophy,' to use Walter Benjamin's phrase; nor do I pretend it displays the scouring thoroughness about the pitfalls of thought
to be found in, for instance, Adorno's *Minima Moralia*, a book
unmatched in its relentless skewering of intellectual and philosophical self-delusion. ('Piety, indolence and calculation allow
philosophy to keep muddling along within an ever narrower
academic groove,' Adorno notes early in that book, 'and even
there steadily increasing efforts are made to replace it by organized tautology.')[2] But it is certainly advanced in what might
be called the *useful oddball* strain of philosophical reflection –

the strain that includes the less programmat.c, often more marginal thinkers whose work tends to figure in these pages: Nietzsche, Rorty, Cavell, Fish, C.L.R. James, Adorno and Benjamin themselves.

Here, as elsewhere, I am mostly interested in exploring (and also acting out) the instability or even discomfort that is a distinctive feature of genuine intellectual undertakings – an instability felt as much within academic disciplines and institutions as against the larger background of mass society and consumer culture, a sort of twin alienation. Since that stance is one frequently misunderstood by forces on all sides, ideologically both left and right, populist and elitist, often including those who see themselves as more 'properly' intellectual, some further *avant la lettre* explaining is perhaps in order here, before we begin. Along the way, I want to implicate myself, and you, in the problem.

II

To that end, I will probe for a moment the very idea of critical engagement in a media-saturated culture. What shape does intellectual life assume today? To what extent, and in what form, is practical judgment possible today? To ask these questions is, in turn, to spend some time sifting through the various representations of intellectual life available to us, and to weigh the differences between what we call practical and what we judge (often dismissively) as impractical. I will initiate that sifting with a significant contemporary depiction of intellectuals in everyday life, taken, as with so much exemplary cultural commentary of recent vintage, from an episode of the animated television series *The Simpsons*.

In an episode from the 2000/1 season Homer, the patriarch of this benighted all-American family, discovers through a convoluted chain of events that he has a crayon lodged in his brain. It has, apparently, been there since a childhood incident in which he attempted to force as many crayons as possible into his head via ears and nostrils. An explosive sneeze brought them hurtling out, but Homer had in the meantime lost count of how many he'd inserted and so continued on, happily oblivious to the remaining foreign object.

Once discovered, the last crayon is quickly removed surgically and Homer discovers, to his surprise, that he is actually of above-average intelligence. This has many positive consequences, not least a new fashion sense involving, among other things, V-neck sweaters, neckties, and smart trousers after the manner of a young Bing Crosby or Archie from Riverdale. He also enjoys a vastly expanded vocabulary, a hitherto absent appreciation of irony, and a greatly improved relationship with daughter Lisa, who has been until now the embattled voice of intellectual conscience in the family's play of signature arias. (In an episode from a few seasons before, Lisa had feared that stupidity was hereditary in the Simpson family, and despaired of an inevitable decline, until confronted by members of the female side of the family, all of whom were accomplished professional women with degrees and thriving, socially conscious careers.)

There are unforeseen difficulties, however. Homer begins to take seriously his job as the safety officer of a large nuclear power plant. His whistle-blowing about safety violations leads to massive layoffs as the plant is shut down. Homer's former friends and colleagues burn him in effigy in the local bar. As he is saying 'I notice a distinct strain of anti-intellectualism in this bar,' they hit him with a plank and throw him out. Homer goes to Lisa and asks her why she never said that being intelligent was so painful. She acknowledges that it is true, and shows him a graph she's plotted demonstrating the inverse relationship between intelligence and happiness. 'I make a lot of graphs,' she says sadly. How does she get through the day? 'Tai chi,' she says dreamily. 'Chai tea.'

Homer goes to a popular movie starring Julia Roberts and Richard Gere, ingeniously titled *Love Is Nice*, and watches in mounting boredom as the clichéd plot lurches towards its banal, unfunny conclusion. His sister-in-law Selma somehow notices that Homer is not laughing along with the others.

'Don't blame me,' Homer says. 'This movie is tired and pre-dictable.' He complains that of course they all know the two main characters are going to end up together, then corrects a nearby audience member who confuses the actors Bill Pullman with Bill Paxton. The audience, shocked by this thoughtless revelation of the conclusion, attack him, hit with a plank, and eject him from the theatre. 'Point out your plot holes else-where,' the pimply usher shouts. Homer wanders the streets in a Forties-style cinematic montage of despair, while neon signs of a dumbed-down culture float past: Smart People Not Wel-come, Dum-Dum Club, Lunkheadz, Disney Store.

At this point, Homer decides that he no longer wants to be intelligent. Rebuffed by the scientists who put him in this new state, who claim they won't play God, he goes to Moe, the local bartender who doubles as an amateur surgeon, to have the crayon reinserted in his brain: a procedure Moe calls 'the old crayola oblongata.' Moe positions it in Homer's nose and begins hitting it with a handy ball-peen hammer; the further it enters Homer's cranial cavity, the dumber he becomes. When he says 'Extended warranty? How can I lose!' Moe knows he has gone far enough and Homer has been restored to his former state of happy stupidity.

Only Lisa is distraught at the return of the familiar Homer. But her father hands her a letter, written before he underwent the back-room operation. In it he explains that he 'took the coward's way out' in returning to his status as an ignorant, bigoted, small-minded poster boy of dumb-ass American manhood. He could not endure the sense of isolation and dis-content, not to mention the plank-blows to the head, entailed by being a smart man in a dumb culture.

III

On the surface, this story neatly illustrates one common view of intellectuals, a view that is, let it be said, highly flattering to their self-image. It is a view that I will return to later, because its oppositional character, even in a satirical treatment, is foremost: the intellectual as cultural rebel. That Homer chooses not to continue in this role, which the story leads us to believe against all previous evidence is his natural one, can only be taken to mean that being an intellectual requires a consistent act of rare courage. It means, among other things, foregoing the simple pleasures of the mass market and enduring the opprobrium of those more complacent, less vigilant than oneself. Whether it is over safety standards or aesthetic standards, the intellectual emerges as a kind of cultural guardian, feared and resented but nevertheless superior.

This is a common piece of intellectual self-congratulation, indeed, ranging over the extant literature in even more respectable sources than *The Simpsons*. Plato's defence of the true philosopher against the false claims of the sophist, in the service of justice and the good, set the agenda early. Here the intellectual is a dedicated esoteric seer, astringent and provocative, who unshackles the chains of delusion, indolence, and common sense. In our own day, that is still very much the view of intellectuals defended by both Richard Hofstadter and Edward Said in their respective influential books on the place of intellectuals in American and mass culture. (These two adjectives have become more or less synonymous in the years that separate Hofstadter's 1963 study, *Anti-Intellectualism in American Life*, and Said's 1994 effort, *Representations of the Intellectual*.)

It is also a view with some measure of truth. To stay with the handy materials of popular culture for the moment, who among us has not sat through a recent Hollywood movie that was rendered unwatchable by weight of cliché and stale characterization? Who has not groaned with apprehension, or perhaps merely sagged inwardly, at the appearance of a character whose very lines could be uttered in advance of the event? As Adorno says in *Minima Moralia*, with trademark bitter and impressive *Weltschmerz*, 'Every visit to the cinema leaves me, against all my vigilance, stupider and worse.'

This cinematic predictability even has a strange self-referential instantiation for intellectuals, as when, in a series of 1990s action movies that includes *Executive Decision* and *The Rock*, formerly nerdy PhDs are disarmed of their critical capacities by being literally armed with automatic weapons. We know the triumph of anti-intellectualism is complete when the way troubling (and presumptively unmanly) men living the life of the mind are brought to heel is by making them into ultra-violent vigilantes. Nicolas Cage, complaining in *The Rock* that he is not cut out for the gunplay antics of Sean Connery, says, 'I can't do this. I drive a Volvo! A beige Volvo!' I have never been able to decide whether this is just a lucky hit or, instead, an extremely savvy reference to Stanley Fish's famous denunciation of falsely modest academic posturing, 'On the Unbearable Ugliness of Volvos.' Here one false self-image meets another, with the final result being some decent jokes and a high body count.[3]

More seriously, the notion of intellectuals 'speaking truth to power,' to use Said's habitual phrase, is still a cherished one among thinkers and writers, even when they are not explicitly engaged in political criticism. Challenging the dominance of given thought-clusters and patterns of discourse is always a political act; it unsettles the taken-for-granted, already-thought aspects of everyday life that are ideological in the structural sense. Often such criticism works by focussing on the nature of discourse, the way language itself inscribes patterns of domination in what it makes sayable or thinkable. Exposing and challenging these presuppositions, whatever they may be, is a cardinal task for the intellectual. It is this fact which gives some credence to the crusading image of the intellectual as a great revealer, a deft surgeon of the commonplace.

I want to complicate that representation of the intellectual, however, for it contains a tendency, or set of them, which may well prove self-defeating in the current cultural landscape. It will be necessary, in other words, to destabilize our presuppositions about the intellectual's self-regard just as much as any other piece of cultural property. Adorno again: intellectuals are 'at once the last enemies of bourgeois and the last bourgeois. In still permitting themselves to think at all in the face of the naked reproduction of existence, they act as a privileged group; in letting matters rest there, they declare the nullity of their privilege.' Perhaps a little more helpfully, Christopher Hitchens likes to remind us that speaking truth to power is actually pointless: power knows all about truth; it just doesn't care. If you want to change the world, you've got to speak truth to powerlessness. And this involves, first of all, keener awareness of the sophisticated dodges and assimilationist strategies of popular culture.

It is significant, after all, not only that *The Simpsons* represented intellectuals in the manner described earlier, but that intellectuals were even represented on *The Simpsons*. It is true that the show is also full of standard anti-intellectual gestures ('Joblessness is no longer just for philosophy majors,' a news anchor says in one episode. 'Useful people are starting to feel the pinch'). But it tends to undermine these jokes even while making them. And so, unlike most earlier forms of cultural seepage, this one has an uncertain or unstable entailment which I believe is new, and worth exploring.

When I learned most of what I know about opera from watching *Bugs Bunny*, for example, high and low culture were mixed but not in a way that actually effaced the boundary between them. Those were straightforward allusions, funny in being out of context, but mostly reinforcing of the existing categories. Now, however – now that *Bugs Bunny* watchers *are* the intellectuals – these categories have little or no purchase on critical discourse. And this new kind of combination, or erasure, of what were formerly labelled 'high' and 'low' cultural elements allows for a new form of the old elitist superiority, say, as represented by Adorno and Horkheimer in their denunciation of the culture industry.

This can be hard to see at first glance, especially insofar as we are immersed in the products of the culture industry rather than disdaining them, because our initial response, as intellectuals, is a form of second-order pleasure that we are, after all, spending that half hour watching an animated television series and not, for example, reading a hundred pages of *Dialec-*

tic of Enlightenment. We say: nobody can accuse us of being ivory-tower intellectuals! At the same time, our self-regard has not been challenged by this engagement, merely reinforced. One reason intellectuals like *The Simpsons*, just as they often like baseball and Las Vegas, is that these are cultural manifestations sufficiently complex, ironized, or simulacral to allow the free play of our particular kind of fun: making connections, noticing allusions, undermining the stability of references, making new ones, seeing hidden agendas, bringing the dominant culture into contact with subtle critique, being sophisticated.[4]

Appearances to the contrary, then, *The Simpsons* is just as elitist *under this interpretation* as any high-culture performance defended in the traditional manner by an old-fashioned cultural elitist. I don't mean here the obvious problem of making academic fodder of popular culture, writing incomprehensible, jargon-ridden articles about television or film. I mean a trickier issue of how an intellectual relates to a dominant culture at all, especially one that is, as now, all pop and no high.

IV

The point here is not to take *The Simpsons* away from us, but to recognize the complexity of the problem of being an intellectual in this culture, which happily, and sometimes confusingly, mixes elements of celebration and critique, dominance and subversion. That complexity has at least three prongs which we can isolate in an effort to think more clearly about the general project of thinking clearly, which is what we ought to mean by intellectual engagement.

In the first instance, we have to recognize that, in such a culture, intellectual interventions are not restricted in their availability. *The Simpsons*, after all, is a widely shared cultural property. Children love it, so do many adults who would never fancy themselves intellectuals, indeed would have no wish to do so. And yet, these people watch the show with evident enjoyment. Are they intellectuals manqué? Does the show work on many levels at once? Is irony so pervasive as to be, now, a habitual response on the part of a general audience, not just a specialized, knowing one? All of these conjectures contain some truth, in my view, and examples of complex, critical, and even subversive elements in the dominant culture would seem to undermine the old idea that there is a duped mass, on the one hand, and an enlightened cognoscenti, on the other.

In a sense, it would all be so much simpler if the crude version of the Adorno/Horkheimer picture were accurate: then we, the 'smart' ones, could set about our projects of critique not necessarily with the confidence that we will succeed in finally enlightening the credulous population (that would put us out of business, after all), but that we hold some kind of master key to the puzzle of cultural domination. We would have the confidence of correctness, if not of effectiveness. And that's a nice feeling to have; but it's just too simple – and frankly too cranky. If the cost of being right in this sense is that, like Adorno, we have to abominate motels and films and jazz on the radio, then I say thanks but no thanks.

This undesirable endgame – which, to be sure, is the merest caricature of Adorno's complex, prickly views – exposes the second prong of our situation now. The old Gramscian image of the intellectual was of a dedicated critic who could, by staying one step ahead of the tide of mass culture, fight off the soft forces of domination. Unlike Adorno, Gramsci was inclusive on the question of who could be an intellectual – 'all men are intellectuals,' he wrote in his *Prison Notebooks*, 'but not all men have in society the function of intellectuals' (I'll leave aside the question of women) – but he nevertheless thought that being an intellectual involved a critical attitude to the whole of one's cultural context. One needed, in a sense, to have one foot outside the bewitched circle, to be *in* the culture but not *of* it.

The trouble with this project is that there is no such outside. This is always true, I suspect, but it is even more obviously true when one inhabits a mass culture ruled by the values of speed, novelty, and knowingness. It is impossible for an individual to move faster, or be more ironic, than the currently hegemonic forces of culture. They always outstrip one's attempts at critical distance, as long as critical distance is conceived in this externalist fashion. The contradiction nestled in the heart of the Gramscian project, then, is one concerning domination. Taking up a critical stance against hegemony is really a form of dominating dominance: it is, to use Levinasian language, totalizing rather than infinitizing. It therefore meets one project of domination (the mass-cultural one) with another (the intellectual one). Even if this move could be effected – and, as I say, I don't think it can – it would still fall prey to self-defeat. Why intellectual domination rather than cultural, after all?

It is even possible, just to add insult to injury, that such a superior attitude fails even to be critical in its own terms. It may, for instance, price itself out of the cultural market, making intellectual interventions into a game for specialists only. That is what happens when intellectuals are tamed and warehoused in universities, made to seek tenure through the publication of impenetrable journal articles, and given just enough salary and self-respect to make them comfortably middle class and therefore no danger to anybody. More seriously, the attitude of superiority with respect to one's own culture can lead to a special form of deception, the kind that Marshall McLuhan warned against and constantly fought off. It is, McLuhan said, precisely when you think you understand what is going on that the culture gets the better of you. Comprehension is the enemy to be feared, because it leads to moralism, and that leads to a special kind of blindness, the smug blindness of having *figured it all out*.

This is really a particular instance of a general problem which intellectuals of all sorts need to be on guard against. Smartness tends naturally to see itself in terms of problem solving. From Oedipus onward, in fact, the riddle has stood for us as an apotheosis of intellectual engagement. Cleverness and tenacity, subtlety and flexibility of mind – these are the things that lead to good problem solving. Of course, we can now recognize the dangers of problem solving's inner logic, the way it facilitates instrumental reason to the detriment of all other kinds, the way it prizes success over wisdom, the way it spins practical reflection into theoretical systems. Being smart is a tricky business: even when apparently deep or critical, it leads us quickly into the heart of the mousetraps of domination and control. 'Nothing is more unfitting for an intellectual resolved on practising what was earlier called philosophy,' Adorno notes,

> than to wish, in discussion, and one might almost say in argumentation, to be right ... When philosophers, who are well known to have difficulty in keeping silent, engage in conversation, they should try always to lose the argument, but in such a way as to convict their opponent of untruth. The point should not be to have absolutely correct, irrefutable, water-tight cognitions – for they inevitably boil down to tautologies – but insights which cause the question of their justness to judge itself.

Here is the central contradiction once again: The world is dominated, we may want to say, by a certain kind of smartness, the smartness of technology and problem solving and method. That is what we must oppose. But then the opposition, so generally pursued, becomes itself a higher-order smartness, a sort of cognitive system, and just as easily succumbs to arrogance and disconnection. And yet, even that is not quite right. Rather, the second-order domination succumbs in a much more pernicious way because it does not recognize its own participation in that which it seeks to dominate through criticism. This, in turn, leads to the need for third-order smartness. Call this Adorno's Ladder.

Such escalating difficulties, possibly infinite regresses, of criticism lead, in turn, to the third prong of complexity, which in a sense merely returns us to the first one. One way of characterizing intellectuals is that they try to be smart about being smart about smartness. And yet, because some of us get paid to be smart full-time, whether in this self-reflexive way or not, we begin to believe that we are the *only* smart ones. This typically just reinforces the elitism and condescension that outsiders view with such distaste and which make them inclined, if they are able, to take our toys away from us. Underfunding of universities is often justified on the basis of their irrelevance, but just as often resentment and hostility are in play. Anti-intellectualism is always a strong force in mass culture.

Unfortunately, the flip side of this hostility is not renewed intellectual energy within universities, but instead more and more rigid specialization, and eventual ossification, of the traditional disciplines. Partly this is simply in the conservative nature of institutions, which tend to discourage eccentricity and work to reproduce themselves in their own image. They also, as much as any corporate structure, facilitate envy and resentment. A department chair of my acquaintance describes our university culture as a large version of the arcade game 'Whack-a-Mole,' in which the object is to bat down as quickly as possible any head that rises above those of its fellows. There is also what we might agree to call the *necromantic temptation* of scholarly discourse: the way ever more arcane and difficult theoretical knowledge can be used to intimidate and, often, exclude those who do not possess it. From this vantage, graduate school is nothing other than an extended initiation into a magical circle of adepts who can command the symbols of theory's magic.

In addition to these long-standing (and well-known) dangers of professionalization, there is the way we internalize the external pressure to demonstrate relevance. My own discipline, for example, is presumptively dedicated to questions which by their nature have no final answers. They are not problems to be solved. And yet the demands of instrumentality see value only in solved problems, not in what I would offer as more subtly articulated unanswerable questions. The dominance of use-values infects all aspects of intellectual endeavour conducted under institutional circumstances: What is it good for? What use is it? But, as Aristotle once said, we need also to ask, 'What is the use of use?' If, instead of asking this question of ourselves and our students, we fall into the mealy-mouthed utilitarian justifications for our undertakings – in philosophy, for example, we are often encouraged to tell students that philosophy is good preparation for a career in law or business – we grant victory before the fact to this scale of value. Responding to the demand for relevance, in other words, becomes a form of self-censorship. 'Priorities of urgency are established,' Adorno notes of this tendency. 'But to deprive thought of the moment of spontaneity is to annul precisely its necessity.' This is what he calls 'the cult of the important.'[5]

To advocate deprogramming of this cult is not to say that no form or manner of relevance is possible, or desirable, only that it must be sought, and given, on thought's own terms. 'The self-criticism of reason is its truest morality,' Adorno notes, implying the necessary immersion and intricacy of all genuine intellectual activity: its values cannot be imported, or imposed, from elsewhere. If they are, we run the risk of becoming second-rate quasi-scientific adjuncts to the larger project of understanding the world by solving all its problems.

This capitulation leads in turn to a curious situation in which the field of intellectual life is cleared for some perhaps surprising figures – though this is only surprising if you have not been paying attention to the general culture over the past fifteen years. Despite laments like those offered recently in *The Nation* by a distinguished panel of public intellectuals, including Christopher Hitchens, Russell Jacoby, and Stephen Carter, the public intellectual has not disappeared. The situation is far more dire than that: nowadays, *everyone* is a public intellectual. A recent issue of the *National Post Business* magazine, for example, featured a cover story on Josef Strauss, the new CEO of JDS Uniphase. On the cover he was described as 'an eccentric icon, a restless intellectual and disruptive thinker.' It turns out that his disruptive thoughts mostly involve aggressive acquisition of failing dot-com companies. No self-respecting CEO can fail to have himself described as an intellectual, perhaps even a visionary. Designers and architects are now intellectuals as well, almost per definition. Columnists and television presenters parade across our papers and screens in the guise of intellectuals, explaining the events of the day in the smooth phrases of punditry. So many intellectuals! This even as, weirdly enough, the culture continues to be, on the surface anyway, hostile to the very idea of them.

It can get even more subtle than that. Consumer brands, which now function almost independently of the products they are used to sell, are the new celebrities of our culture, tracked and discussed after the manner of a sports hero or reckless minor royals. But they are also by the same token the new public intellectuals, appropriating formerly robust and independent ideas as part of their narratives of commercial success: Ikea means democracy, Starbucks means community, Nike means transcendence, IBM means communication, 3M means innovation. This displacement is not really new, of course, though it has perhaps spiralled into the stratosphere during the last fifteen years. A few of us are old enough to remember (or, if not that, to have seen in Don DeLillo's novel *Underworld*) that DuPont long ago promised us 'Better Things for Better Living through Chemistry.' And Coke didn't just add life, or offer the real thing; it made the world sing, and reconciled youthful energy with peace and harmony. Can we name a single intellectual who could hope to do as much?

These developments have only a little to do with the defection of cultural studies graduates to the advertising and marketing industries, where they can make far more and live far better, speaking of better living, than revealing the same secrets to an audience of students even poorer than themselves. That is certainly a genuine and deplorable (though probably overestimated) factor in the mounting sophistication of branding, but of far greater importance is the fact that intellectuals (and artists and teachers and writers) have allowed it to happen by failing to make ideas interesting in non-commercial terms. That, after all, is the other side of the intellectual's oppositional responsibilities: critique cannot be an end in itself, it must issue in compelling thought and action that at least tries to change the world for the better – a prospect about which I am, I confess, a cynical optimist: someone who hopes for the best even while expecting the worst.

We have retreated from our own cultural responsibilities, in short, and the result is not that there are no intellectuals but that there are no emancipatory ideas. That will mean, ultimately, that we have no culture other than commercial culture, and then our self-defeat will be complete.

V

At this point, you may well be wondering what *my* agenda is here, and in the essays that follow. How do the present interventions fit into the field I am seeking to describe? What intellectual status do they have? Am I, in other words, merely being smart about being smart about being smart, seeking to dominate those who seek to dominate domination?

Allow me to attempt to answer those questions by probing, for a brief moment, my own representations as an intellectual. Said notes in his study that 'representation' can mean, variously, intervening, being present, speaking for, appearing as, and seeing oneself as. It can also mean, as in contemporary street slang's verb form 'represent,' to be strong and committed, to rise to the challenge. More deeply, if we accept Baudrillard's warnings about the simulacral tendencies of postmodern culture, we have to add a new level of caution about the very idea of representation: those things we call representations are not actually re-presentations of some authentic original at all, but instead proliferating and interrelated tokens with no originary type standing behind them and giving them point. It can also simply mean the danger of succumbing to the economic world's imperatives of interchangeability, speed, production, and advertising: in the commercial world, after all, one is *represented* by an agent. Adorno therefore offers his tart 'advice to intellectuals: let no-one represent you.'[6]

My own suggestion is that all these meanings of 'represent' are compressed, sometimes confusingly and always inevitably, when one's intellectual work spills outside the confines of an institution like the university. This is not really an issue of one's primary source of income, however; Adorno, like many independent thinkers, had no fondness for academics, and yet if anything he maintained an attitude of even more aggressive aloofness than they typically do.[7] The real issue is how one addresses oneself to a culture, and the dangers lurking therein. If one appears on television, for example, it is well to remember that inordinate attention will be given to one's personal appearance and clothing. If one continues to have a presence in that weirdly visual medium (McLuhan said that television is actually tactile, not visual: we lower ourselves into it like a warm bath), changes in hairstyle or fashion sense may become matters of discussion, at least among people with nothing more important to distract them. Soon enough, one's party-going habits, cocktail preferences, and sexual orientation may become fodder for gossip magazines and society pages.

This is perhaps surprising, but it is hardly news. The real question is, how does one negotiate that knowledge? It cannot be ignored, since that too is a response. And contrary to much costless wisdom, it cannot be managed easily. A media-saturated culture is always trickier to navigate than it seems to those who have not tried to do so. It can be hard to resist the temptations posed by outside interest and minor-league celebrity. There is always, furthermore, the danger of being assimilated and smoothed over despite one's best intentions. For many, these dangers are sufficient to render the entire notion of wider engagement a non-starter. But that has the usual consequence of inaction, namely to leave everything as it is.

Now, this is not the place to rehearse the arguments about whether or not intellectuals should appear on television (I have in any event made my position clear elsewhere; see 'Fear and Self-Loathing in Couchland'). That is just a minor part of a much larger issue. I am interested, instead, in what this particular challenge says about how intellectuals fit into everyday life, especially the everyday life dominated by mass media and mass culture. Most of us are familiar with the figure of, if not the label for, what Pierre Bourdieu felicitously called *le fast-thinker*, or professional pundit; some of us are familiar, further, with the challenge of not becoming one.[8] Without indulging in self-aggrandizement – and, as I will suggest in a moment, that is almost always the before-the-fact objection raised against even talking of these matters – I want to suggest that my own case might be considered a small-scale example of the larger issue.

So, for the record, here is a sample of some of the things I have been called over the past five years, mostly as a result of talking about ideas in non-academic fora: a popularizer, a pop philosopher, a hip philosopher, a celebrity philosopher, a made-for-TV philosopher, a philosopher-journalist, a 'philosopher,' not a philosopher at all, a rock-and-roll philosopher, a fashion-plate philosopher, a philosopher king, a hip philosopher prince, a gendernaut, a pundit, a philoso-pundit, a pundit-du-jour, a talking head, a media king, a media master, a media slut, a media whore, a swinger, and (last but certainly not least) a ubiquitous bore. My appearances have been parodied in magazines and web sites and, in what was to me an extraordinary development, an online publication called *Good Magazine* devoted an entire week of entries to fictional deconstructions of my life, including one where I quit philosophy in order to be a Canada Post letter-carrier, another where I was part of the cast of *Law and Order*, and a third where I was the object of secret improper advances known as 'palming' (I will leave the details of that as an exercise for the reader's imagination).

I must hasten to add that all of this is offered purely in the spirit of the present investigation. In fact, if I don't add that – and perhaps even if I do – there is a clear danger of merely perpetuating the cycle of reaction I am trying to analyse. This, after all, is one of the ways structural goals are achieved in a mediated culture, namely, by making all discursive moves, even attempted critical ones, contribute to the cult of personal celebrity. So don't get me wrong: I am certainly not complaining about the attention, and I am not interested in levelling particular blame. Indeed, to me personally, this sort of attention is funny and strange and oddly flattering. (One probably never gets tired of being thought hip, for instance, no matter what it actually means and no matter how square the person applying the label. And as one magazine editor said of the online parodies, irony about irony is the new sincerity: one has to accept the implied compliment.) To be sure, I have to some extent invited these reactions, if only in the sense of allowing myself to become a very, very minor-league public figure whose intellectual opinions have been quoted now and then on television.

The real issue is what these reactions say about how intellectual interventions are handled by larger cultural forces. And on that score it seems to me that there is evident here a strong stake in *reducing* or *deflecting* the deeper possibilities of critique, the possibilities where imagination is stretched and new forms of life or thought entertained. This is what I want to analyse here. While these developments may seem to suggest a new ease of entry – a new level of comfort – with the prospect of intellectuals swimming in the cultural mainstream, appearances can be deceiving. The background judgment that an intellectual is merely a pundit or a celebrity is part of a larger ideological project of not taking intellectual work seriously: it is anti-intellectualism masquerading as cultural sophistication. In fact, the reactions betray an anxiety about the possible challenge that, in this case, philosophical reflection poses to everyday life. There is a clear *need* here, an overwhelming desire, to belittle, and so apparently defeat, the intellectual's attempted challenge.

In the old days, this would have been done by ridiculing the intellectual's other-worldliness, his or her ivory-tower status. That started with the way the Athenians handled Socrates, and it still happens often enough today. But if an intellectual is *not* other-worldly – if he or she is comfortable speaking of television and fashion and popular music, as well as Aristotle and

Habermas and Wittgenstein – then he or she must be attacked a different way. Such a figure must first be degraded to the status of bare personality, and then eliminated *as necessarily no more than a personality*, that is, a shallow seeker-after-attention. That attack has two related fronts. One is the implied reduction of all claims, whatever their nature or cogency, to instances of personal advancement or punditry; this effectively defangs any publicly offered intellectual challenge by folding it down to the same flat status as any other claim or position made in the mediascape. The other front involves the sneakier, and more cynical, tactic of denigrating any and all public interventions in the name of 'traditional' intellectual standards (usually those of the cynic's imagined academic past); this in effect makes the intellectual a traitor to his own commitments for having the temerity to venture outside the 'proper' sphere of intellectual activity.

VI

It is never easy to know precisely how to deal with these pressures, and I acknowledge I have not always done as well as I might in that regard, but what I want to emphasize in conclusion is that this is really just an instance of the general quandaries intellectuals now face in everyday life. I said earlier that I wanted to destabilize standard-issue intellectual self-congratulation concerning superiority to one's dominant culture. That destabilization is important, indeed crucial, because a stance of superiority simply will not serve us anymore in the business of cultural criticism. For one thing, it is the quick route to a self-nullifying obscurity where one is read only by the entirely like-minded, and perhaps not even by them. That may be comfortable, but it is a failure of intellectual duty – admittedly using 'duty' here as a handy word for what I would like to see happen, what I think is valuable and good. Realizing this possibility of failure, then, one might be tempted simply to fly to the opposite extreme and embrace the dominant culture with gusto, becoming a dedicated celebrant of its smooth and shiny surfaces. But that, too, is a failure of duty because it abandons the possibility of a searching critique of dominant values, the possibility which is alone the justification for our existence as intellectuals and critics.

Instead, one has a much harder course to pursue, which is to accept one's place within a reductive, speedy, unjust, and media-driven world. 'There is no way out of entanglement,' Adorno reminds us. 'The only responsible course is to deny oneself the ideological misuse of one's own existence.' That strikes me as true, but it is more complicated than it sounds. We may dispute what follows from an attempt to deny mis-use – Adorno, like the many less talented thinkers who imitate him, deliberately vacillates between engagement and detach-ment, irony and passion – but I think it means, above all, striv-ing to remain oppositional and marginal without becoming marginalized. Crucially, this must not be merely a pose, the sort of self-congratulation of the imagined outsider, actually a smooth insider, condemned by Russell Jacoby in his sour assessment of the current academic jet set, with its lucrative conference circuit and first-class air miles privileges.[9] It is, rather, an attempt to put oneself in question at every moment, never to rest easy with one's own sense of engagement and representation.

That in turn means using the available means of communi-cation even while knowing the grave risks involved, trying (perhaps with only limited success) to say something rough and unsettling on airwaves too often dominated by everyone saying the same thing. It means creating an alien figure in the media landscape, a dandy or punk or swinger, as it may be, who upsets the existing categories of judgment, if only slightly. It means being unpredictable, ironic, satirical, playful, and prickly.

Is this merely subversion for its own sake, just another pecu-liar form of cultural posturing? No. As I suggested earlier, crit-icism is always a political act, and in a world increasingly dominated by the neo-liberal orthodoxies of global capitalism, it becomes ever more overtly so. Unlike Stanley Fish, for example, who would condemn a commitment to principle – any principle – as just another form of genteel self-justification, I believe ideas cannot be meaningfully advanced without some basic commitment to regulative ideals. These ideals are not metaphysical in the sense that I would ever claim they embody 'nature' or 'destiny' in human affairs; they are, rather, orienting hopes that work to guide and assess our (for the moment, my) intellectual interventions. Call the resulting formula *critical immersion guided by the norm of justice*, and the resulting condition a form of the exile that Said sees so clearly as a necessary part of intellectual engagement.[10]

By justice I mean very much what Habermas meant when he formulated, in various disputed versions, the principle of universal access: no decision can be legitimately taken without the participation of all those affected by it. Democracy, in short. In long, there is of course a great deal more to be said, and argued; but I will not do that here. Suffice to say that there is implied here a commitment to social hope but without the rigidity of a specific teleology.[11] Justice is not best conceived as an end-state to which we philosophers have some privileged epistemological access and about which, if once it were realized, we could simply inform our fellow citizens. Justice functions, always, as a regulative ideal with critical purchase on our actual social and discursive practices.

Such an intellectual commitment to justice should, above all, be dedicated to no particular group or body, certainly to no set of professional constraints or disciplinary goals. There is a profession of philosophy, certainly, but as the philosopher Jonathan Lear reminds us, the idea of a profession of philosophy is actually a contradiction in terms. We can professionalize the practice of careful reflection, but the result will never capture what is essential to that project. It might even be dangerous to try. '[W]e want to pass on fundamental truths,' Lear writes, 'and in our attempts to do so truth becomes rigid and dies.' That is alarming but, as Lear wisely concludes, the 'only remedy' to philosophy's in-built impossibility 'is to treat this as a comedy rather than a tragedy.'[12] Or, better, to treat it as both simultaneously, like so much of human life.

We do well, finally, to remember that intellectuals are after all human, subject to all the usual frailties and delusions and pleasures of the species, sometimes more so (in vanity and touchiness, for instance). 'Abstruse thought and profound researches I prohibit,' wrote David Hume, assuming the voice of the spirit of life, 'and will severely punish, by the pensive melancholy which they introduce, by the endless uncertainty in which they involve you, and by the cold reception which your pretended discoveries shall be met with, when communicated. Be a philosopher; but, amidst all your philosophy, be still a man.'

That is excellent advice, but of course it does not really *solve* the larger problem of how intellectuals relate to culture, so much as add nuance to our imprisonment within the problem. We cannot escape contingency and finitude, and we should probably give up the attempt, whether it is theological or philosophical or scientific. Hume knew this very well, and yet rightly feared the consequences of his commitment to philosophical scepticism: 'I am at first affrighted and confounded with that forlorn solitude in which I am placed by my philosophy,' he wrote, 'and fancy myself some uncouth monster, utterly abandoned and disconsolate. Fain would I run into the crowd for shelter and warmth.' Nowadays, the shelter and warmth offered by the crowd are no less tempting, and maybe even more powerful. In a no-brow culture, it is so much easier to be Homer than to be Lisa.

So, in conclusion, we must ask once again: performed by humans or otherwise, sceptical or fideistic, is philosophy even possible anymore? Sadly, looking at both the academic discipline and at the various extra-academic reactions to that discipline – both the risible pedantry of the academics and the sorts of metaphysical nonsense that crowds the bookstore shelves labelled 'Philosophy' – we can have no lively expectation of a simple affirmative on that score. Or perhaps any other

kind of affirmative. And if philosophy in general looks impossible, a fortiori the prospects of any form of *political* philosophy
seem worse. Here, before we have even fairly begun, we are
forced to wonder if theoretical work can ever really issue in
effective practical judgments, judgments that can impinge
upon and change the world for the better (whatever we mean
by better – I mean less ignorant and more democratic).

Well, these are the difficult, perhaps unsolvable difficulties
at the heart of all the reflections that follow, as of all reflection
worthy of the name, no matter which voice or tone is adopted
at a given moment. My sole conviction here – if it deserves to
be called a conviction – is that it is never possible to decide, in
some impenetrable theoretical manner, whether intellectual
interventions have a worldly point. Aristotle wanted to distinguish *theoria* – getting things right in general – from *phronesis*:
practical deliberation about particular ends. But this is a distinction we can, and must, jettison. We need not have a clear
and complete theoretical picture before we begin; we probably
don't need it at all.

We cannot know how much the world is changed by our
reflections. We cannot know if a given argument plants its
hooks deeply, or at all. But we can know that every intellectual
intervention adds something new to what was there before,
and may be, if communicated well, the one that helps build a
bridge to those who can use the ideas to change the world.
Every critical sortie has a chance of success, in other words,
meaning a chance to decrease the evident levels of misunderstanding, ignorance, injustice, and oppression in the world. At
the very least, it has a chance to make things more fascinating.
For better or worse, possibly sometimes both, no discursive
foray leaves the world intact.

And that is a great deal – enough anyway to allow us to get
on with the things that interest us, the things that feel like
they need saying. Comfort has many forms, some of them
cold; and in any event comfort is not always what we should
be seeking. You may find consolation here, in other words,
but let me express the hope that you will not – that you will

find, instead, something more unsettling and more important: uncertainty.

What more could anyone reasonably say before the fact, or by way of introduction?

Notes

1 See Mark Kingwell, *A Civil Tongue: Justice, Dialogue, and the Politics of Pluralism* (University Park, PA: Penn State University Press, 1995) and *The World We Want: Virtue, Vice, and the Good Citizen* (Toronto: Viking, 2000; revised ed., New York: Rowman & Littlefield, 2001).

2 Theodor Adorno, *Minima Moralia: Reflections from Damaged Life*, trans. E.F.N. Jephcott (London: Verso, 1974; orig. Frankfurt: Suhrkamp Verlag, 1951), p. 66.

Adorno is repeatedly concerned here to identify and think through the hostility between professional scholarship and extra-academic intellectual engagement; he is, by the same token, preoccupied with the cultural postures or stances available to the intellectual in an era of mass culture, and the culture industry. 'Nothing less is asked of the thinker today,' he writes at another point, 'than that he should be at every moment both within things and outside them – Münchhausen pulling himself out of the bog by his pig-tail becomes the pattern of knowledge which wishes to be more than either verification or speculation. And then the salaried philosophers come along and reproach us with having no definite point of view' (pp. 74–5).

At the same time, he is well aware that these arguments are often the very thing that perpetuates the hostility: 'Intellectuals, who alone write about intellectuals and give them their bad name in that of honesty, reinforce the lie. A great part of the prevalent anti-intellectualism and irrationalism ... is set in motion when writers complain about the mechanisms of competition without understanding them, and so fall victim to them' (p. 28).

3 I have written elsewhere about another, more complicated appropriation of intellectual self-image, the television sitcom *Frasier*. On the surface a fairly straightforward (if gentle) mocking of the pre-

tentious Harvard-educated radio psychiatrist, played with great
skill by Kelsey Grammer, the show is actually in its basic structure
a celebration of his social status. This is effected by, among other
things, the ongoing struggles for insight between Frasier and his
father, Martin (John Maloney); and by the delicate wit and co-
dependency of the relationship between Frasier and his younger
brother, Niles (David Hyde Pierce). See 'The Uneasy Chair,' in
Mark Kingwell, *Marginalia: A Cultural Reader* (Toronto: Penguin,
1999).
4 Adorno was well aware of the dangers inherent in this particular
form of diversion: to 'call philosophy – as I once did myself – the
binding obligation to be sophisticated, is hardly better' than pursuing faux-naiveté. 'Even when sophistication is understood in
the theoretically acceptable sense of that which widens horizons,
passes beyond the isolated phenomenon, considers the whole,
there is still a cloud in the sky. It is just this passing-on and being
unable to linger, this tacit assent to the primacy of the general over
the particular, which constitutes not only the deception of idealism
in hypostasizing concepts, but also its inhumanity, that has no
sooner grasped the particular than it reduces it to a through-
station, and finally comes all too quickly to terms with suffering
and death for the sake of a reconciliation occurring merely in reflection – in the last analysis, the bourgeois coldness that is only too
willing to underwrite the inevitable' (*Minima Moralia*, pp. 73–4).
5 *Minima Moralia*, p. 125.
6 *Minima Moralia*, p. 83.
7 The very first entry in *Minima Moralia*, 'For Marcel Proust,' establishes the tone and themes, as well as the intricacy of negative-
dialectic thought, to be found throughout that idiosyncratic collection of cultural critical remarks: 'The occupation with things of the
mind has by now itself become "practical," a business with strict
divisions of labour, departments and restricted entry. The man of
independent means who chooses it out of repugnance for the
ignominy of earning money will not be disposed to acknowledge
the fact. For this he is punished. He is not a "professional," is
ranked in the competitive hierarchy as a dilettante no matter how
well he knows his subject, and must, if he wants to make a career,

show himself even more resolutely blinkered than the most inveterate specialist.'

In this way, professionalization of thought has a doubly negative effect, restricting both insiders and outsiders: 'The departmentalization of mind is a means of abolishing mind where it is not exercised *ex officio*, under contract. It performs this task all the more reliably since anyone who repudiates the division of labour – if only by taking pleasure in his work – makes himself vulnerable by its standards in ways inseparable from elements of his superiority. Thus is order ensured: some have to play the game because they cannot otherwise live, and those who could live otherwise are kept out because they do not want to play the game' (p. 21).

Later, Adorno makes the point with greater simplicity: 'Even the so-called intellectual professions are being deprived, through their growing resemblance to business, of all joy. Atomization is advancing not only between men, but within each individual, between the spheres of his life' (p. 130).

8 Bourdieu merely follows Adorno in seeing speed as a danger in intellectual life. 'The shadow of [haste and restlessness] falls on intellectual work. It is done with a bad conscience, as if it had been poached from urgent, even if only imaginary occupation. To justify itself in its own eyes it puts on a show of hectic activity performed under great pressure and shortage of time, which excludes all reflection, and therefore itself. It often seems as if intellectuals reserved for their actual production only those hours left over from obligations, excursions, appointments and unavoidable amusements' (*Minima Moralia*, p. 138).

9 See Russell Jacoby, 'Intellectuals: From Utopia to Myopia,' in *The End of Utopia: Politics and Culture in an Age of Apathy* (New York: Basic Books, 1999), especially pp. 119–23. Jacoby is typically excoriating, without being at all helpful or anywhere positive, in his denunciation of overprivileged academic intellectuals who go on and on about their 'marginality' even while enjoying all the benefits of cultural success: applause, attention, fame. Nevertheless, his chapter is a good primer on what we might call the 'handwringing' genre of intellectual assessment. See also Jacoby, *The*

Last Intellectuals (New York: Basic Books, 1987) and Richard Posner, *Public Intellectuals: A Study in Decline* (Cambridge, MA: Harvard University Press, 2002).

10 It is always difficult to avoid a higher-order assimilation when one makes intellectual work explicitly political, which is one reason I offer this claim is such an open-ended way here. 'Even those intellectuals who have all the political arguments against bourgeois ideology at their fingertips undergo a process of standardization,' Adorno writes, 'which – despite crassly contrasting content, through readiness on their part to accommodate themselves – approximates them to the prevalent mentality to the extent that the substance of their viewpoint becomes increasingly incidental, dependent merely on their preferences or the assessment of their own chances' (*Minima Moralia*, p. 206).

11 Compare, on this point, the essays in Richard Rorty's collection, *Philosophy and Social Hope* (New York: Penguin, 1999). I am less concerned than Rorty to distance myself from any sort of principle-based political commitment, a concern which leaves his various pronouncements on the desirability of the classless democratic society sitting oddly with a consistent refusal to make a validity claim. Rorty gives with one hand what he takes away with the other. A much more compelling version of the hope-without-telos position is articulated by Ernst Bloch in his *The Spirit of Utopia*, trans. Anthony Nassar (Stanford, CA: Stanford University Press, 2000). And my own attempt at being utopian without being teleological is contained in Kingwell, *The World We Want*, especially ch. 5.

12 Jonathan Lear, 'Introduction,' *Open-Minded: Working Out the Logic of the Soul* (Cambridge, MA: Harvard University Press, 1998).

PART I
FOUNDATIONS

The Plain Truth about Common Sense: Scepticism, Metaphysics, and Irony

A historically minded reader will see that my title is a cobble of titles: both the famous pamphlet by Thomas Paine and the less famous objection to that work which indicated how, in political argument anyway, *Plain Truth* and *Common Sense* need not always be in agreement.[1] The title is also meant to recall Thompson Clarke's influential dissection[2] of that quintessentially plain philosophical man, G.E. Moore – whose 'Defence of Common Sense'[3] is taken by Clarke to get some airplanes off the ground of the plain and, therefore, unwittingly to inspire an uncommonsensical scepticism about them.

The title is meant, further, to express a wish which most thinkers who ally themselves with common sense share, namely, that what I have to say will strike you as commonsensical. The precariousness of that wish, furthermore, its instability within the context of a philosophical argument like this one (and like Moore's, and in a much different way like Reid's and Berkeley's), is the last thing, by way of introduction, that the title is meant to say.

I Plain Common Sense

What is the plain truth about common sense? It is surprising, though perhaps not to philosophers, that this question has no easy answer. We all think we know what common sense is until we begin either (a) to reflect critically on it, in which case we have arguably ceased to be commonsensical, or (b) to conflict with others about certain elements of it, casting parts of our own common sense into question.

This of course will not do, for among other things common sense must be common; it must also, I could add, be stable, and these disagreements appear to threaten that stability. Sometimes such disputes proceed from category mistakes and a rather common (if not a sensible) unwillingness to draw distinctions. If it is true, as Timothy Sprigge suggests, that 'we will only be able to articulate clearly what the common sense view of the world is when we do not have an inordinate respect for it,'[4] then a degree of justified violence is in the offing. To get at common sense, we must do some conceptual carving. Whether this will *ex hypothesi* bar us from speaking, later, of the plain truth about it is the central question I want to raise in this discussion.

Some distinctions may help immediately. A great deal of what we commonly speak of as common sense is better described as 'common nonsense': I mean the tenets of folk wisdom, old wives' tales, traditional remedies, received lore, and the like. With I hope no disrespect to old wives, much of what passes for sense in this realm is, and has been shown to be, false; and whatever else is true about common sense, it must not be known to be false. In other words, it survives as sense only to the extent that its falsity does not arise. It is very possible that its truth does not come up either, in any verificationist sense, but that does not pose a threat to sense – at least not yet.

But beliefs on the order that colds are contracted by sitting in draughts, that butter is good for blistered burns, or that philosophers cannot master worldly tasks are both false and elements of a certain kind of common sense. We need not trouble to distinguish here – though we surely could – among superstition, pseudoscience, delusion, prejudice, and sheer bloody-mindedness, all of which may be found represented in this realm. Nor am I suggesting that the realm is itself a stable one, presenting a unified face to the world. We all have our own stores of this common (non)sense, sometimes defined by family or group solidarity, usually determined by cultural background, and almost always of little lasting philosophical interest when we want to isolate common sense for bigger fish-frying.

To do *that* we have to draw at least one more distinction, though I don't pretend it will deal decisively with the elastic nature of common sense. The distinction, borrowed from Marcus Singer, is between common sense as what we might call *basic knowledge*, and common sense as *sound judgment*. In the first sense, common sense 'is ordinary, normal, average understanding – common understanding – without which one is foolish or incompetent or insane. In the other, common sense is thought of as good, sound, practical sense.'[5] The distinction, Singer adds, is among other things useful for showing that '[i]t is one of the anomalies of common sense that, in one sense, common sense is something common, while, in another sense, common sense is something uncommon.' I propose to leave the uncommon sense of common sense aside[6] and concentrate now on those elements, or at least those we can easily isolate, of the sense without which we court folly or insanity.

Once more, here we normally think we know what common sense is, but our thinking so can rapidly lead us into trouble. *Common* common sense (which I will call, with Thompson Clarke, 'plain common sense') is thought to be something shared by all human agents. It is sense both in the sense of being based on sense (the sensory receptors through which we experience the world) and in the sense of being common (it does not depend on particular experience or background). So it would not, could not, make sense to cut against this common sense, at least in those realms we call the everyday or the ordinary or the plain. That is, we would make ourselves out to be fools or madpeople if we did that. We would lack what Herbert Fingarette has called, with reference to insanity, a 'grasp of essential relevance.'[7] That much is clear enough, I think, to stand.

Yet it is possible that, from some points of view (both plain and philosophical), we have left common sense behind even in saying this small amount. That is, by speaking of something common to all, have we left the realm of plain common sense and ventured into the realm of philosophical prejudice, the marshalling of universal categories and the bending to them of already historicized experience? Perhaps. An even more pressing objection is that our small clearing of common-sense space is always going to be a false achievement, for we cannot ever fully specify what the elements of plain common sense must be. In other words, all talk of plain common sense becomes, like it or not, talk of *philosophical* common sense – and, whatever its charms, that is not the plain truth that we wanted.

The reason for this claim, which I think is not quite commonsensical, is that plain common sense will by its very plain nature defy strict determination. Because it is a basic feature of – or perhaps 'background to' – experience, our normal methods of investigation will fail when we attempt to isolate its *general* features and state them clearly. The common-sense view of the world is, as Hobhouse said, 'the result of thought acting on masses of experience too great to be perfectly articulated.' So any articulation will be partial (not whole) and therefore partial (prejudiced).[8] Thus the second objection really becomes a version of the first.

Yet I don't think these objections are entirely convincing, and for a fairly commonsensical reason, namely, that whatever difficulties we may observe in the prospect of giving a full description of plain common sense we can, without inordinate difficulty, say what some of the *main* features of plain common sense are. If we could not do that, it would not, I think, remain common sense. It's true that it will, at a later stage, prove necessary to stop the investigation of the plain, but not for these reasons exactly, and certainly we will not stop before we have fairly begun.

Therefore, with apologies to these qualifying warnings, and with a measure of awareness about the dangers courted, I want to claim that the essential features of plain common sense are the following: (1) that there is an objectively existing world external to me; (2) that it has existed for some long time in the past and will so exist in the future; (3) that I exist as both a subject and an object in this world; (4) that I existed in the past and will exist in the future; and finally (5) that there are numerous others like me, both subjects and objects, who exist in time and the external world.

There is a great deal more I could say about plain common sense, shadings of detail and complex relationships, with exceptions and qualifications of varying degrees of interest. I could, in addition, speak like William James of common sense's pragmatic value: 'Common sense appears,' he writes, 'as a perfectly definite state in our understanding of things ... satisfies in an extraordinarily successful way the purposes for which we think ... It suffices for the necessary practical ends of life.'[9] To speak this way is not necessary, however, and it may be misleading, for all of these details may be seen either to follow from my five common-sense propositions, or to extend beyond them to our goals and actions. What is plain, I think, is that those goals and actions could not succeed without a view of the world as it is essentially described by my five propositions.

Stated *as propositions*, of course, they have an odd flavour: the oddness of the move from plain common sense to philosophical common sense. It is an oddness which can lead us to wonder for what reason, in what sense, or in response to what challenge such propositions would or could be relevantly uttered. More on that later. For now I think it is plain that anyone who doubted the truth of any of these propositions would be, as Bradley once put it, either a fool or an advanced thinker. Let us consider the advanced thinker.

II Metaphysics/Scepticism

Common sense has been both a source and a target of scepticism. It has also been both an enemy and a friend of certain metaphysical doctrines, sometimes at the same time. It is these varied uses that will show us, I think, just why the philosophical truth about common sense is that there is none, and the plain truth about it is that there is no more to say, except ironically. What do I mean?

I mean first that many uses of common sense are tropic. That is, they post an appeal to common sense as part of a rhetorical strategy or course of argumentation. Thomas Paine did it, and so did his pamphleteering opponent, and disagreement here no more indicates the incoherence of common sense in the plain sense than such appeals ever do. These opposing appeals can indicate genuine disagreement about a proposition, but it is not necessarily or even often a common-sense one. For example, I may think it is only common sense that taxation without representation is unfair. You counter that it is only common sense that colonies cannot have the full rights of a home nation. Neither of these views is common sense, let alone 'only' common sense – as if to quibble indicates a troubled mind, or a foolish one. Both speakers want to appear realistic, hard-nosed, and sensible; both want to suggest that any opposing view courts incoherence, if not outright insanity. But this is not strictly speaking true, for sane people may disagree about certain matters, especially in politics.

The same rhetorical strategy is evident in what might be called common-sense, or plain, scepticism. I say I am, for example, sceptical of the efficacy of placing purple rock crystals in my pockets during a viva voce examination. Here the tropes are a little harder to untangle. Plain sceptical appeals are usually scientific ones, finding superstition and widespread delusion full of error. This is not, it goes without saying, what we think of as philosophical scepticism; but neither is it, and this may require saying, a straightforward appeal to plain common sense – though it is allied with it. We might say that science is systematic and reflective common sense, but it will therefore conflict with undifferentiated or truly plain common sense (as in, e.g., the heliocentric model of the universe, which seems to confound the solid common-sense perception that the sun rises and sets) as well as with what I called earlier common nonsense (as in, e.g., the non-falsifiable nature of astrological claims).

Despite the close relationship between them, then, straightforwardly to call this scientific attitude 'common sense' is no more than to attempt an argumentative stamp of approval. Hence the rhetoric is not very different from the political example, though the appeals may be more resistant to objection. Plain common sense and science do run on some kind of line: 'the way things really are' and 'the way we commonly see them' are linked together, but never simply or without further ado. For one thing, plain common sense appears to require and admit of no particular theory or paradigm, whereas science always will. (At the very least, there must be a theory of experimental proof.) Theory provides access to the reality described in the 'really' of the phrase 'the way things really are.'

It is perhaps *this* link between common sense and science which leads a certain kind of philosopher to make an appeal to common sense. Indeed, as in politics and other spheres of conceptual dispute, the appeal is frequent and may even provide a master trope for philosophical argumentation. Because there is, as Montaigne reminded us, nothing so absurd that some philosopher has not thought it, it has long been the habit of philosophers to decry the excesses and absurdities of their predecessors. This is most commonly, and most easily, accomplished by showing (or anyway saying) that the predecessor has deviated from common sense in some ridiculous manner.

'From Descartes onwards,' says Jonathan Rée, 'the habit of decrying the wayward voyages of old philosophers who, as represented by Milton, "found no end, in wandering mazes lost," became a pervasive mannerism of philosophical writing; and it enabled philosophical authors to make an intriguing invitation to their readers, that they join a democratic, commonsensical alliance against the baseless, self-deceiving conspiracy which philosophers had imposed upon an over-indulgent public opinion in the past.'[10] The starting point Rée chooses ('from Descartes onwards') is not idle. For it is characteristic of philosophy in the mood inaugurated by Descartes – a mood where the possibility of perceptual error is a great

enemy – that questions of doubt and certainty, partiality and
generality, assume an awful importance. Appeals to common
sense, then, assume an authoritative status in what can be
called traditional epistemology, the branch – though mood,
again, is better – of philosophy in which knowledge is thought
to be (required to be) both certain and general. As we shall see
shortly, to just the extent that this thought (or requirement) is
present, so is the spectre of scepticism: but not now of the plain
or common-sense variety.

In my view, claims to accord with common sense really perform a rhetorical role even greater than that suggested by Rée.
For, in addition to distancing themselves (often, though not
always, explicitly) from earlier or anyway other systems of
firm knowledge, they also distance themselves (often, though
not always, implicitly) from suggestions that firm knowledge
cannot be had. Thus, to take one prominent example, we have
Bishop Berkeley's much-quoted avowal: 'I side in all things
with the mob,' he says, pledging himself 'to eternally banish-
ing Metaphisics, &c., and recalling Men to Common Sense.'
Lest this statement appear incongruous with Berkeley's celebrated idealism, one has only to recall that a thesis about the
grounds or dependency of knowledge may, possibly should,
in no way affect the contents of knowledge. The reader of Berkeley who doubts his sanity with respect to the presence of the
table in front of us (as students are sometimes inclined to) has
failed to see that the *metaphysical* claim he makes is not only
not in conflict with the *commonsensical* claim, but is in fact
dependent on it.

Hence, to the extent that they attempt to provide solid
grounds for belief or knowledge, and not change or perhaps
even challenge the content of it, all metaphysical claims
revolve on appeals of greater or lesser degree to the status and
authority of plain common sense. George Pappas notes that
both realism and idealism can therefore be of the common-
sense variety, claiming (a) that common-sense propositions
are, in their own sphere, true and certain; and (b) that common
sense is a reliable criterion for assessing metaphysical theories,

if not the sole or strongest criterion.[11] Divergences in metaphysical commitment result not from variable views of common sense as such, but rather from variation on what to do
with it, what to make of it, how to relate it to truth or how
things really are. In Berkeley's case, *versions* of the two claims
are accepted. He might, of course, quibble that it makes no
sense to speak of 'truth' or 'certainty' within the common-
sense sphere, but he certainly does not doubt the stability of
the mob's view of things for their purposes. He might also add
that, given this, common sense can be only a *touchstone* to
metaphysical evaluation, not a strict determinant. In short,
Berkeley's 'weak' common-sense metaphysical view entails
that philosophy should accord with common sense only if it is
also already superior to its metaphysical rivals in offering
greater explanatory ability. Put oppositely, metaphysics should
only contradict common sense when it thereby provides a
superior explanation of the world's true nature.

'Strong' common-sense claims will argue by contrast that,
given common sense's presumptive truth, anything that does
not accord with common sense must be false, and cannot be
countenanced in a metaphysics. Thus the no-nonsense realism
of Thomas Reid, the Scottish 'common-sense' philosopher who
wished to tie all metaphysical judgments to the putative
authority of common sense, is only the most extreme version
of a philosophical strategy intrinsic to all metaphysical system-
building. That extremism is dangerous, though, for it can lead
to contradictions: common sense may change, or be effectively
reformed by science. And a variable realism no longer looks so
hard-nosed and sensible. Reid makes the mistake of thinking
that common sense is a firm category and therefore a suitable
sole basis for his philosophical position. But '[t]he common-
sense view of the world is a mass of contradictions,' Sprigge
reminds us, 'and one who wants to know how things really are
must move on from common sense, to some view of the world
which will clash with it at points. Since common sense clashes
with itself the requirement of consistency with common sense
rules out common sense itself.'[12] Like the scientist, the respon-

sible metaphysician *begins* with how things appear and moves from there to how things really are, based on a theory that is, by degrees, more or less responsive to the imagined firmness of the original appearance. Or, put in different philosophical vocabulary, the philosopher begins with the *contents* of common-sense beliefs and from there moves to query the *grounds* of those beliefs, hoping either to establish the firmness of those grounds or discover the manner in which belief of some (any) kind could be firmly grounded.

Thus it has always been philosophically fair to claim that, though the table appears to be really out there in front of us, it is not (i.e., not really). Or that, though we believe the table to be there, we do not know it (or know it justifiably). What it is *not* fair to claim is that the table does not even appear to be there, that we don't believe it to be. That claim is insane. *Of course the table is there; open your eyes and look!* Metaphysical systems may bring on themselves all manner of tortuous apparatus and system machinery in a drive to say how things really stand; but if they do not, at some level, begin with how things commonsensically stand, they are no good even as metaphysics. The traditional appearance/reality distinction and the more nuanced contents/grounds of belief distinction are, from this point of view, versions – perhaps the governing ones – of the move from the plain to the philosophical.

In sum, responsiveness to common sense, true to philosophical argumentation's overarching strategy of claiming to side with the mob against absurdity, is a necessary condition of a successful metaphysics, though (as the example of Reid shows) it is not a sufficient condition.[13] Singer puts the matter this way: 'Although a metaphysics too literally attached to [common sense] may be false as metaphysics, no metaphysics that contradicts it *in its context and about its proper business* can be true.'[14] Still, metaphysics often invites misunderstanding as a result of its alleged responsiveness to common sense, and it may in addition be motivated by urges that can be (should be?) resisted. Common sense, it is commonly thought, remains unimpressed by, and shows no need of, the saving systems constructed by metaphysics to save or explain it. It has no desire to move outside itself, and consequently its impatient replies to the metaphysician are usually on the order that he or she is not an advanced thinker but, in fact, a fool. You argue that there is no table really there? I just told you there was. How do I know? I opened my eyes and there it was before me. What – of what peculiar kind – is your problem?

Speaking now diagnostically, the metaphysician's problem is a *philosophical* one, and like many others of the same kind, it has the peculiarity that it cannot be felt to be a problem unless one has already assumed the one and only odd position from which it can arise as a problem. Put another way: to get the plain man to see a problem with his common sense is already to demand a surrender of his plainness in favour of the philosophical, a surrender he will resist insofar as he has common sense. What is the problem with untutored common sense? That it does not see its own weakness – but therein lies also its strength. Common-sense metaphysics, and metaphysics of many other kinds, are from this vantage responses to a certain kind of vulnerability that is felt to exist in plain common sense – but felt only philosophically.

What is that vulnerability? It is that common sense is not immune from a sceptical challenge of Cartesian provenance – not the dubiety of our senses on certain occasions (for we have common-sense, and also scientific, ways of dealing with that), but rather the dubiety that can arise even in cases of otherwise perfectly clear knowledge, namely that I might be dreaming, or might be a brain in a vat.[15] It is understanding the true force of this doubt, understanding it in a sense where it cannot simply be waved impatiently away, that motivates the metaphysician.

Yet here, as it has often been remarked, especially in the recent diagnostic moods of philosophy, the metaphysician cannot succeed. In order to refute the doubt introduced by Descartes, the metaphysician must resort to just the sort of system which common sense will find hard to countenance. Berkeley siding with the mob is all very well, but they will want none of him and his principled anti-realism. The low opinion of the common-sense world would be a small price to pay in exchange for certain knowledge of that world. But it is the worse fate of the metaphysician to find that all quests for certainty will of necessity fail to rid themselves of the doubt introduced by Descartes. Any degree of knowledge that falls short of laying to rest the dreaming doubt cannot be called certain; and that doubt cannot, in the sense imagined by Descartes (i.e., under conditions of perfect knowledge, while I otherwise think myself clear-headed and with eyes peeled), be laid to rest.[16] The ingenuity of metaphysicians in seeking this good riddance of doubt may know no bounds, but their efforts are Sisyphean. Metaphysician and sceptic are locked in eternal struggle, a dance to the death that shall consume them both in claim and counterclaim.

No wonder, then, that the common-sense response to these disputes of traditional epistemology has been to leave the disputants to their own perverse devices and desires. There are, after all, lives to be led, houses to be built, meals to be savoured, warm afternoons to be enjoyed in good company. And who, in his right mind anyway, could doubt that the world is right where it appears to be, moreover is *really* there, and requires no defence and succumbs to no challenge? Who could doubt that I am here, and so are others like me? That we have been in the past and will continue to be, though not for long, in the future? Though common sense might not put it this way, traditional epistemology is language on extended holiday, a long and fruitless journey to a world other than this one, a fanciful Club Med of the mind.

III The Plain Man

This plain impatience with the traditional philosopher becomes the plain patience of Moore in his 'Defence' and 'Proof.' But here the complications of plain and philosophical proceed in a reverse direction: not the metaphysician who claims plain authority for his system (like Berkeley or Reid), but the system-busting plain man who inexplicably writes as a philosopher.

Moore convincingly shows that common sense of the plain variety is immune from the sceptical challenge, and concomitantly is uninterested in the system-building of the metaphysician. For Moore, as for common sense generally, these two warring figures are two sides of the same foreign coin. And yet Moore's defence, and his proof, are generated by a philosophical intelligence, given philosophical window dressing of the usual kind (rigour, argumentation, plodding qualification), and ultimately thought to be philosophically worth saying. He says his 'philosophical position' is that certain common-sense propositions are ones he 'knows, with certainty, to be true.'[17]

These are, with some variation, the propositions I enumerated earlier. Moore's 'defence' of these propositions is to point out what we might call a 'performative contradiction' in those who persist in denying them. Any philosopher who has, for example, denied the existence of what are usually called 'other minds' has at the same time assumed their existence in the people he is addressing. Moreover, because the propositions of common sense are known, with certainty, to be true, they cannot be consistently denied. 'Some philosophers,' he says, therefore find themselves in the unenviable position of affirming some (metaphysical) propositions that are incompatible with common sense, even while they *must* at the same time affirm the propositions of common sense.

Matters are likewise in Moore's 'proof' of the external world. Here the existence of external objects is proven by demonstrating that we know at least two external things exist, namely my left hand and my right hand. I prove it by saying 'Here is one hand' (with a suitable gesture) and adding – though this is really philosophical overkill – 'Here is another' (gesturing now with my other hand). Since we know this is a hand, to offer it to view is to *prove* its existence: that is, to generate a conclusion that is not contained in the premises, and goes beyond them.

It is with this 'going beyond' the premises that the picture begins to get confusing. Our dissatisfaction with Moore's sleight of hand is the clue to this confusion, for it is only here that it is obvious just how Moore has failed to hit the mark in his remarks.[18] The problem, I take it, is not so much with him as with the status of the claim he thinks he is refuting. But Moore shares the blame in thinking that the sceptical claim (which may not be one) is even capable of refutation in the way assumed. In short, by ceasing *for even one moment* to be the plain man (the patience he displays is evidence of this ceasing), Moore succeeds only in giving his remarks a peculiar plain/philosophical status that is no better (though no worse) than the peculiar plain/philosophical character of the traditional epistemologist's remarks. Moore protests too much. Instead of offering a philosophical defence where one is neither needed nor possible, Moore might have been better advised to introduce his metaphysical foe to a sceptic, and sent them both off to another room.

I believe the picture of Moore is therefore relevantly as Clarke sees it. Moore, 'the inveterate plain man,' is fending off doubts that from the point of view of common sense are not serious: 'these implained doubts are ignorable – either absurd, irrelevant, or out of place.'[19] Yet Moore's foible is to attempt a defence of common sense in terms of very general propositions (that is, propositions of philosophical common sense). This attempt leads him beyond the security of the plain. He can – he must – be forgiven. It is not simply Moore's desire to philosophize that led him astray, but the nature of common sense itself. '[U]nder a certain conception of common sense,' says Clarke, 'reality exceeds this daydream' of a plain man simply defeating always implained doubts. Our view from the plain extends past its limits, in other words, and this of necessity. Here we have not only the roots of the sceptical problem, but also the first indication that common sense is, contrary to common sense, not immune from doubt *from its own standpoint*.

How does reality exceed the plain, and in what sort of direction? Consider Clarke's misleading and misled plane spotters, who discern features of warplanes on the basis of partial information. From the position of greater information (knowledge of a little-used type of airplane, similar in most respects to another), certain judgments of the spotters begin to appear doubtful. Though for practical (military) purposes the spotters do not need to know of the additional possibility – the little-used airplane is not as threatening as its near-twin – it is nevertheless the case that grounds for doubt can be introduced. But only, of course, from the position that is detached from those practical purposes.

Clarke and Barry Stroud believe the sceptical doubt is like this: a function of a detachment view of objectivity. It is only in wanting to step back, and back again, and again, that Descartes's dreamer enters the picture. As Clarke puts it: 'We want to know not how things are *inside* the world, but how things are, absolutely. And the world itself is one of these things.'[20] The desire to detach from practical purposes, and therefore from all imaginable contexts, is the engine that drives Cartesian doubt. (Certainty and doubt always come together, two modalities of the same desire.) It is the peculiar virulence of the sceptic's challenge that, though it arises only at the furthest reaches of the backward dance, it appears to have an effect on all subordinate positions too. That is, philosophical doubt casts aspersions on all knowledge, though not usually for practical purposes. Hence drawing the line of doubt from context to context, and out of all context – the move from partial to general to universal – is tantamount to surrendering the certainty common sense led us to believe we had.

Is this a false trail, however? Is the line really connected, or is the philosopher instead doing something so different from the plane spotters that imagining the wider circles of possibility is a mug's game, the pathology of some few twisted minds? We may be inclined to think so. If we just say no to objectivity (of the detached sort), can we not forestall doubt at just that point where we might otherwise threaten to tumble into the dreaming question? Then the question looks mad, or ill posed, or abusive of grammar, or falsely motivated, or excessively general – in short, a fetish of a strange minority of the population, deviant and ignorable. In Stroud's example, a party guest, told another guest has just seen a goldfinch in the garden, is moved to ask 'How does he know he's not dreaming?' We might take this as a feeble joke, of the kind often enough made at philosophy parties. If the guest were to persist in her question, however, past the point where we all laughed dutifully in recognition of her attempt at wit, we might begin to wonder just what was wrong. Was she ill? Tired? Or worse, gone off her rocker?

Yet these responses will not do, ultimately, in laying her question to rest – though we may lay *her* to rest in a quiet corner. Certainly her question is indeed ill posed, perhaps pathological, in this context. But there is little question that we can pose her question otherwise, in other places, in a way that makes it immune from routine dismissal. Doing philosophy is one of these ways, perhaps the only one. For this reason, the impatience of some ordinary-language philosophy, confronted with a sceptic, begins to look similar to Moore's patient handwaving. Yet, because ordinary-language philosophy is still philosophical, it is subject to the same limitations as Moore, ultimately locking itself in an eternal struggle of claim and counterclaim.

It is Stanley Cavell's genius to describe this moment in the struggle over common sense, to suggest that the recovery of the ordinary is more problematic than the brisk ordinary-language philosopher sometimes assumes. (Scepticism's legacy, as Clarke suggests, may lie in its ability to force us to come to grips with, give a better characterization to, the plain.) What, after all, is the basis of a claim to ordinariness? It is trivial, but true, to say that the ordinary-language claim is always already extraordinary, just as Moore's common sense is already too uncommon to avoid philosophical countercharge. Hume argued that, to recover the world we all know, one had to work through the false metaphysics of his predecessors; it was not enough merely to start with the everyday and remain there. Why not? Why not, from another vantage, simply dispense with the quest for certainty, the drive to detach, that leads us down that well-trodden garden path of doubt?

The reason, I think, is clear. Common sense itself demands it, rests happy with nothing less. The line of back-stepping is contained in the very claim to certainty of itself that makes common sense commonsensical. Do we know that the world is out there? Of course we do. Is it really there, are you certain? Of course I am. How do you know you're not dreaming? ... I may reply that I simply know, or that I've just awoken, or I pinched myself: but these are all consistent with the dreaming possibility. It is possible, as Clarke argues, that 'we are forced winetasters of the conceivable' and will therefore reach the limits of what we can imagine, where the detached doubter will begin to collapse in on himself. Stroud does not think so, partly because his hard objectivity is consistent with all of us being dreamers, with no one around to say so, or stand where one could say so. True detachment means never having to say (never having to have at least one agent who can say) the rest are dreamers. And that is precisely the version of objectivity contained in common sense. Common sense is a time bomb of certainty whose own desires set it always on auto-destruct.

IV Irony

The plain truth about common sense, then, is that it cannot restrict itself to the plain. That is also, I think, the philosophical truth about common sense. Common sense is not, contrary to itself, immune from sceptical doubt in its own sphere, or from its own inbuilt instability. The plain and the philosophical run together whenever we stop to speak of the plain, whenever common sense pauses to say anything about itself. Moore's dilemma is therefore ours. Common sense appears to entail, in its nature, what Stroud calls 'the conditional truth of scepticism': if the Cartesian question can be posed, it leads to doubt of a kind we cannot coherently master, or defeat. Can the question be posed? Or better, must it be? Or is the real question ultimately, as Hume suggested, one of how to *live with* our (always inevitable) scepticism, given that we cannot *live* it? Is philosophy, and common sense too, always about forging deals with doubt?

Consider two possibilities. Stroud concludes his assessment of scepticism's philosophical significance, after demonstrating the inadequacy of Kantian and Carnapian (i.e., very roughly, both metaphysical *and* anti-metaphysical) strategies of defeating the sceptic,[21] with a claim made current by Cavell: the 'not fully natural' nature of the sceptic's doubt, evident in our reactions to it, resides in its having been made in 'a non-claim context.' This is not to say what the ordinary-language philosopher sometimes says, namely, that the doubt simply cannot be raised (there is no context for raising it). That objection to the sceptic is only useful, I suggested, in locking the ordinary-language philosopher and the sceptic in a mortal, and unwinnable, battle. Talking that way, they talk past each other: 'What do you mean I cannot (we don't ordinarily) talk that way? I just did.' The context in which the dreaming doubt is raised is the philosophical, and while we may be inclined to call the move to that context pathological or perverse, it remains to be explained why so many otherwise responsible people go there so often and stay there so long. We cannot explain the philosopher away by claiming that 'we' do not ordinarily talk that way.[22] Philosophical appeals to the ordinary cannot be authoritative if they are merely appeals to what *we* consider worth, or not worth, saying.

Cavell notes that such appeals are really about making sense, about the relation of speech-act to the sphere of its occurrence. And he concludes from this that the philosophical context is an odd one, perhaps the oddest.[23] The oddness lies in the kind of desire that operates here, the desire that finds the dreaming doubt so necessary and so difficult. At work here is the philosophical desire for *completeness* (knowledge of the whole world – that is why, for example, the philosopher's chosen object is always a generic macro-object, a table or chair and not, say, a Louis XV gilt escritoire); and for *certainty* (sure knowledge of the world). Though Cavell finds this desire natural enough – the philosopher is not making the simple-minded error of perversely raising standards of knowledge too high to be met, or twisting language to his own malicious purposes; he is somehow compelled to raise these doubts – the investigation it leads to is, as a result of its peculiar context, locked in a dilemma.

The traditional investigation of knowledge, Cavell says, 'must be the investigation of a concrete claim if its procedure is to be coherent; it cannot be the investigation of a concrete claim if its conclusion is to be general. Without that coherence it would not have the obviousness it has seemed to have; without that generality its conclusion would not be skeptical.'[24] The dilemma is captured by the suggestion that 'the example the philosopher is forced to focus upon is considered in a non-claim context,'[25] and therefore can never be vindicated coherently. Thus the inherent *instability* of the philosopher's position, which oscillates between a desire for certainty and the debilitating doubt that comes with it. The only thing that can or should be said in response is that the philosopher is no longer making sense. He is being odd in a way that incidentally demonstrates the dispensability of doubting. For, though the desire to be certain and complete may be natural, it is not necessary: the philosopher discovers nothing about the world, only finds what he has put there.

We will be inclined, I think, to regard this as a rather hollow victory (Cavell himself only hazards that he might be willing to call it a 'refutation').[26] Commonsensically, the *oddness* of the sceptic has never been very far from view, and gaining some fine-tuning on that oddness does not lay to rest the power of philosophical doubt as long as we share even a vestige of the desire that brought it on. That is, as long as we presume a common-sense world that is really out there existing, the dreaming doubt will have a hold on us. At most, Cavell has succeeded in getting rid of an unwelcome party guest; but her odd question hangs in the air, disturbing us whenever we pause to remember it. We can ignore the sceptic, put her doubts aside for now, even think she is crazed and peculiar; but for common sense the doubt she has raised will, now and then, arise as something that makes sense. And insofar as that is true, no genuine and final refutation of the doubt is possible.

It is for reasons like these, among others, that Quine attempted to naturalize epistemology[27] and Rorty felt compelled to argue that the world was something well lost.[28] For it is only by dispensing with the very desires for completeness and certainty about our knowledge that the grounds for doubt are systematically removed. It is only by no longer seeking the world through ever-better descriptions (i.e., descriptions that approach greater correspondence to what is out there, or even greater coherence among claims about what is out there)[29] that we can free ourselves from the shackles of Cartesian doubt and, as Wittgenstein suggests, stop doing philosophy when we want to. In the terms of a later discussion the problem is, according to Rorty, the following:

> ever since Plato we have been asking ourselves the question: what must we and the universe be like if we are going to get the sort of certainty, clarity, and evidence Plato told us we ought to have? Each stage in the history of metaphysics – and in particular the Cartesian turn toward subjectivity, from exterior to interior objects of inquiry – has been an attempt to redescribe things so that this certainty might become possible.

But each of these attempts has failed, getting us no closer to the imagined world of true knowledge we set out to find. 'The only things that are really evident to us' in this long history of fruitless searching, says Rorty, 'are our own desires.'[30]

It follows from this, I think, that the philosophical quest for a general theory of knowledge is similarly up for retirement. For it was the desire to provide such a theory that, according to Stroud, underwrote the worst excesses of the metaphysician. The desire for generality and certainty that generates scepticism is not a desire that arises for practical purposes, only for philosophical ones.[31] The theoretical part of this desire, the wish to codify and defend, is not commonsensical – indeed, it is partly in opposition to theorizing that common sense remains commonsensical, happily implained as Clarke says. Is this *theorizing* wish the wish to be cured, then? This too may seem a little too easy. Philosophy in this charming therapeutic mood may appear simply to be waving a magic wand or the healing hands of a televangelist ('Evil metaphysical delusions ... come out!'). What is of lasting interest is the diagnosis concerning the impulses and desires, including those of cleaving to a tradition of inquiry, that lead us to the quandary characteristic of the sceptic's challenge. It is partly Rorty's willingness to look to other traditions, including the tradition of recovery associated with Husserl's reconstruction of the natural attitude and Heidegger's emphasis on everydayness, as well as the tradition of American pragmatism, that allows him to find his kind of anti-representationalism convincing.[32] There is also, not to be underestimated, an Ockhamist flavour to our salutary losing of the world: in terms of elegance and explanatory adequacy, Rorty's pragmatism and theses about contingency may be considered theoretically superior to the muddles of metaphysics.[33] (Whether they are superior on other counts is a separate question.)

Still, plain common sense will balk at this prospect of ironical (and therefore uncommon) common sense.[34] The sceptic's challenge seems to induce a kind of epistemological vertigo, but so does Rorty's dispensing with the world. Whither the firmness of my ordinary experience? Are we doomed, philosophically, to find the world dissolving between our fingers, either in sceptical doubts or (little better) in cheerful anti-foundationalism? Is this, perhaps, just another reason why common sense should steer clear of philosophers, those malpracticing surgeons of the obvious? Cultivate irony, someone could suggest, for we cannot avoid acting just as though the world is already out there now. But what advance is this over the sociability of Hume, never troubling to doubt in the midst of backgammon? Both attitudes, underwritten by a putative recovery of the everyday on the other side of philosophizing, may leave the commonsensical cold. Yet how can they be avoided without compromising our very common-sense awareness of the world? Can we simply keep our heads down, ostrich-like, and get on with things, untroubled?

Common sense would have us think so, but on this count, as on others, it is at war with itself. I suggested earlier that philosophical systems built on appeals to common sense were not structurally sound; on the other hand, no straightforward philosophical defence of the propositions of common sense could hope to succeed. Such defences might even be systematically incoherent, arguing specifics in terms of generalities or mixing the plain with the philosophical. Now it seems likewise true that no common-sense avoidance of philosophy can hope to succeed, for the drive to philosophize is inscribed in common sense, even (or especially) when it is most strenuously avoiding the quagmires of philosophy. Philosophical appeals to common sense – both Berkeley's and Reid's sort, and Moore's very different sort – are not stable. But this is because common sense itself is not stable, not because philosophy and common sense have nothing to say to each other. Quite the contrary: they have, perhaps to the chagrin of both, all too much.

So I am moved to say, in conclusion, that the plain truth about common sense is ... we have no way of talking philosophically about it. The recurring oddness and confusion of our attempts so to talk stem from the dual fact that the plain actively resists philosophical defence (indicating a decisive break between the two realms), and yet inevitably demands the philosophical whenever plain-dwellers stop to think (indicating a continuity between them). The image of vertigo is well chosen: it's not simply that our heads spin when we pause to think about the world and our knowledge of it; more to the present point, we can only avoid that spinning by not looking down, not pausing to think about the status of our common-sense achievement, but instead walking blithely on, eyes front.

It is true that for most people, most of the time, this blitheness comes naturally. They put one foot in front of another without apparent effort. Some of us, cursed with a peculiar kind of curiosity, will insist on gazing into the abyss. Our best hope then is that we can, though unavoidably dizzy, avoid falling into it – and do so in interesting ways. I hope, plainly, that this has been one of them.

Notes

1 This objection to Paine's tract may remind other readers of a different text, the magazine of that name distributed by an organization called The Worldwide Church of God.
2 Thompson Clarke, 'The Legacy of Skepticism,' *Journal of Philosophy* 69 (1972): 754–69. Clarke's central example of pragmatic scepticism concerns the issue of plane spotters attempting to distinguish between near-identical silhouettes of two enemy airplanes, one lethal and one harmless.
3 G.E. Moore, 'A Defence of Common Sense,' in *Philosophical Papers* (London: Allen & Unwin, 1959), pp. 32–59. See also 'Proof of an External World,' in ibid., pp. 127–50.
4 Timothy Sprigge, 'Philosophy and Common Sense,' *Revue Internationale de Philosophie* 158 (1986), p. 204.
5 Marcus Singer, 'Ethics and Common Sense,' *Revue Internationale de Philosophie* 158 (1986), p. 227. I am also indebted to Singer's analysis in this paper of folklore as 'common nonsense.'
6 I think, however, that Singer is convincing on the point that this species of common sense has a considerable moral significance. This is true of the 'sensus communis' thinkers discussed, for example, by H.-G. Gadamer in *Truth and Method*, trans. Garrett Barden and John Cumming (New York: Crossroad, 1988), I, 1, i.e., Vico and Shaftesbury; it may be equally true, in the guise of the virtue *phronesis*, of Aristotle.
7 Herbert Fingarette, 'Insanity and Responsibility,' *Inquiry* 15 (1972): 6–29.
8 L.T. Hobhouse, *The Theory of Knowledge* (London: Methuen, 1896), p. 377.
9 William James, *Pragmatism* (New York: Longmans, Green & Co., 1907), pp. 181, 182.

10 Jonathan Rée, 'The Story of Philosophy,' in *Philosophical Tales* (London: Methuen, 1987), p. 41.

11 George Pappas, 'Common Sense in Berkeley and Reid,' *Revue Internationale de Philosophie* 158 (1986): 292–303.

12 Sprigge, 'Philosophy and Common Sense,' p. 203.

13 A failure to appreciate this instance of necessity/sufficiency has led some metaphysicians to discard common sense too quickly. 'Very little can be done with common sense,' said C.D. Broad. 'Any theory that can fit the facts is certain to shock common sense somewhere; and in face of the facts we can only advise common sense to follow the example of Judas Iscariot, and "go out and hang itself"' (*The Mind and Its Place in Nature* [London; Routledge & Kegan Paul, 1925], pp. 184–6). Or compare F.H. Bradley's pronouncement that 'I see no way ... by which the clear thinking which calls itself "Common Sense" and is satisfied with itself, can ever be reconciled with metaphysics ... And for "Common Sense" also it will remain that we shall be able to live only so far as, wherever we feel it to be convenient, we can forget to think' (*Essays on Truth and Reality* [Oxford: Clarendon Press, 1914], p. 444). What is distinctive about these complaints is that they arise from the philosophical realm – where one is in possession of 'the facts' – looking back on the plain from which they have only just come.

14 Singer, 'Ethics and Common Sense,' p. 234. The italics in the quotation are mine – this phrase, I want to say, captures what the plainness of plain common sense is all about.

15 Rée says, of the latter possibility, that of course we *are* brains in vats. Our vats happen to be bodies situated in the world. I take it that the point of saying this is to show that the force of the Cartesian doubt does not depend on a peculiar science-fiction imagination, or the 'intuition-pumping' efficiency of some ingenious thought-experiment.

16 This dilemma of certain knowledge has been much remarked on, and it is, among other things, what Barry Stroud means by *The Significance of Philosophical Scepticism* (Oxford: Clarendon Press, 1984), esp. ch. 1. Stroud's study is a book-length reply and commentary on Clarke's 'Legacy of Skepticism.' See also Stanley

Cavell, *The Claim of Reason* (New York: Oxford University Press, 1979), chs. 6 and 8.

17 Moore, 'A Defence of Common Sense,' p. 32.

18 Thomas Nagel (in *The View from Nowhere* [Oxford: Oxford University Press, 1986], p. 69) expresses this dissatisfaction by saying that Moore, confronted with the epistemological abyss between the content of belief and grounds of it, turned his back and announced he was on the other side.

19 Clarke, 'The Legacy of Skepticism,' p. 755.

20 Ibid., p. 762.

21 I cannot here provide the details of these demonstrations, but put briefly: Kantian transcendentalism, which attempts to save empirical certainty with idealism at another level, can provide no motive for its two-worlds thesis independent of its desire to defeat the sceptic. Likewise with Carnap's verificationism, which cannot adequately take account of the objective world – that is, the reality of a world independent of our verifications. Stroud's insistent realism, which underwrites both criticisms, may certainly be challenged, but it *is* consistent with common sense.

22 This summary undersells the force of ordinary-language responses to the figure J.L. Austin calls 'the wily metaphysician.' In 'Other Minds' (*Philosophical Papers* [Oxford: Clarendon Press, 1979], pp. 76–116), Austin makes the point with the subtlety it deserves: the metaphysician's claim, and the sceptic's attendant doubt of the claim, are 'outrageous' because they never specify in what sense 'real' or 'certain' is meant in their tussles; no conditions are given which could possibly satisfy the claim, and therefore the claim is not sensible. Cavell's discussion is predicated on the force, as well as the limitations, of this view.

23 Cavell's debt to Wittgenstein is evident here, though he seems insistent in the Preface to *The Claim of Reason* that he has not looked at Wittgenstein's remarks in *On Certainty*, and relies instead on thoughts gleaned from *Philosophical Investigations*. Wittgenstein at times seems to make the apparently ordinary-language claim that the sceptic's doubts are not 'real' – i.e., they cannot be sensibly raised (though 'unreal' and 'senseless' may be different notions). It is this claim that fuels criticism of Moore's

argument provided by followers of Wittgenstein, notably Norman
Malcolm. Stroud (*The Significance of Philosophical Scepticism*, ch. 3)
gives a good defence of Moore against these claims that he is
doing something hasty, illjudged, dogmatic, or linguistically
incorrect. For a comparison of Wittgenstein and Moore on the
issue of whether the sceptic's doubt is senseless, see Alan R.
White, 'Common Sense: Moore and Wittgenstein,' *Revue Internationale de Philosophie* 158 (1986): 313–32.

24 Cavell, *The Claim of Reason*, p. 220. I am not able here to give
Cavell's enormously suggestive and nuanced account of the
ordinary-language/scepticism encounter its due. In its depth of
detail and witty attention to the integrity of conflicting positions,
it is the best such account in the literature.

25 Ibid., p. 218.

26 Ibid., p. 223.

27 See Quine, 'Epistemology Naturalized,' in *Word and Object*. Quine
argues that the detachment view of knowledge is incoherent:
'There is no such cosmic exile' as the detached viewer, he says.
The reason is simple – we cannot ever stand elsewhere than in our
own standpoint. The image of Neurath's ship is a favourite here:
the world, like the mythical sailing vessel, can be rebuilt in places,
but never from the ground up, and we can never stand elsewhere
than on it. From this point of view, the sceptic is not *incoherent*,
he's simply *overreacting*. (See Stroud, *The Significance of Philosophical Scepticism*, ch. 6.)

28 Richard Rorty, 'The World Well Lost,' *Journal of Philosophy* 69
(1972): 649–65.

29 Rorty suggests that a correspondence theory must be abandoned
as a result of its failure to gain true access to the real world (the
metaphysical project, or in typical Rortian caricature, 'Platonism').
A coherence theory must likewise be abandoned because it is in
fact predicated on pragmatist desires – desires to cope better with
ourselves-in-environment.

30 Richard Rorty, 'Heidegger, Contingency, and Pragmatism,' in
Essays on Heidegger and Others, Philosophical Papers Vol. 2 (Cambridge: Cambridge University Press, 1991), p. 29. Rorty suggests
that, since 'Plato set things up so that epistemological skepticism

would become the recurrent theme of philosophical reflection' (p. 32), the only choice lay between Platonism and some sort of Deweyan pragmatism. He sees Heidegger as torn by the choice – unable to accept Platonism, yet unwilling to accept pragmatism wholeheartedly. As elsewhere, Rorty counsels us to relax and accept pragmatism – including the 'contingency' of our moral and philosophical vocabularies – without unnecessary (and futile) hair-pulling about losing the reality of the real world.

31 This is perhaps overly crude. Rorty himself, in 'Cavell on Skepticism' (in *Consequences of Pragmatism* [Minneapolis: University of Minnesota Press, 1982], pp. 176–90), criticizes Cavell for conflating three *different* versions of the sceptical challenge: (a) the technical, Reid/Berkeley worries generated when perception is analysed in terms of a 'theory of ideas'; (b) the Kantian worries about whether we can overcome the gap between the world and our descriptions/knowledge of it; and (c) a 'Sartrean' worry that incomplete knowledge generates a contingency about the world, which we find threatening. Rorty chides Cavell (pp. 180–3) for not seeing that, though there may be a link between (b) and (c), there is no obvious one between (a) and (b) – certainly not simply because there is one between (b) and (c). But Rorty is being too reductive: there is no prima facie reason against seeing (a) as a species of a more general worry. Cavell's problem in *The Claim of Reason* isn't, as Rorty suggests, that he is hung up on certain 'classic' philosophical positions; Rorty's problem is that he doesn't want to see these 'Anglo-Saxon' positions as part of the bigger picture.

32 Rorty's precise relationship to these traditions is not easy to nail down. For example, he wants to follow Heidegger's criticism of metaphysics some distance, part company with Heidegger on the question of pragmatism, and arrive at a position even more deeply historicized than Heidegger's own. See Part 1 of *Essays on Heidegger and Others*, especially 'Heidegger, Contingency, and Pragmatism,' pp. 27–49.

There is some misleading talk of 'common sense' in this last article. Rorty quotes Heidegger as equating common sense with sophistry, and contrasting true thinking with this sort of unquestioning refusal to 'hear the call of Being' in our language. Rorty agrees, only suggesting that we are not as bad (and the Greeks not as good) at challenging this sort of complacent common sense as Heidegger suggests. I believe this use of common sense as sophistical received opinion is not simply equatable with the 'basic knowledge' use I have adopted in this discussion, though there is a connection. Plain common sense does, to a large extent, succeed only by fending off the challenges of (philosophical) thinking. Yet, as I have been suggesting, this success is not stable, for thinking enters the picture like it or not.

33 The richness of this complex of theses, and their significance for political life, is suggested by Rorty's recent collection *Contingency, Irony, and Solidarity* (New York: Cambridge University Press, 1989).

34 Stroud notes, I think correctly, that Moore is decidedly not an ironical defender of common sense – and that is partly why Moore looks so odd to us. The oddness lies in, among other things, Moore's unwitting demonstration that philosophical defences of the plain are self-contradictory.

Husserl's Sense of Wonder

The experience of astonishment before the world – 'wonder' – demands serious investigation. That investigation may be hampered by vagueness, disagreement, or obscurity; and no final illumination may prove possible. But these difficulties have not deterred previous wonderers. Indeed, it is perhaps *because* of its lack of ultimate success that the investigation of wonder is so long-standing – at least as old as Plato and Aristotle, who held *thaumazein*, wonder at the fact of the world, to be the beginning of philosophy.

It is important for my present purposes, purposes that will emerge as we go along, that Edmund Husserl was occupied with wonder. Husserl believed he had found an enduring answer to the question of wonder in a return to 'the Greeks.' I want to examine that claim in what follows. Within Husserl's larger phenomenological project, there lies an illuminating but not final analysis of wonder as a threefold structure: the wonderer, the wonderful, and wondering as the relation between them. For Husserl, as for many others, wonder is the experience that prompts philosophy, a doorway to pure theory. But also like many others, Husserl's account of wonder faces difficulties of specificity and exactness. Because he failed to make much of his sense of wonder, we may frequently feel as though we are grasping at straws. And if we are to say what a phenomenology of wonder is, it will involve going beyond what Husserl has given explicitly.

In discussing Husserl's sense of wonder, then, this paper will address three general questions: (1) What have philosophers thought of wonder? (2) What is distinctive about Husserl's contribution to this thinking? And (3) what shortcomings are there in that contribution? The discussion will show that, because Husserl's analysis lacks specificity in saying what wonder is – especially in saying who the wonderer is – he remains unclear on the important relation between wonder, theory, and daily life. He also fails to work out in detail a phenomenology of wonder, a failure we may go some distance in remedying as part of a larger project of recovering a sense of wonder before the world.

The essay falls into six parts. I look first at a number of philosophical characterizations of wonder, in an attempt to say what wonder is and why it should concern us. Next, I rehearse Husserl's remarks, from *The Crisis of European Sciences* and the 'Vienna Lecture,' on the role of wonder in ancient Greece. The third section discusses in some detail Husserl's sense of crisis, which is bound intimately to his sense of philosophical history. Section IV then discusses his proposed solution to this crisis, and its shortcomings. I return in the fifth section to the specific role of wonder in that solution, while the sixth section attempts to set out – with all this background in place – the distinctive phenomenology of wonder suggested in Husserl's late work. Here, though Husserl himself has failed to say in much detail what wonder is, I think it is possible to offer an adequate interpretation in the spirit of Husserl. The route may appear circuitous, but I think it will become clear that what is distinctive about Husserl's 'sense of wonder' cannot be approached in any other fashion.

I Why Wonder?

Why should wonder be of any philosophical concern? And is there a single experience, or set of experiences, that the word describes? We may find that there is no consensus on these questions, partly because strict analysis of wonder is so difficult. Looking critically at the experience of astonishment may be something that began with (some) ancient Greeks – though this is a claim more often asserted than argued for – but wonder itself is not restricted to the intellectual and methodological heirs of those Greeks. The experience of wonder is, we might think, basic to human consciousness. In one of its most important manifestations, wonder prompts a question every child has asked, the same question Leibniz felt compelled to begin with: 'Why is there something rather than nothing?'[1] Most children, unlike Leibniz, are not encouraged to pursue the question and discover where their primitive sense of wonder can lead them. Most children, in other words, do not become philosophers: early wonderers at the fact of the world, they are trained to forget the questions that have no clear answers. The experience of wonder may continue to visit many, but pursuit of the question is left to a few.

Ernst Bloch notes this basic aspect of wonder, that it begins with the apparently naive but actually profound question. Philosophers are all children when it comes to the origin of that investigation now called philosophical; they must start from scratch. And while they may turn their investigation to particular, quite sophisticated purposes – thereby obscuring its origin and ground, perhaps as something embarrassing – its structure is still visible to those prepared to ask the child's question. But '[i]f the intellectual shock of first amazement, together with whatever provoked it, does not last,' Bloch says,

the unremitting uniqueness of the first question disappears ... [A]ll specific, particular and empirical questions are modifications of the unique impact of the basic wonder-arousing question. Admittedly, in their tangible substance they have become specific, but they are also estranged from their critical stimulus and concern. (PF, 7)[2]

This estrangement leads, as we shall see, to a series of problematical developments which culminate in Husserl's sense that the Western world is in a general state of crisis with regard to philosophy and science.

Bloch would not challenge such a claim in outline, but his emphasis differs. Without wanting to open up a detailed comparison of Bloch and Husserl, three things might be noted briefly. First, like many others, Bloch sees the origin of philosophizing in the experience of 'wonder and amazement, not merely at something, but at the that and the specific what of so much of the somewhat, and in its very midst' (PF, 4). Second, he notes that the effacement of the sign of this origin in the specific questioning of science has led to developments culminating in a radical and *in its own terms unsolvable* mind-body split. Third, then, humankind is suffering basic alienation from its own nature and possibilities – alienation which is not merely personal but threatens the vitality of a human future and of the peculiarly human 'principle of hope.' What we have lost is, at base, our regard for amazement, that 'more searching investigation' which occurs 'not so much in a difficult as in a strange environment that is not necessarily inconsistent with us – for often the reverse is true.' Bloch goes on: 'Precisely quite simple, even insignificant and transitory impressions can provoke the amazement in question, and start the cracks and crevices in ordinary, conventional perception' (PF, 4).

In losing our ability to be amazed in a strange environment, or indeed to see a familiar environment as sometimes very strange, we may have obscured the origin of philosophizing. But an obscuration of origin does not mean we have lost philosophy. Modern philosophy – now made traditional, ruled by convention, canonical – continues without full regard for the experience that gave it rise. Wonder, even if in reality the origin of philosophy, may not be considered an experience deserving philosophical attention. On the other hand, simple wonder cannot be viewed as sufficient of itself to be the philosophizing it sets in motion. The tradition, with its conventions and rules, must be evaluated *alongside* the experience of wonder. Such a tradition may be rejected as ossified, conservative, or misleading, as Husserl attempts to do, but it cannot simply be ignored. The relation between original wonder and theory as it now operates is thus more complicated than Bloch suggests here and, while his approach to the issues is pleasantly radical, it appears to lack context.

By contrast, the analytical philosopher Ronald Hepburn demonstrates how far one can investigate the experience of wonder within traditional conventions, without ever touching on the limits of philosophy or its world. True wonderment in its philosophical connotation, says Hepburn, must be distinguished from astonishment at 'mere novelty' – a distinction to be found not only in Kant (*Verwunderung* vs *Bewunderung*) but also in Heidegger (curiosity vs marvel). The thrust of Hepburn's distinction is thus that 'legitimate' wonder must always be wedded to a concern for truth, ultimate causes, reasons; the wonderer wonders only to the extent that he gets his 'real' inquiry going. 'Existential wonder' at the sheer facticity of the world may not be of legitimate interest, Hepburn suggests, since it opens up no set of reasons to be investigated. It is a kind of wonder, but not one that leads to anything further. In other words, Leibniz's question is one we may ask but from which we must expect no true propositions. What other philosophers have labelled the central experience of wonder – wonder at the world as simply there – Hepburn wants to set on one side as unworthy of serious philosophic interest. For him, the wondering Kant may remain enduringly in awe of the starry heavens above him and the moral law within, but he is not at the same time constantly astonished at the fact of the world.

But it is not obvious that existential wonder *cannot* prompt a new way of looking or awareness of the world. It is neither 'mere novelty' nor the sort of limited, specific wonder Hepburn wants to emphasize (what he calls, for instance, 'logical wonder'). Therefore, the stone that remains unturned in his careful analysis is the unacknowledged primacy of one's confrontation with the being of the world. Articulating at least seven different kinds of wonder – most of them concerned with obscured causes or the temporarily astonishing – Hepburn has only this to say about the kind of wonder which excites basic interest in less stringent wonderers:

> We can give no reason for the world's being rather than not being. We can meaningfully ask why it exists, but we have no resources for answering the question. Wonder is generated from this sense of absolute contingency; its object the sheer existence of a world. I shall call it 'existential wonder.' All reasons fall away: wondering is not a prelude to fuller knowledge, though the generalized interrogative attitude may persist. (W, 140)

There would appear to be some confusion in this. If such wonder is not a prelude to a fuller knowledge of causes, a clearer science, what is it? Hepburn allows that the 'generalized interrogative attitude' existential wonder excites may remain, but it is not clear what structure he sees operating here. Is this attitude what Husserl calls the 'theoretical attitude,' which he attributes first and foremost to a transformation of perspective 'beginning with a few Greek eccentrics' (VL, 289)? Or would Hepburn wish to place the motor of philosophizing in some other position, agreeing at least partially with Bacon that amazement is 'broken knowledge' and that, where possible, knowledge displaces it (W, 137)? Even allowing room for 'existential wonder,' this Baconian attitude – wonder not as the prelude to inquiry, but a deficient mode of it – would be wholly at odds with what Husserl, Bloch, and others wish to say about wonder.

Perhaps more to the point, it is an inadequate philosophical response to the difficulties wonder raises. As a pure experience, as simple astonishment at the fact of the world, wonder precedes both its flowering into philosophy and its investigation *by* philosophy. As I mentioned, our difficulty with wonder is not only that we have lost sight of it in the flush of investigative success – until, as Bloch writes, it ceases to be an investigation or even an experience we take seriously. We also must face the difficulty that wonder *by its very nature* is pre-theoretical. Of itself it is not equal to the task it inspires;

wonder and philosophy are related, but not identical. It is easy to see the source of Hepburn's difficulty, then, his sense that 'all reasons fall away.' But that does not justify his analytical response. True, wonder seems to defy our reason, seems to bring with it the ineffable and demand the mystic's silence. Wittgenstein placed the issues raised by wonder out of bounds in the *Tractatus*, stating: 'It is not *how* things are in the world that is mystical, but *that* it exists' (TLP, 6.44). Like Hepburn, the early Wittgenstein recognizes Leibniz's, and the child's, question as one that cannot be answered by philosophy as he conceives it. Propositions say nothing about *why* or *that* the world is, they only give us a picture of it in language.

'What we cannot speak about we must pass over in silence' is thus one way of responding to these difficulties (TLP, 7). Seven types of wonder is another. But more radical options exist, and here Bloch's investigation points the way. The crux of our apparent inability to talk about wonder lies not with wondering but with what we take as admitting of talk. And, if we must face the fact that wonder is fleeting, a different approach – Husserl's approach, broadly – may prove helpful. What is wonderful, Husserl suggests, is not simply the oak leaf I look at, making me wonder why there is not nothing, for this feeling soon ceases. *What is also wonderful is this experience of wondering itself, and myself as the person in whom astonishment before the world is felt.* Wonder invites not only investigation of the world, but also reflection on the subject who experiences it, and on his experience itself. In short, the phenomenon of astonishment cannot be seen as one aspect to the exclusion of others: 'wonder' is altogether the experience of wonder, the world it points to (as astonishing), and the subject who feels the astonishment.

What, then, can be said about wondering to conclude these first remarks? Even if no definite conclusions are yet available, it is clear that wonder is an experience worthy of investigation. Indeed, this may be an investigation all philosophers must occasionally undertake, to one degree or another. As mentioned, thinkers since Plato and Aristotle (and Descartes) have thought wonder the very origin of philosophy. Socrates advised his young pupil Theaetetus that philosophy could start nowhere else than in astonishment:

> Socrates: I fancy, at any rate, that such [logical] puzzles are not altogether strange to you.
> Theaetetus: No, indeed it is extraordinary how they set me wondering whatever they can mean. Sometimes I get quite dizzy with thinking of them.
> Socrates: That shows that Theodorus was not wrong in his estimate of your nature. This sense of wonder is the mark of the philosopher. Philosophy indeed has no other origin, and he was a good genealogist who made Iris the daughter of Thaumas.
> (*Theaetetus*, 155d)

The reference here is not entirely clear, since Socrates and Theaetetus are referring to logical problems of the kind that often get people interested in mathematics or logical theory. (In Hepburn's example, it is the kind of wonder that visits the person astonished to find that not one bachelor of his acquaintance is married.) But we need not restrict Socrates' remark so; indeed, the same dialogue provides us with a better image of the wondering that leads to philosophy: the young philosopher Thales who fell off the wall in his single-minded efforts to observe the stars.

As Heidegger noted, wonder is not mere curiosity or the desire for the novel (BT, 216 ff.). Thomas Aquinas thought it was a kind of desire for knowledge. Scientists from Bacon onward have thought it imperfect knowledge, though sometimes useful in starting one on the path to scientific truth. Always it has been dear to philosophers both amateur and professional. Gabriel Marcel said, 'A philosopher remains a philosopher only so long as he retains [the] capacity for wonderment ... despite everything ... that tends to dispel it.'[3] This statement accords with Husserl's strong sense, with the Greeks, that wonder is the origin and ground of the 'theoretical attitude.' I now turn to an examination of his thoughts on the subject.

II The Beginning of Origin: Wonder in Greece

Husserl's remarks on the role of wonder in the historical/ teleological coming-to-be of the Western world – which for him goes by the convenient name 'Europe' – are contained primarily in his May 1935 lecture to the Vienna Cultural Society on 'Philosophy in the Crisis of European Mankind,' now commonly known as the 'Vienna Lecture.' Here, as Husserl struggles to come to grips with his sense of crisis in science and philosophy, he is thrown back to ancient Greece as the source and guiding light of Western philosophizing.[4] And here he rediscovers wonder, what the Greeks called *thaumazein*, as a central notion for his phenomenological project. It would be too strong an assertion to say that wonder is the central concept of Husserl's phenomenology, but not perhaps to say that the world exposed by wonder, and the attitude shifts occasioned by it, are central. Without *thaumazein* there is no theoretical attitude, and hence no philosophizing; without philosophizing there is no thematization of the world as an object of investigation; without this investigation, in Husserl's view, there is no coming-to-be of humankind at large.

Husserl adopts the notions, unfashionable today, that Western humanity represents true human nature, and that without philosophy such a nature is never wholly realized. His sense of crisis, then, has to do with the fact that, for reasons we shall investigate below, even *with* philosophy that nature may fall short of fulfilment. The return to Greece is for him an effort to recover the original questions of philosophy and the attitude that went with them. It is a return that creates difficulties, not least (a) that it may prove impossible or undesirable, and (b) that Husserl's history of philosophy is highly prejudiced and inaccurate. There is no such group as 'the Greeks' who had a single notion of wonder and its relation to philosophy; nor is it obvious that, even if there was such a group, their notion of wonder is the one we should emphasize today.

These difficulties will show themselves in what follows. But what is the theoretical attitude Husserl sees beginning in basic wonder before the world? 'The theoretical attitude has its historical origin in the Greeks,' says Husserl, and it amounted to a 'thoroughgoing transformation,' 'the breakthrough of a completely new sort of spiritual structure' (VL, 279–80). This transformation of how individuals saw themselves in relation to the surrounding world grew rapidly 'into a systematically self-enclosed form; the Greeks called it philosophy' (VL, 276). The occasion for the alteration in attitude is *thaumazein*, wonder at the world the individual encounters. Husserl contrasts the theoretical attitude with an earlier norm to which it perforce refers back, 'the natural primordial attitude' – the world seen as ruled by mundanity, practicality, and the various goals and interests of everyday social living.

There is some confusion in Husserl's account of how these attitudes relate, and therefore where wonder fits in. He wants to say that the natural attitude is not wholly 'repudiated' or 'passed beyond' in the philosophical transformation; it is rather changed into new attitudes which, however important, are not possible without reference to the natural attitude. More deeply, he does not take the world of everyday to be illusory or deceptive; it is not *maya*. It is, in phenomenological terms, *unthematized*, unexamined in its primordiality. That examination comes only with phenomenology and its method of 'bracketing' the everyday in a series of *epochés*, or abstentions. I will return to this point later; for the moment let us observe the transformation for the Greeks of the natural attitude into the critical theoretical attitude.

Husserl refers to the change occasioned by wonder as a 'reorientation,' one which is limited and periodical. The first philosophers could not answer the 'call' to theorize at all times. They had to continue to live in the world, building ships, managing farms, trading goods, and so on. They could not help, however, the change that came over them in the way they regarded the world. Husserl suggests two paths open up:

One is that the interests of the new attitude are meant to serve the natural interests of life or, what is in essence the same thing, natural praxis ... But in addition to the higher-level practical attitude ... there exists yet another essential possibility for altering the general natural attitude, namely, the *theoretical attitude*. (VL, 282)

Vocational and impractical, the theoretical attitude suggests itself to the Greeks as a *critical* reorientation. It is not the thematization of the world which may take place within a mythical-religious attitude, that higher-level practical praxis bent to community needs. Rather it is the non-referential, anti-pragmatic attitude which thematizes the world *as such*, taking at first the form 'of the universal critique of all life and all life-goals, all cultural products and systems ... of mankind and of the values which guide it explicitly or implicitly' (VL, 283).

This general critique therefore follows from the experience of wonder, that foundational 'Why?' that stands like a brightly lit question mark over every aspect of the world and over the world as a totality. Husserl clarifies what is at stake here:

Man becomes gripped by the passion of a world-view and world-knowledge that turns away from all practical interests and ... strives for and achieves nothing but pure *theoria*. In other words, man becomes a non-participating spectator, surveyor of the world; he becomes a philosopher. (VL, 285)

How does this happen? How is the transformation effected from *thaumazein* felt within the natural attitude to the drive to increase theoria which *is* the theoretical attitude? What structure is in place here? Husserl states that this is of basic importance, yet there is little in the 'Vienna Lecture' or elsewhere to suggest his sense of the precise steps in the historical transformation. The only real evidence provided is a questionable argument by analogy. Husserl wants to say that the reorientation of some early Greeks toward *theoria* is closely related to the reorientation of some moderns toward phenomenology. If this is so, then Husserl's illumination of the phenomenological attitude will be an analogue of the Greeks' reorientation to the theoretical attitude. The structures, though distinct, will not be contrasting. Non-relative *theoria* in ancient Greece will be exposed as parallel to non-relative phenomenological knowledge in modern Europe.

But is it so? Central to the question is Husserl's characterization of science, ancient and modern. Wonder, he says, led the Greeks to science because it exposed the possibility of non-relative truth. From the adoption of the theoretical attitude,

> there soon results a far-reaching transformation of the whole praxis of human existence, i.e., the whole of cultural life: henceforth it must receive its norms not from the naive experience and tradition of everyday life but from objective truth. (VL, 287)

This last distinction is, in principle, a central one we have learned from the Greeks, between *doxa*, or opinion in relation to the world, and *epistēmē*, non-relative knowledge of the world – science. In Husserl's view, then, science begins indispensably with *thaumazein*, the wonder we see as 'incipient theoretical interest,' 'a variant of curiosity.' Wonder may lead to *doxa*, which he describes as 'fully disinterested seeing of the world'; but only in *epistēmē*, 'genuine science,' do we pass beyond the relativity of our own seeing to *the way the world is*. If *thaumazein* is the reorientation toward a new attitude, theoria is the filling out of that attitude and episteme its ultimate goal. *Doxa* and *epistēmē* may both be characterized as theoretical, but only *epistēmē* is scientific (VL, 285).

In Husserl's view, however, modern science has lost sight of the fact that *epistēmē* does not oppose *doxa*, though it is distinct from it. The failure of modern science, as the next section attempts to show, therefore lies in opening up an unbridgeable chasm between *epistēmē* and *doxa*. Husserl wants to show that *epistēmē* in its sense is not opposed to *doxa*. The non-relativity of phenomenological knowledge, then, does not suppress or denigrate the doxic – as, Husserl suggests, modern science does. In this sense, Husserl sees phenomenology as closer to the original intent of the wondering Greeks, to maximize *theoria* in all its forms in an 'infinite task' of accumulating knowledge.

This may seem paradoxical, and there are enduring confusions in Husserl's views here, but we cannot approach them without examining more closely his sense of crisis in European science. Three questions now become foremost: (1) What is the crisis Husserl is concerned with? (2) Is the structure of phenomenological reorientation as closely related to Greek theorizing as Husserl suggests? I.e., does phenomenology provide the only non-relative knowledge? And (3) what role does wonder play in the crisis Husserl wishes to expose? We will find that Husserl does not provide satisfactory answers to these questions.

III The Structure of Crisis: Wonders Lost, Artfully

It would be possible, even relatively easy, to discuss Husserl's sense of crisis in the sciences without ever referring specifically to their origin in simple wonder. Easy, but not complete, since a close examination of material in the 'Vienna Lecture' shows that the notion of *thaumazein* is central for Husserl. In this section of the paper I want to say a little more about the shape Husserl believes the scientific crisis to be taking. This will involve a fairly long excursus into the internal argument of Husserl's *Crisis*, necessary because the investigation of wonder could not go forward unless we canvassed at least some of the reasons Husserl points to for the modern 'crisis of the European sciences.' Sections IV and V are then concerned with the possibility of recovery from crisis and the task of philosophy and the philosopher within that recovery, while Section VI marks a return to the phenomenology of wonder.

It is important to see first why Husserl thinks that scientific crisis – the alienation of science from its task – is a necessary implication of scientific success. Science as such, he suggests, branches into 'the sciences'; the overarching theoretical task is divided up, delegated to specialists in parcels. While the sense of absolute or objective truth sanctioned by the theoretical atti-

tude is not lost, the notion that there is a single task of philosophy is obscured. This process of combined loss and success is
demonstrated most forcefully by Husserl's understanding of
the concept of infinity. As useful surveying and the numbers of
daily living are transformed into geometry and arithmetic, he
says, 'intuitively given nature and the world are transformed
into a mathematical world, the world of the mathematical
natural sciences' (VL, 293). This is a world that admits theoretically the concept of infinity in all aspects of the world. Infinitely accurate measurement is always in principle possible,
since it is only limited by human perception and technological
development. All lines we naturally take to be straight are
merely approximations of straight lines which asymptotically
approach, over time, the *ideal* of the straight line.

It is this very idealization of the world that Husserl wishes
to point to, since it represents a turning-point in the development of human theorizing. We must note here the variety of
dualisms that Husserl runs together in his analysis. Broadly
speaking, he wants to point to a single chasm opening up
between:

science	and	philosophy
natural science	and	metaphysics
the natural	and	the psychic
objective	and	subjective
body	and	mind
ideal	and	real
world of scientific inquiry	and	world of daily experience

Husserl's failure to distinguish adequately among these various oppositions leaves his sense of crisis somewhat confused.
It is clear that for Husserl there are two main prongs of experience, but unclear just what are the parameters of each. He also
asserts, sometimes without adequate argument, that one pole
of this opposition – on the left above – actively suppresses and
denigrates its opposite, while maximizing itself. In tactics now

familiar in deconstruction, he will reverse the split and then show it to be illusory. This strategy is, however, not always clear. Some approach can nevertheless be made to what implications this split – or series of them – might have for humankind.

What we forget, Husserl suggests, in the rush of modern (that is, post-Galilean) scientific success is that the ideal world of geometry and mathematics is not the world in which we live (C, 29). Its relation to the world of daily experience is always problematic, something scientists may refuse to dwell on. Our world of daily living is not an approximation of the perfect world we find on three planes in Euclid and Galileo. For that is a world where points have no dimension, lines are pure infinite extension, and planes are perfectly flat in all directions. It is an *abstract* world. The early triumph of the natural sciences, therefore, was

> the surreptitious substitution of the mathematically substruc-
> tured world of idealities for the only real world, the one that is
> actually given through perception, that is ever experienced and
> experienceable – our every-day lifeworld. (C, 49)

What are the consequences for us of this idealization of the lifeworld and of the ascendancy gained by the ideal world through science? First, it might be noted that it is structurally here that Husserl locates the separation of natural science and metaphysics – elsewhere called, perhaps misleadingly, 'science' and 'philosophy' – is effected. How?

Husserl, focussing on the figure of Galileo, thinks that this results from a particular failure of Galilean science: to ask the simple question of how abstract geometry originated. That this was not an issue for Galileo, indeed that he never had the condition for the possibility of asking it, shows to Husserl the thoroughgoing idealization of the lifeworld (C, 29–34). Galileo, Husserl suggests, did not question the idealized world he investigated in his masterful experiments, nor did he conceive that this might be a 'created' world that existed only within experimental method. All subsequent inquiry of a 'scientific' kind is concerned with measurement, exactness, infinite perfectibility (C, 36). Questions of experience, life in the world, are not only separated off, they are relegated to an inferior status because they cannot be investigated by science's chosen methods.

This opposition of a 'natural' world (where science can perform its task) and a 'psychic' world of experience (where science throws up its hands) is also, says Husserl, the opposition of objective and subjective. Remembering only part of what the Greeks told us, 'science' has to do with non-relative, objective truth; forgetting the rest, 'metaphysics' is criticized as subjective and hence of no general interest. Husserl notes that '[t]he world splits, so to speak, into two worlds: nature and the psychic world, although the latter, because of the way it is related to nature, does not achieve the status of an independent world' (C, 60). A second consequence, then, is that the realm of the psychic is so dominated by naturalism that it loses its own self-defining character (C, 60–9). If personal experience is judged to be 'merely' opinion, then it is no longer of interest to those concerned with the non-relative.

This development is further worked out by another decisive figure in Husserl's history of thought, Descartes – 'the primal founder not only of the modern idea of objectivistic rationalism but also of the transcendental motif which explodes it' (C, 73). Descartes is central to Husserl for many reasons, but for the moment it is enough to see one thing: it is decisive for subsequent philosophical and scientific development that Descartes performed the radical doubt for which he is known, but also that he failed actually to 'carry through the original radicalism of his ideas' (C, 78). Dominated by a Galilean picture of the world, Descartes's investigation stopped with the world of evidence. He did not think to extend his sceptical *epoché* to the subject who doubts, the ego – though he did expose that ego as never before. Descartes is thus able to reconstitute the world he inherited virtually unscathed, and yet leave the 'transcendental motif' open to further development.

Husserl is thus convinced that the 'crisis' of the sciences stems from Descartes's attempt to ground certainty, an attempt based on the method of early modern scientists. The results of this attempt include a radical mind-body split that philosophers have been attempting to repair, without success, for centuries. They also include the radical separation of objective and subjective, a polarity that results from early theorizing turning its back on the individual experience which gave it rise. Concomitant with this is a separation of the world of daily experience from the world of scientific inquiry, a split that also manages to give a superior position to a world in fact based on a more primordial structure. The ideal, mathematical world, the world of rationalism's 'reason,' cannot escape its origins in the lifeworld, it can only obscure them. Like an ambitious man who outstrips his poorer brothers, it scorns the stuff of which it is made, looking on daily subjective experience as not only inferior but in some cases an impediment to its 'real' work. That work, as Husserl notes, is really work of and about idealities, not realities.

Is this picture accurate? There are at least three points at which the question can be asked. Is Husserl's history of science and philosophy true to the facts, or is it rather an attempt to provide justification for a conclusion reached already? Is his sense of separation between the lifeworld and the idealized world of science a good picture of how science operates? Surely scientists begin in the lifeworld as much as philosophers do, beginning there an investigation that sometimes (but not always, e.g., mechanics) takes them into idealizations. Finally, we must question the accuracy of Husserl's charge that the sciences actively suppress the lifeworld, making wonder impossible. This appears simply untrue. Though wonder in its phenomenological sense may be rare, other kinds of wonder certainly motivate scientists in their investigations. And in this they may show themselves to be legitimate heirs of the Greek theorizing tradition. Husserl can only maintain the contrary by leaning hard on questionable historical analysis. It might still be opaque to us, then, how it is that Husserl can speak of a 'crisis' in the sciences. Their advances and achievements are everywhere obvious, and so far there is no evidence that they actively suppress the world of daily experience.

These questions do exercise Husserl, and he has no particular wish to contend with those who note advances in biology, medicine, physics, and other natural sciences (see, e.g., C, 118 and VL, 270). His concern is rather with attitude. The sickness to be faced, he says, has to do with the 'naive' rationalism he sees beginning with Descartes, and with the problematical 'naturalization of the psychic' begun earlier. The sciences are in crisis because they refuse to recognize their origin in the lifeworld; more than this, Husserl suggests that the sciences seek to suppress the lifeworld by labelling it not worthy of investigation.

But Husserl wants not to denigrate the achievements of science, only to have them seen as essentially spiritual events, events of human life in essence. Indeed, in the present climate of thinking – where the body can be separated from the spirit for investigation but not vice versa (VL, 271) – it is a fatal error for humanism to tangle with the sciences on their own ground:

> Only in the knowledge belonging purely to the science of the spirit is the scientist not open to the objection that his own accomplishment conceals itself. Accordingly, it is a mistake for the humanistic disciplines to struggle with the natural sciences for equal rights. As soon as they concede to the latter their self-sufficiency, they themselves fall prey to objectivism. (VL, 297)

Husserl wants to revitalize – to thematize once more, in a complicated fashion – the world on which science is based, but which natural science now conceals just as it reveals it. This world of daily experience is a more complex and miraculous place than we seem to imagine, he says, and a return to it will be no easy task.

This is of course where wonder enters the investigation once more. Wonder, Husserl suggests, exposes a threefold structure: the wonderer, the wonderful, and wondering. The wonderful is precisely the world as we find it, the world of daily experience. Despite science's primal origin in wonder, Husserl insists that the idealization of the world in *modern* science effectively closes off the experience of wonder we came to know via the child's question. Indeed, the question is relegated precisely to children and other naive metaphysicians. Since 'Why is there something rather than nothing?' cannot be answered (as science and some kinds of philosophy now conceive answers), it is a question of no interest. Perhaps more than this, it is a question that gets in the way of science's attempts to categorize and explain its idealized world.

The scientist might insist, however, that wonder is not lost on him, that the fascination with the oak leaf or the workings of his hand grip him too, on occasion. He might even hold that these momentary feelings of astonishment contribute to his curiosity and desire for scientific knowledge – so that he will examine the capillaries of the oak leaf under a microscope, or dissect a corpse's hand to observe the finely tuned anatomical wiring within. This looking 'inside,' however, is not the response wonder demands of us; it is a deflection that slides back into the view of the world as idealized, mathematized, capable of infinite measurement. The world that wonder exposes is not the idealized world, and it does not submit to investigation as the sciences conceive of it. The world of everyday is both more simple and far more complicated than we usually imagine. We need only reflect on the feeling we have when the scientists respond to wonder with a disquisition on capillary action in plant tissue or microanatomy: 'No, that isn't what I meant. I'm really talking about something else.' What that 'something else' may be will become clear in the next two sections.

IV Radicalizing Radical Doubt: The Ego in Question

Accepting for the moment a crisis of the proportions described by Husserl, what are we to do? This is a question for which we have no previous experience, and it cuts to the heart of the way our world is understood and typically investigated. 'We are absolute beginners here,' says Husserl, 'and have nothing in the way of logic designed to provide norms; we can do nothing but reflect' (C, 133). While reflection may seem a poor excuse for a philosophical method, and something hardly equal to the present task, Husserl is convinced that

> only through the highest form of self-consciousness, which itself becomes one of the branches of the infinite task, can philosophy fulfill its function of putting itself, and thereby a genuine humanity, on the road [to realization]. Only through this constant reflexivity is philosophy universal knowledge. (VL, 291)

As explicated in the *Crisis* and elsewhere, the rigorous application of various kinds of self-reflection is a method able to tackle the present crisis in some sense, able to extend the radical turn of Cartesian philosophy so that, as a beginning, the ego is bracketed just as completely as the external world. In this task, the individual examines his own ego 'purely as performer of all his validities, of which he becomes the purely theoretical spectator' (VL, 298).

How is this accomplished? As elsewhere, Husserl's method depends on a series of *epochés*, or abstentions, with regard to aspects of the world as experienced. These are not abstractions from the world, even less are they denigrations of it; the *epoché* sets off a part of the world as *not under consideration now*. It is the conscious resolve not to let that part of the world matter to me as I perform some other investigation. In this understanding, then, Husserl speaks of an *epoché* of the natural sciences as a first step (C, 135). This involves placing the concrete nature and results of the natural sciences in brackets, having them not matter to me, the point of the procedure being largely to turn away from the idealized world that the sciences force upon me – a world in which subjective is contrasted with objective, and found wanting. Husserl notes of his method that:

> The Delphic motto 'Know thyself!' has gained a new signification. Positive science is a science lost in the world. I must lose the

world by *epoché* in order to regain it by a universal self-examina-
tion. 'Noli foras ire,' says Augustine, 'in te redi, in interiore
homine habitat veritas.' (*Cartesian Meditations*, p. 157)

For phenomenology, all methodological moves are reflective
moves which expose not the poverty of objectivity but the confusion evident in the separation between objective and subjective. Radical self-reflection makes this possible in a way the
science of psychology never can: 'Because of its objectivism,
psychology is completely unable to obtain as its subject matter
the soul in its essential sense, which is, after all, the ego that
acts and suffers' (VL, 296).

This move back into the ego and away from the objective
sciences may accomplish a bracketing of the idealized world
of science, but it does not take me out of the world. Instead it
serves to point out a central paradox in human experience as
Husserl explores it. How is it that I am both a subject experiencing the world and an object within the world? (See C, 104
ff.) The method Husserl suggests for dealing with this paradox is the 'transcendental *epoché*,' a 'total change of the natural
attitude of life' (C, 148). This change in attitude thematizes the
world as never before since, performed in one fell swoop and
made permanent, it completely alters the way the subject
experiences the world. 'Through the *epoché*,' says Husserl, 'a
new way of experiencing, of thinking, of theorizing is opened
up to the philosopher ... [H]e simply forbids himself ... to
continue the whole natural performance of his world-life'
(C, 152).

But this no mere intellectual parlour trick. It exposes to the
subject the world *as phenomenon*, lays bare its essential structure, and points out the phenomenal features of the world
obscured by natural living: the intentionality of consciousness
(every experience is experience *of* something), intersubjectivity
(the phenomenal world as a 'reciprocity of perspectives,' in
Alfred Schutz's phrase), the grounding function of time, kines-
thesis, and so on. The *epoché* also opens up new reflective possibilities with reference to the subject/object dilemma, since

'by virtue of [this] present method of *epoché*, everything objective is transformed into something subjective' (C, 178). How is that? Briefly, it hinges on Husserl's understanding of consciousness as divided into ego-pole and object-pole.

The world is objectively real, but experience *of the world* may be investigated in its separate aspects: the world as constituted, experienced thing(s) (*noema*, the noematic pole); and acts of experiencing (*noesis*, the noetic pole). 'Everything is subjective' in that all things are known through subjective experience, though they retain their status as objective things without question. Husserl rejects any sort of idealism such as Kant's where the noumenal resides 'beneath' phenomenal experience, as it were, to prop up the phenomena which present themselves to the subject as the only things that can be known. Husserl countenances no such separation, maintaining instead that there is no 'outside' to human experience towards which we vainly strive, nor an 'inside' which is thus cut off from 'objective reality.' Subjective experience is experience of the world, first and foremost, since 'all this [in the world] belongs to the "phenomenon," to the world as constituted pole' (C, 183).

This goes some way to explain what it might mean for phenomenology to see *episteme* and *doxa* as distinct but not opposed. There remains a further difficulty, however, one which Husserl never satisfactorily deals with in his writings. In order to start up the stalled investigation of Descartes, to efface the naiveté that led to the 'deluge of scepticism' and rationalism, Husserl must attempt an *epoché* of the ego itself. He must extend self-reflection back into the self as such. And this is not as easy as simply saying that transcendental phenomenology is not Cartesianism. Husserl maintains the difference lies in the fact that his point 'is not to secure objectivity but to understand it' (C, 181). His understanding of objectivity, of the structure of intentional consciousness, is tied up with the notion of the life-world. But it is not clear here – and it remains unclear, I think – that Husserl is thereby able to answer the fundamental transcendental question: 'Who is the ego?'

Nevertheless, in reactivating the transcendental subject via the *epoché*, and exposing the world as phenomenal, Husserl's method goes some distance in characterizing the strange nature of the world in which we live. Only by stepping back in the *epoché* is the natural world shown to be the lifeworld as Husserl understands it, the world seen together as world-consciousness and world itself. This new attitude exposes the world as always already present, pregiven, the 'sedimentation' of historical occurrences which inescapably suffuses our actions and experiences. We do not come to the world afresh, but rather we come to it as a conditioned and structured thing – an accomplishment, we might say – of all those who came before us and exist with us. The world is a more complex and *achieved* structure than we usually imagine, especially in the mundane realm of daily experience. Husserl wants to suggest that the rules governing daily life and the intricate infrastructure of interpersonal relations are more miraculous and mysterious than immediate experience of the world might indicate.

The philosopher – or, as we should now call him or her, the phenomenologist – does not go unchanged by the alteration of attitude achieved in the transcendental *epoché*. In an oft-quoted passage, Husserl likens his transformation to a religious conversion:

> [T]he total phenomenological attitude and the *epoché* belonging to it are destined to effect, at first, a complete personal transformation, comparable in the beginning to a religious conversion, which then, however, over and above this bears within itself the significance of the greatest existential transformation which is assigned as a task to mankind as such. (C, 137)

Husserl is at pains to show how this 'existential transformation' fits into a life lived perforce in the natural, mundane world. Tied in here is his sense of phenomenology as *vocation*, as something to which one is called but which does not take one from the world – as, by contrast, a mystic's divine revelation might do. The next section addresses this notion of vocation and its relation to the Greeks, and attempts a return to the experience of wonder.

V The Task of Philosophy and Wonder, Its Propaedeutic

Describing the crisis he sees in the objective sciences, Husserl writes, in terms we have already discussed:

> Skepticism about the possibility of metaphysics, the collapse of the belief in a universal philosophy as a guide for the new man, actually represents a collapse in the belief in 'reason.' ... If man loses this faith, it means nothing less than the loss of faith 'in himself,' in his own true being. (C, 12)

The stakes could be no higher, as far as Husserl is concerned, and they demand radical action. Husserl's judgment may be questionable in this, and indeed his assertions concerning human teleology – that it is only truly represented in the West, 'Europe,' and can be nowhere else – may appear prejudicial, tradition-bound, or simply wrong.

However, it is important to see *within his own terms* the aptness of the solution Husserl offers, one whose force might still be considerable even if the terms of reference are mistaken. Husserl believes the state of crisis demands a rejuvenation of the original philosophical impulse evident in the Greeks, a rejuvenation intended to reform metaphysics and establish once more the universal, infinite task of philosophizing, the search for *episteme* or absolute truth. Without such a revitalization, he suggests, humankind is doomed to descend into barbarity on the back of naive objectivity and rationalism (VL, 299). In this sense, then, the philosopher who genuinely faces the crisis – the phenomenologist – is truly acting as 'a functionary of mankind' (C, 17).

Here Husserl's understanding of philosophical vocation engages with the *epoché* of transcendental phenomenology described in the previous section. Phenomenology is, for its progenitor, no mere alternative system of thought to be evaluated coolly and assimilated by modern philosophy. Rather it is intended as a radical, provocative challenge for modern philosophy to open its eyes to the infinite task from which it is descended. That is only possible via the *epoché*, via the transformation and alteration of attitude that comes over the phenomenologist when he sees the natural world *as* the lifeworld. Husserl's understanding of vocation (*Beruf*) is tied to his insistence that the *epoché* takes the phenomenologist not out of the world but, in a sense, more deeply into it. So that 'this newly established vocational interest, whose universal subject matter is called the "lifeworld," finds its place among the other life-interests or vocations and it has "its proper time" within the one personal time' (C, 136).

While this may be so, it is still true that the one who is 'called' experiences the world differently than before, since his attitude to it has changed. This person may not be acting as a phenomenologist at all times; that is, he or she must perform a sort of reverse *epoché* whenever performing some piece of the business of everyday: paying the bills, cooking dinner, taking the family dachshund for a walk, and so on. But the phenomenologist does not escape the attitude in which the lifeworld is a theme for him or her. These remarks on phenomenology as vocation can be compared with those sections of the 'Vienna Lecture' in which Husserl looks to the vocational aspect of the Greeks' theoretical life. In choosing not the 'higher-level practical attitude' but instead the theoretical attitude, the early philosophers characterize philosophy as vocational and non-practical. They dedicate their lives in advance to the accumulation and refinement of *theoria*. Their new attitude '[i]n the sphere if its own vocational life ... is based on a voluntary *epoché* of all natural praxis, including the higher-level praxis that serves the natural sphere,' in favour of the new 'theoretical praxis' (VL, 282).

Discovery of this sense of phenomenological vocation is possible within daily life only through 'a radical enquiry back into subjectivity [which will] make objective truth comprehensible and arrive at the ultimate ontic meaning of the world'

(C, 69). As mentioned, what is being sought is not a 'new objectivity,' but an understanding of objectivity *in relation to* the world – a sense of how the capacity we call 'reason' is related to the world we experience (C, 13). The important question at this juncture is, How does the experience of wonder fit into Husserl's newly elaborated scheme? What role does *thaumazein* play here, where the potential phenomenologist is poised on the edge of becoming a 'functionary of mankind,' a searcher after human telos?

Husserl never addresses the question explicitly, but strong conjectures can be drawn on the basis of what he said about the importance of *thaumazein* for the Greeks. Certainly wonder at the world's being – and being the way it is – retains its strength through the ages. It is just as capable of inspiring the theoretical attitude in the Toronto of 2002, say, as it was in the Athens of the fourth century. More fundamentally, it is, as Marcel urged, a feeling that never deserts the philosopher as long as he remains a philosopher. It may seem to come and go, but it never really leaves. Or, as Eugen Fink has maintained (in this case speaking about a particular kind of philosopher), the phenomenologist is actually *defined* by his 'astonishment before the world.' It is therefore not too ambitious to call wonder the propaedeutic to the task of philosophy, nor to situate it centrally in the development and maturing of the theoretical attitude.

In saying this, we need not go as far as Husserl in linking the theoretical to both a severe crisis, or loss of theoretical faith, and his sense of the functional task of philosophy subsequent to that crisis. For myself, I am content to leave this question open and neither insist on nor deny the structural connections Husserl mentions here. In particular, however, I am uncomfortable with the notion of the Greek entelechy representing a lost teleological pole for all of humanity, and with Husserl's denigration of non-European philosophies as not philosophy at all. But none of this affects the role of wonder in inspiring reflection on oneself and the world – and oneself in relation to the world – and hence of the philosophical attitude in general.

The next section, which concludes this investigation of wonder and its place in Husserl's late thinking, attempts finally to say how a phenomenology of astonishment is structured. In particular, I want to show that wonder succeeds in thematizing the world, however fleetingly and imperfectly, and thus shows forth the way to concrete theorizing and more sophisticated investigation of the world in which we live. Here we must go beyond what Husserl has offered us, but with confidence that this can be done in a phenomenological spirit. As with any investigation of wonder, however, this remains in the realm of tentative exploration.

VI My Wonder Before the World

In what does wonder consist, finally? We have already noticed several features that appear necessary, if not sufficient: fleetingness; the 'standing out,' in relief we might say, of some feature of the world and thus the world itself; the more basic structure thus exposed – experience of the world and the world as experienced; and so on. Following Husserl's lead, I have resisted the analytical categorization offered by Hepburn and others, not because I think it is wrong but because I think it get us no closer to the structure of wondering than any other investigation that is scientific in style. Hepburn comes perilously close – though, to his credit, never succeeds – in taking the wonder out of wonder.

I began this investigation with a child's question – 'Why is there something rather than nothing?' – and I return to it now because it has retained its force throughout. The question stands, and will go on standing as long as there are people around, children and philosophers, to ask it. But what is the peculiar force of this question? What does it bring out that nothing else can? First, wonder succeeds in thematizing the world in an non-specific, pretheoretical, and unrigorous way. It is the very rough first stab at thematization, the experience that first admits the world in which living goes on *as an issue*. It may be the natural world or it may be, in more rarefied species of wonder, the lifeworld or the question of the meaning of

Being. Wonder sees the world of everyday as suddenly strange and mysterious, obtrusive, standing out. The question has been opened up by the momentary experience, the question that is honed into the 'infinite task' of *theoria* and shows itself working out its praxis in the theoretical attitude. Wonder may be a transitory first cousin of the transcendental *epoché*, which sets off the concerns of daily living from the world in its pre-givenness and the relation of my consciousness to it. Wonder exposes the rather startling fact of the horizon of meaning which surrounds me at every point in life.

It is appropriate to ask at this point some apparently naive questions. How does one invite the experience of wonder? Indeed, can one invite it or does it simply visit us unbidden? What features of the world are more wonderful than others? Are the starry heavens more astonishing, in themselves, than the deep blue sea? Should I attempt to lead a life of rapt attention at nature to invite wonder? I may think it appropriate to walk up in the hills, perhaps with a set of paints, seeking landscapes or waiting for sunsets. I may try to make myself more childlike, rejecting the social pressures that prevent me from seeing things as wonderful. (My friends will find me worse company, perhaps.) What precise steps can I follow to make wonder more likely to happen to me, assuming it is an experience of which all of us are capable? Most importantly, what is the proper object of wonder? The natural world? Some particular aspect of it, 'the sublime,' say? Or is it something else?

The questions appear naive, but they are to the point. Husserl has suggested that wonder is an experience we can all share, but that certain forces now inhibit that experience. Implicitly, then, we must seek to minimize those inhibiting forces and cultivate and seize on the experience of wonder. But without a clear sense of the object of wonder it is not clear how this is to be done. So one problem with wonder in a phenomenological context is whether there is an adequate way to get it going. As I noted earlier, Husserl accepts the importance of seeing the structural links between *thaumazein* and *theoria* but never actually discusses them in detail (VL, 285). His understanding of wonder, beyond the various features I have stated, remains a little opaque.

Now it might be wondered if another approach to wonder is more fruitful. For instance, Hepburn refers not to Husserl but to his renegade pupil, Heidegger, whose reflections on astonishment are to the point. Compare this passage from *Being and Time*, which famously contrasts wonder with mere curiosity (one of the modes of everyday Being of Dasein):

> Curiosity has nothing to do with observing entities and marvelling at them – *thaumazein*. To be amazed to the point of not understanding is something in which it has no interest. Rather it concerns itself with a kind of knowing, but just in order to have known ... Curiosity is everywhere and nowhere. (BT, 216–17)

By contrast, of course, Heidegger's *thaumazein* is focussed, rapt attention on an entity that astonishes, that provides no immediate or instrumental knowledge. It does tarry, for as long as its fleeting character makes possible, and has the peculiar effect of throwing the person back on himself – taking him away from chatter and idleness, exposing his horizon of concern. In this analysis, that before which I feel wonder is the Being of beings; this is the proper object of my wonder. Like Husserl, Heidegger seizes on a Greek experience of wonder, intending to revitalize and thematize it, but his Greeks are not necessarily Husserl's Greeks. Anaximander and Parmenides are arguably the guiding lights of Heidegger's question of the meaning of Being. Who are Husserl's? Aristotle? We cannot be sure. One thing we can be sure of is that Husserl's wonder, though focussed and rapt like Heidegger's, has a different object. Instead of Being, Husserl is astonished before the world *and* the ego – and the relations between them. This is a point that needs now to be examined.

Bloch relates that one associated question of wonder – some way past 'Why is there something rather than nothing?' – has to do with the astonishing fact of the ego: 'How is it that I have *I* tagging along with me? How strange to have my *horizon* of experience travelling about with me at all times!' (PF, 5). Bloch expresses this strangeness with an example from anthropology: a group of Fijians being 'discovered' by European sailors showed no reaction when the big frigates hove to in their harbours; but the reaction was enthusiastic and extensive when the ships' boats came into shore bearing men. The Fijians, unable to escape their own horizons of experience, acted under a fundamental, unwilled *epoché* that exposed itself in the fact that ships meant nothing to them, while the smaller boats retained meaning. The large objects were a mystery, therefore of no interest, while boats were those things that took men upon the water. Similar stories abound in journals of 'discovery.' Bloch's point is that an individual never escapes the fact of his horizon, a fact which remains in general transparent to him. It works by means of *epochés* of a kind – I automatically abstain from noticing things for which I have no frame of reference – and is also laid bare by more rigorous and radical *epochés*. But we never escape it. In Bloch's succinct formulation: 'Wherever we go, we go too' (PF, 10).

Wonder, then, can be as much before the ego who experiences it as before the world he experiences. The two – indeed, these plus the *act* of experiencing itself – are not fundamentally separable. That is why Husserl's investigation is as much about the lifeworld as it is about the transcendental ego at its centre (centre for each one of us). Three things thus become exposed: the miracle of the world before us, both seen as natural and seen as the lifeworld; the mystery of the ego who experiences the world; and the enigmatic relation that exists between them in complex structures of phenomenal experience. Seen in this way, Husserl approaches as closely as anyone a coherent thematization of wonder itself.

Phenomenology does not tell us the whole story about wonder. It may be the case, as I have suggested, that it is not, in principle, capable of telling the whole story. Whole stories are, by their nature, elusive. But this need not worry us unduly. As I mentioned at the outset, the force of wonder's central questions does not waver. My own experience – that final phenomenological appeal! – indicates that it is indeed the spur of theoretical activity, the kick-start on the motor of philosophy. That does not commit us to Husserl's program any more than it does to Aristotle's. As mentioned, the teleological thrust of Husserl's argument fails at several points to be convincing. Moreover, it is not obvious that *epistēmē* is the theoretical possibility he held it to be. Finally, Husserl's own procedure remains in large part unthematized by phenomenology, a problem of self-reflexivity that vexed this master of reflexivity to the end of his life.

I mention these critical points mainly in the interests of completeness. A full treatment of them would require more, and more detailed, investigation, and I have certainly taxed the patience of our wonder quite enough already.

Notes

1 Gottfried Leibniz, *Philosophical Papers and Letters*, ed. Loenker (Chicago: University of Chicago Press, 1956), II, 1038. It has been suggested that the modern philosopher who reactivates Leibniz's question is Heidegger, not Husserl. To the extent that Husserl's wonder is not confined to the extent that wonder is always before the Being of the world, this is so. My suggestion in what follows is that Husserl saw himself doing something more fundamental than his breakaway pupil: thematizing wonder in the world, in me, and also in the relation between us. This may not answer, however, the critic who finds Husserlian wonder still on the level of beings and not Being. Both Husserl and Heidegger wanted, for different reasons, to return to 'the Greeks.' Their divergence on this issue shows that they indeed had different Greeks in mind in that return.

2 The following abbreviations are used in this paper:

PF   Ernst Bloch, *A Philosophy of the Future*, trans. John Cumming (New York: Herder and Herder, 1970).

W   Ronald W. Hepburn, 'Wonder,' in *Wonder and Other Essays* (Edinburgh: Edinburgh University Press, 1984), pp. 131–54.

BT   Martin Heidegger, *Being and Time*, trans. John Macquarrie and Edward Robinson (New York: Harper and Row, 1962).

C   Edmund Husserl, *The Crisis of European Sciences and Transcendental Phenomenology*, trans. David Carr (Evanston, IL: Northwestern University Press, 1970).

VL   Edmund Husserl, 'Vienna Lecture,' original title: 'Philosophy in the Crisis of European Mankind,' in *Crisis*, pp. 269–99.

TLP   Ludwig Wittgenstein, *Tractatus Logico-Philosophicus*, trans. D.F. Pears and B.F. McGinnis (London: Routledge and Kegan Paul, 1961).

3 Gabriel Marcel, *The Existential Background of Human Dignity* (Oxford: Oxford University Press, 1963), p. 12.

4 It is a frustrating but perhaps typical habit of Husserl that he offers no argument in favour of this 'return' beyond a general lionizing of the first Western philosophers. One can only speculate whether this move is the result of Husserl's immersion in the Western tradition. Today, when that tradition is challenged on all sides, we may be less comfortable with having 'the Greeks' represent the highest in human development. But perhaps not. Either way, Husserl never makes it clear which Greeks he really means to indicate here, and this enforced homogeneity is itself problematic. As Heidegger could have told him, Anaximander is not Aristotle when it comes to wonder.

Phronesis and Political Dialogue

I

Consider one recent version of the claim that we[1] badly need the Aristotelian virtue of *phronesis* in order to make sense of our ethico-political lives. '[M]odern critical theory which envisages an emancipated society based on our interest in autonomy vastly overestimates the role of reason in human affairs,' Steven Smith argues.[2]

> It avers that through the power of their own self-critical rationality people can come to an understanding of themselves and their affairs and thus reorder their collective lives to express better their desire for freedom. But what this demand conceals is the problem of exactly how the insights of universal reason are to be applied to particular situations. What is absent from the modern critical project is a theory of political judgment, or *phronesis*, a form of reason or ethical know-how which involves complex judgments specific to the particular practices or situations at hand.

It follows, in Smith's view, that '[w]ithout some notion of political judgment, the Habermasian ideal speech situation, like the Hegelian end of history, remains an empty possibility.'[3]

Especially as directed against Habermas, this complaint has

a familiar ring. The charges of emptiness or transcendentalism that are brought to bear on Habermas's discourse ethics – charges that, despite Habermas's own efforts to fight them off, recapitulate Hegelian criticisms of Kantian moral theory – frequently turn on a demand for practical application. According to these critics, discourse ethics comes up short when faced with the demands of practical ethical and political situations. With its ideal speech situation (the presuppositions of rational speech modelled in a counterfactual regulative ideal) and the allied 'D' and 'U' principles (revisions of the categorical imperative that derive a dialogic test of universalization from the more general commitment to discourse arising out of disagreement), Habermas's theory is, the charge goes, too universalistic, too rationalistic, for us to expect meaningful practical results. Its model of unconstrained justificatory discourse is still too much allied with what Bernard Williams labelled 'morality, the peculiar institution.'[4]

The fairness of these charges can be assessed in several ways. One might, for example, delve more deeply into discourse ethics to see whether the charges stick. This would involve following the numerous elaborations and nuances of the theory that Habermas has offered, especially in the recent works published in English as *Justification and Application*[5] and *Between Facts and Norms*.[6] In the former, Habermas usefully distinguishes among three uses of practical reason – the pragmatic, the ethical, and the moral[7] – and so provides a taxonomy that sets limits on what discourse ethics can do. This goes some distance in illuminating the issue of practical-political application.[8] In the latter work, the interconnections between discourse ethics and law are systematically addressed for the first time in Habermas's work, clarifying the relationship between idealized normative conversation and the real demands of political life.

A complete treatment of the issues raised by these works would take many pages; my present ambition is much narrower in scope. In this paper I will focus attention only on the issue of the demand for *phronesis* as the proper corrective to the universalism of discourse ethics. Indeed, if Smith is right, *phronesis* ought to be seen as a necessary corrective to modern critical theory generally. *Phronesis* here takes on the critical role of a saving gesture, a necessary addition, that might be capable of delivering the modern critical-theoretical project – a project that is, in Habermas's hands, necessarily dialogic – from what threatens it, namely, well-meaning rationalistic irrelevancy. Without that corrective, the dialogue conceived by discourse ethics begins to seem either pointless or unattainable.[9] The central questions before us are therefore the following: What is *phronesis*? (Section II). Is it recoverable in our own day, and how? (Section III). And can it save discourse ethics from itself? (Section IV).

It is of course possible that this is the wrong way to look at the question, that is, as one in which we rescue a universalistic dialogue of legitimation by adding elements of justification by way of *phronesis*. According to Williams, Hegel had it right when he proceeded in a different manner: Hegel 'asks how a concretely experienced form of life can be extended, rather than considering how a universal program is to be applied.'[10] Instead of reforming universalistic moral assessment with particularistic ethico-political application, in other words, perhaps we should give up the universalism altogether in favour of something *sittlich* and ethically real. Then the relevant question for present purposes would be this one: what role, if any, does *phronesis* play in this other kind of political dialogue? I will address that question only in the conclusion of this paper (Section V).

II

Definitions of *phronesis* abound, but Smith's captures the conventional main points. '*Phronesis*,' he says, 'is the Aristotelian virtue especially required in political decision making and is akin to the quality of moral reasonableness, which consists of knowing the myriad details relevant to a case and what the parties to it would be likely to accept as a solution.'[11] Other definitions emphasize more clearly the crucial role of *phronesis* in mediating between universal moral laws and particular practical situations. Some go even further. Stanley Rosen, in the course of rejecting Heideggerian fundamental ontology as an ethics, notes that Heidegger 'fails to capture the living nutrient of human existence: *phronesis*. Heidegger cannot distinguish, as we do in everyday life, between a good and a bad man.'[12] For Rosen, *phronesis* seems to stand for moral judgment as a whole, and that is much more than a virtue of thought concerned with application. It may also be more than Aristotle intended with his original discussion of *phronesis*. To sharpen our sense of what *phronesis* is, we can do no better than return to Aristotle's treatment.

In Book VI of the *Nicomachean Ethics*, which discusses the intellectual virtues, Aristotle makes the familiar fivefold distinction to categorize 'the ways in which the soul arrives at truth,' giving us the following aspects of mental activity: science (*episteme*), skill (*techne*), practical wisdom (*phronesis*), intuition (*nous*), and wisdom (*sophia*) (NE 1139b17–1141b20). The man of *phronesis* is, he tells us, 'able to deliberate rightly about what is good and advantageous for himself,' but 'not in particular respects, e.g. what is good for health or physical strength, but what is conducive to good life generally' (1140a25). Because it concerns itself with variable things, *phronesis* is distinguished from *episteme*; it is also distinguished from *techne*, since *phronesis* issues in action and not production. The proper end of practical wisdom, then, is action: doing well, based on the available evidence and reasoning about my human purposes.

Aristotle goes on to mention that 'political science and *phronesis* are the same state of mind, though their essence is not the same' (1141b25). That is, there is a part of political science that is scientific – the kind of investigation Aristotle himself undertakes – but the remainder, what we might call practical politics, is governed by *phronesis*. Thus, though it appears prima facie an individual virtue, *phronesis* does not remain divided from wider political concerns. This point is most obvious when we consider that an ethical life cannot be led in a tyrannical society, which does not support but undermines its pursuit of the good. After some further discussion of other virtues, Aristotle concludes Book VI with a statement of the centrality of *phronesis* in the ethical life. It is, he says, the governing virtue, the one without which the others remain impossible, for without correct practical deliberation there is no ethical action, and hence no ethical character. 'It is not possible to be good in the true sense of the word without *phronesis*,' he says, 'or to be practically wise without moral goodness' (1144b10).

Pace Rosen, Aristotle's discussion does not provide warrant for the view that *phronesis* is synonymous with moral judgment in general. What does emerge very clearly in Aristotle's treatment is the strong ethico-political connection of *phronesis*. Practical wisdom may be a virtue of individuals, but since those individuals realize the end of human flourishing (*eudaimonia*) only in a city of just and friendly association, there is no sense in which the *phronimos* is involved in private or personal projects of virtue. That provides at least preliminary evidence for taking seriously the calls for *phronesis* as a crucial corrective to critical theory, especially as that theory relates to central questions of political legitimacy. And the need for *phronesis* to weigh in with critical theory is all the more obvious if that theory labours under vestigial Kantian influences, for here, as noticed, we may be in grave danger of losing sight of the particular. More up-to-date support for these claims, assuming we require it, can be found in Hans-Georg Gadamer's deft discussion of *phronesis*, which focuses clearly on the stakes for interpretive critical theory.

Though Gadamer admits that 'Aristotle is not concerned with the hermeneutical problem and certainly not with its historical dimension, but with the right estimation of the role that reason has to play in moral action,' he claims that 'if we relate Aristotle's description of the ethical phenomenon and especially the virtue of moral knowledge to our own investigation, we find Aristotle's analysis is in fact a kind of model of the problems of hermeneutics.'[13] Thus, keeping in mind that 'the central problem of hermeneutics' is for Gadamer the issue of application, we begin to see the decisive role *phronesis* has to play not only in critical social theory oriented around interpretation – critical theory, that is, seen as part of what Georgia Warnke has aptly called 'the hermeneutic turn in recent political philosophy'[14] – but also in the general theory of interpretation associated with philosophical hermeneutics.

For Gadamer, the key to genuine interpretation is the attention given to its threefold structure. That is, acts of true interpretation always involve the exercise of three faculties or means of distinction: the *subtilitas intelligendi* ('understanding'), the *subtilitas explicandi* ('interpretation'), and the *subtilitas applicandi* ('application'). All true understanding necessarily involves application, according to Gadamer, because we can only put an interpretation into play by applying understanding to the thing interpreted. The means of such application is a form of *phronesis*, mediating universal and particular with a form of knowledge that, as in Aristotle, is distinct from both *episteme* and *techne*. Understanding that remains on the level of *episteme* or *techne* would lack something crucial, namely the sensitivity to context and flexibility of application that Gadamer crucially identifies as essential elements of true acts of interpretation. It is precisely the modern disregard of the phronetic that leads to strong but misguided claims in favour of method and algorithm. It also supports, among other things, a debilitating distinction between the 'firm' *Naturwissenschaften* and the 'soft' *Geisteswissenschaften* – a distinction that has the ultimate effect of barring truth claims to humanists and social scientists or, what may be worse, forcing them to adopt the methods of natural science to vouchsafe their intellectual respectability.

Gadamer explains the key role of *phronesis* by following Aristotle's brief discussion (1140b20–5) and distinguishing it from the other forms of knowledge along three dimensions.

(1) *Phronesis* by its very nature does not face the usual problems of acquisition and application associated with a body of technical or scientific knowledge. 'We learn a *technē* and can also forget it,' Gadamer says. 'But we do not learn moral

knowledge, nor can we forget it. We do not stand over against it, as if it were something that we can acquire or not, in the way that we can choose to acquire or not an objective skill, a techne. Rather, we are always already in the situation of having to act ... and hence must already possess and be able to apply moral knowledge.'[15]

(2) *Phronesis* demands a different conception of relation between ends and means than that associated with other kinds of knowledge. *Phronesis* does not exist a priori, nor is it specifically goal directed. 'Moral knowledge can never be knowable in advance in the manner of knowledge that can be taught,' says Gadamer. 'The relation between means and ends here is not such that knowledge of the right means can be made available in advance, and that is because the knowledge of the right end is not the mere object of knowledge either. There can be no anterior certainty concerning what the good life is directed towards as a whole.'[16] It follows that we must complete moral knowledge with knowledge of the particular situation, and this latter knowledge is a form of experience – for which, as they say, there is no substitute.

(3) *Phronesis* is therefore a form of self-knowledge, or 'knowledge-for-the-sake-of-oneself.' It is a matter of self-reflection and the accumulation of insight into my own concerns and abilities, and the sorts of situations in which those concerns and abilities are appropriately exercised – and how. It is, says Gadamer, 'the virtue of thoughtful reflection.'[17]

Gadamer's concern, as stated, is the hermeneutical relevance of Aristotle, and his discussion clarifies the crucial role of *phronesis* in interpretation. 'We too,' he says, 'determined that application is neither a subsequent nor a merely occasional part of the phenomenon of understanding, but codetermines it as a whole from the beginning.' Application is not performed *afterward*, in an act separate from the apprehension of a pregiven text. That view of understanding distorts both the process of application and the nature of the text under consideration. Rather, '[t]he interpreter dealing with a traditional text seeks to apply it to himself' *at every moment* in his struggle to understand. That, indeed, is what it is to struggle to understand. 'He must relate the text to this situation, if he wants to understand it at all.'[18]

These points naturally carry interpretation well past its usual 'merely literary' scope, and squarely into the realm of the practical. In this sense, then (as Richard Bernstein and Stanley Rosen, e.g., have noticed), philosophical hermeneutics extends beyond understanding and into praxis – the sphere of ethico-political deliberation and action. Of course, we may have differing views about whether this is a good thing. 'What Gadamer seeks to show is that authentic hermeneutical understanding truly humanizes us,' says Bernstein; 'it becomes integrated in our very being just as *phronesis* itself shapes the being of the *phronimos*.'[19] Therefore the *Geisteswissenschaften* – when practised authentically – are themselves ethico-practical undertakings. 'As hermeneutical disciplines, they are not concerned with amassing "theoretical" knowledge of what is strange and alien. Rather they involve the type of appropriation characteristic of *phronesis*. The type of knowledge and truth that they yield is practical knowledge and truth that shapes our praxis.'[20]

But we might, on the other hand, view this politicization of interpretation with alarm. It could indicate the failure of our highest rational aspirations, the collapse of the Enlightenment search for truth into sectarian political debate. 'The popularity of hermeneutics in our own time is thus a mark of singular political as well as theoretical importance,' Rosen remarks. 'It is a sign not of our greater understanding but of the fact that we have lost our way, that we understand nothing, to the extent that we adopt rules and principles, which, however, must be supported by an interpretation that hangs in the void [...] Every hermeneutical program is at the same time itself a political manifesto or the corollary of a political manifesto.'[21] Lest that begin to sound promising or liberating, Rosen reminds us that there will always be manifestos we find threatening, regardless of our own ideological commitments. For every Maoist Michel Foucault there is a reactionary conservative Leo Strauss.[22] Our resort to interpretation is, he finally suggests, an act of fear: frightened of the tyranny of truth, we tacitly agree to dismantle it – and thus open the door not only to a cacophony of claims, but to the destruction of the very bourgeois liberal society that claimed a principled openness to those claims.[23]

These are strong arguments. Before assessing them, the logically prior issue must be dealt with. Can we even recover *phronesis* as a meaningful ethico-political category? In what form might it shape the political dialogue of legitimation?

III

Habermas, for one, thinks we cannot recover *phronesis* in a meaningful form. Struggling with the complex issue of ethical cognitivism – and fighting off numerous criticisms of his own universalist form of cognitivism – Habermas challenges a basic presumption of his critics: that ethical know-how can be straightforwardly defended as a remedy for discourse ethics' well-meaning practical nullity. Habermas rejects the move largely because he finds the implicit contrast between *phronesis* and *episteme* no longer meaningful. 'Aristotle,' he says, 'defines this faculty of *phronesis* (*prudentia*, "prudence") in a negative fashion in contrast to the strong claims of *episteme* – the faculty of knowledge concerned with the universal, necessary, and supratemporal dimension of existence and, ultimately, of the cosmos – but without completely denying its cognitive status.' That is, *phronesis* was for Aristotle a form of knowledge and could only be defended as such by referring to another form, *episteme*, with which it was not identical.

'However, *modern* Aristotelians can no longer uncritically appeal to such a faculty of metaphysical knowledge as a point of contrast,' Habermas continues.

The fallible conception of knowledge that informs the sciences involves the renunciation of all metaphysical aspirations, and it is not clear that significant modifications could still be made to this weak, postmetaphysical conception of knowledge without jeopardizing its fundamental cognitive status. On the other hand, the theoretical knowledge secured by the modern empirical sciences can no longer be employed in genuinely practical contexts; at best, it permits calculations of means and ends (technical and strategic recommendations) that are indifferent to moral concerns. On these premises it becomes questionable whether our everyday ethical knowledge can be viewed as genuine knowledge.[24]

In other words, having lost their meaningful point of contrast, modern defenders of *phronesis* are set adrift. They cannot define *phronesis* as commonsensical without losing their claim to normativity. But they cannot define it as cognitive without having to cash out its validity in terms that, according to Habermas, will prove him to be right about the rational presuppositions of discourse – i.e., those presuppositions that are modelled in the ideal speech situation.

Thus, for example, Bernard Williams's attempt to post the limits of philosophy by an emphasis on non-rationalistic practical know-how is not only stalled, it is reduced to incoherence. Says Habermas: 'Williams is compelled to attribute to practical reason a form of rationality that goes beyond sheer common sense but whose difference from scientific rationality remains to be determined.'[25] This middle ground of knowledge collapses under the two sides of a cognitivist dilemma. 'Without metaphysical backing, what Aristotle called *phronesis* must either dissolve into mere common sense or be developed into a concept of practical reason that satisfies the criteria of procedural rationality.'[26] If the claims of *phronesis* are really *claims* – that is, if they possess rational force – that force must be susceptible to (and perhaps only to) just the kind of validity reasoning characteristic of Habermas's recent work.

No doubt this is a satisfying result from Habermas's point of view, but (some of) the rest of us may feel less triumphant. The dilemma sketched between 'mere' common sense and a necessarily 'procedural' rationality is false. Nor is it obvious why we would need a strong metaphysical version of scientific knowledge against which to sketch any notion of practical wisdom or prudence. True, Aristotle defines *phronesis* in the first instance by means of such a cóntrast; but his discussion of *phronesis* does not end there, for he goes on crucially to define the place of practical wisdom within the pursuit of the good life and ethics more generally. This is more than common sense, if that phrase is taken to indicate that which is cognitively so basic as to require (and possess) no further explanation; but that notion of common sense cannot be identical with notions of practical rationality if Aristotle's claims about habituation, indeterminacy, and practice are meaningful. There is no algorithm for practical wisdom, no precise means by which the one right answer is generated. But this does not mean – cannot mean – that there are no right answers, that the status of phronetic claims are necessarily non-cognitive and therefore non-normative. Inexplicit knowledge can guide us just as well, sometimes, as explicit knowledge. Indeed, sometimes explicit knowledge is not what we require. The realm of the practical may be where this is true more often than not.

These points – I do not call them an argument, precisely – may still leave Habermas unmoved. As more nuance is added to his discourse ethics, and more distinctions made, it becomes clear that Habermas's procedural account of rationality, including practical rationality, is not as formal and abstract as it might at first have appeared. (I cannot address here whether the initial appearance was deceiving, or whether Habermas is just good at incorporating critical insight, but the undertaking would prove interesting.) That being so, is it not possible that the cries for *phronesis* have already been answered, that the neo-Kantian peculiarity of discourse ethics has been softened by a growing acknowledgment of the real difficulties of discourse? Perhaps. But then it is hard to make sense of the refusal to grant us even the coherent notion of practical wisdom in terms like Williams's or, indeed, Smith's as quoted at the beginning of the present essay.

Habermas claimed we could not recover *phronesis* because

notions of general rationality had themselves been rendered post-metaphysical and fallible – 'weak,' in his language. This, of course, is one of the things that the call for *phronesis* was supposed to aid, or hasten. Habermas's attitude to these developments remains ambivalent. He sometimes seems to view with misgiving the loss of strong truth-claims of the old-fashioned kind. Yet his own procedural notion of rationality, with its origin and justification in discourse, abandons all form of external support except the minimal ones associated with communicative competence. And it is far from clear that the features of that competence in any way warrant the label 'metaphysical'; if anything, the contrary. Therefore the question of whether we can today recover *phronesis* must remain open, for Habermas has not convincingly argued the case against recovery. But we purchase that victory only at the cost of seeing that the initial attraction of *phronesis* – its alleged ability to rehabilitate Habermasian universalism – is now itself an open question.

Where does this leave contemporary political theory that is interested in understanding the role of dialogue in political decision making? Are the calls for *phronesis* in political dialogue unnecessary, because already effectively answered? Or are they unsupported, because no coherent notion of *phronesis* is there for the taking?

IV

Richard Bernstein is one contemporary thinker who views the emphasis on *phronesis* – associated, in his view, with the rise of philosophical hermeneutics – as a kind of evolutionary shift in philosophical concern. '[W]e are witnessing a new turn in the conversation of philosophy and in the understanding of human rationality where there is a recovery and appropriation of the types of practical reasoning, knowledge, and wisdom that are characteristic of *phronesis*,' he has said.[27] This is to the good, since the notions of rationality characteristic of the Enlightenment have shown themselves to be at best problematic, at worst positively threatening. But Bernstein worries that the particularism associated with *phronesis* remains unclarified because the universals with which it is supposed to interact are unstable. As we shall see in a moment, I believe this worry will resolve itself in what amounts to a slightly more positive version of Habermas's dilemma – and that clarification will help us see what shape a valid political dialogue of legitimation must take.

Phronesis was supposed to help us solve problems of practical application because, as in Aristotle and Gadamer, it remained inexplicit and concrete. It preserved the 'realness' of the practical world without surrendering our ability to have knowledge and make binding choices – to be cognitive and normative. But *phronesis* performs these tasks by making reference to standards of goodness that are thought to be firm and, moreover, knowable. It is possible, as Aristotelians habitually claim against their Kantian rivals, that we need no transcendental telescope to see these standards. We need only a living, breathing community – a form of ethical life. It must, however, be a stable form of life. '[W]hat Aristotle stresses and Gadamer realizes is that what is required for the exercise of *phronesis*, and what keeps it from degenerating into the mere cleverness of the *deinos*, is the existence of such a *nomos* in the polis or community,' Bernstein says. 'Given a community in which there is a living shared acceptance of ethical principles and norms, then *phronesis* as the mediation of such universals in concrete particular situations makes sense.'[28]

The problem, of course, is that this does not describe the societies most of us live in. '[W]hat has become so problematic for us today, what is characteristic of our hermeneutical situation,' Bernstein goes on,

> is that there is so much confusion and uncertainty (some may even say chaos) about what are the norms or the 'universals' that ought to govern our practical lives. What Gadamer realizes (but I don't think he squarely faces the issue that it raises) is that we are living in a time when the very conditions required for exer-

cise of phronesis – the shared acceptances and stability of universal principles and laws – are themselves breaking down.[29]

This means, then, that the mediation of universal and particular is also breaking down. Bernstein is here speaking of a sociopolitical fact – the disintegration of values – but the upshot is substantially the same as in Habermas's refusal to allow neo-Aristotelians a recovery of *phronesis* because of changes in the status of science. *Phronesis* will not save us. Indeed, for Bernstein it seems paradoxically true that *phronesis* remains a possibility for us, a constantly beckoning goal, at the same time that social and political conditions of contemporary society act to undermine the possibility of *phronesis*. He suggests rather bleakly that this is just part of the tragedy of the human condition – an illuminating comment on human limitation and our thwarted innermost desires.

Still, all is not lost. Our desire for *phronesis* is not doomed to unfulfilment simply because we inhabit unavoidably pluralistic societies. There is yet one more commonality between Bernstein and Habermas and it points the way forward. 'Furthermore,' Bernstein says, 'Gadamer does not adequately clarify *the type of discourse* that is appropriate when questions about the validity of basic norms (or universals) are raised [nor] how we are to evaluate a situation in which we are forced to question the validity of such norms.'[30] To be sure, when Bernstein makes this nod in Habermas's direction he is, as always, wary of the transcendentalism to which Habermas is sometimes prey, and he presumably wants us to understand his point in terms of the *interpretive* possibilities inherent in discourse ethics. Questioning the validity of general norms is part of the ongoing conversation of a society, and a centrally important part if the practical-political problems of the society are to be met. Yet that discursive activity is not the only way we have of going on, and so it is equally important to put general norms in contact with the phronetic means of bringing them to the world. If the problem with Gadamer is that he ignores the possibility of instability in the universal realm, the problem with Habermas is that he ignores the reality of political issues in the sub-universal realm. And in both cases we need to remember that 'universal' here means no more – but no less – than 'acceptable to all affected participants.'

We seem to have come full circle. The original calls for *phronesis* were prompted by, among other things, felt inadequacies in Habermas's rationalistic critical theory. As we tried to give *phronesis* character, it acquired its own problems – problems severe enough to lead Habermas, for one, to deny our desire's coherence. But he was biased, and it seemed that some fine-tuning would get us the *phronesis* we wanted. Yet the instability of the universals to which *phronesis* must appeal led us inexorably back to Habermas and the original limitations of his theory.

Is this circle a vicious one? Assume for a moment it is, and consider a different sort of prospect for critical political theory.

V

According to Hegel, and Hegelian-minded critics of modern ethico-political discourse, our desire for *phronesis* is crucially misplaced, a false craving. It is so because it misconceives the problem of ethical (and by extension political) choice, for understandable historical reasons, as one in which too-abstract normative prescriptions require the sensitivity of practical wisdom to be applied properly. The wedge driven between justification and application – a wedge evident most recently in the title of Habermas's collection, but arguably characteristic of all Kantian-style moral thinking – misconstrues the task of critical theory. The desire for practical wisdom arises only from an initial mistake, namely the abstraction typical of rationalistic procedures of moral assessment. The resulting two-stage theory, complete with an airtight separation between the moments of settling on norms and putting them into action, brutally misrepresents ethical reflection and any political dialogue of legitimation that emerges from ethical reflection. And that misrepresentation takes overt form when we demand a recovery of *phronesis* understood as a means of application only.

The alternative, then, must be to reconceive the project of ethical inquiry in such a way, as Williams puts it, that 'a concretely experienced form of life can be extended.' This was surely Gadamer's view as well, insofar as he insisted on the inseparability of application from all acts of interpretation. We might say that the task is to be more Aristotelian even than the initial calls for *phronesis* imagined: we need to return to a sort of pre-Enlightenment conception of understanding that does not seek validity in detachment from the practical.

But then, unfortunately for the happy neo-Aristotelians, Habermas is proved right, for this 'thick' community-specific kind of *phronesis* apparently cannot be recovered today – not, at least, without recovering an entire form of pre-modern ethical life to ground it and give it point. Stopping short of that, and looking to *phronesis* as a kind of ethical knowledge recoverable anytime and anywhere, on the model of scientific knowledge, only ensnares us in the difficulties noticed above. Indeed, Bernstein provides an echo of the dilemma. If we cannot articulate stable universal norms – meaning 'universal across a relevant community' – we cannot expect to have a functioning virtue of thought that captures Aristotle's sense of practical wisdom. Without that base agreement about the good, including especially about the good life for citizens, no amount of sensitivity to context and particularity will save us. The outlook for such community is not good, especially in modern pluralistic societies like our own which begin with an awareness of difference in ethical aspiration. Little fundamental agreement exists on questions of the good except in small subsocial groups whose identity cannot ever extend to society-wide dimensions without tyrannical effects.

Are we doomed, then, to a choice between fractured and isolated like-mindedness on the one hand, and abstract, formal (and therefore potentially brutal, dehumanizing – or perhaps simply empty, pointless) norms of justice on the other? Is there not some basis for talk among the divided groups of a pluralistic society?

I confess I am not as pessimistic as some about this prospect. In fact, there is reason to think that the circle sketched above is virtuous, not vicious. We may not accept Habermas's own claim that his discourse ethics is immune from Hegelian criticisms of Kantian morality,[31] but we can note that the emphasis placed in discourse ethics on inter-citizen communication marks the horizon of a possible community. Because these citizens are engaged in conversation, their ongoing social project retains the possibility of approaching the ideal of a community united in agreement on all its relevant norms. That such an ideal can only ever be approached, and never finally reached, may be a mark of frustrated human aspiration; but it might also be a mark of the continuing openness of any worthy social project. Norms advanced in justificatory discussion are not pulled from thin air; they have their roots in our real *sittlich* concerns.

From the other side, not even Aristotle expected to find the good without reference to the views and actions of those around him – on the contrary. We cannot do otherwise than start from where we are. Indeed, given the very pluralism that poses this challenge for political theory, the countervailing dangers – social chaos based on divergent conceptions of the good, the moral balkanization of society – may itself provide all the pragmatic motivation we need to begin this conversation. But that is not to say that the conversation will produce only pragmatic results over time; convergence on values is possible, in other words, though perhaps not at the beginning – and anyway not necessary there.

Where does this leave our desire for *phronesis*? Habermas's protestations to the contrary, there is a need to actualize and particularize notions of practical reason. The details of ourselves and our situation matter deeply in normative discourse. But in all fairness, even as Habermas has fought off the demands for *phronesis* as a corrective to this theory, the theory itself has mutated into ever more actual and particular forms. Whether this means that it now captures the reality of practical politics must remain a question for another time. The desire for *phronesis* can seem foiled, or deferred, by these latest manoeuvres. But our disappointment at this development must be modified – and here the circle closes once more – by a sense that the very desire for *phronesis* was (and is) instrumental in the creation of a more adequate critical social theory. The project of articulating that theory, like the political dialogue it inscribes, continues.

Notes

1 The suggestion is usually twofold: we political philosophers need *phronesis*, but so do we citizens.
2 Steven B. Smith, *Hegel's Critique of Liberalism: Rights in Context* (Chicago: University of Chicago Press, 1989), p. 245. For a more extensive discussion of the same point, see Charles Larmore, *Patterns of Moral Complexity* (Cambridge: Cambridge University Press, 1987), ch. 1.
3 Smith, *Hegel's Critique of Liberalism*, p. 246.
4 Bernard Williams, *Ethics and the Limits of Philosophy* (London: Fontana, 1985), ch. 10.
5 Jürgen Habermas, *Justification and Application: Remarks on Discourse Ethics*, trans. Ciarin P. Cronin (Cambridge, MA: MIT Press, 1992).
6 Jürgen Habermas, *Between Facts and Norms: Contributions to a Discourse Theory of Law and Democracy*, trans. William Rehg (Cambridge, MA: MIT Press, 1995).
7 Pragmatic uses of practical reason concern problem solving and uses of skill; ethical ones concern the choice and realization of a good life; moral uses concern issues of justice. The categories parallel Kant's discussion of imperatives in the *Groundwork* as broken into (1) hypothetical-instrumental, (2) hypothetical-prudential, and (3) categorical. Habermas's claim, like Kant's, is that only the third kind of use of practical reason – the moral – makes a *univer-*

salistic demand. This is the realm of justice, where we appeal to all rational agents (Kant) or all affected speakers (Habermas) in order to justify a norm under consideration.

8   Goes some distance, certainly, but enough to be convincing? I discuss this issue of Habermas's problems with practical-political application at greater length in chapter 5 of my *A Civil Tongue: Justice, Dialogue, and the Politics of Pluralism* (University Park, PA: Penn State University Press, 1995).

9   To mention just two of the possibilities. Such responses to discourse ethics – by now quite common – are sometimes part of a more general suspicion of dialogue as a site of political legitimacy. See, e.g., Michael Walzer, 'A Critique of Philosophical Conversation,' *Philosophical Forum* 21:1–2 (1989/90): 182–96. See also Georgia Warnke's reply, in the same volume, 'Rawls, Habermas, and Real Talk: A Reply to Walzer,' pp. 197–203.

10   Williams, *Ethics and the Limits*, p. 104.

11   Smith, *Hegel's Critique of Liberalism*, p. 245. We might compare, on this point, John Rawls's important use of the distinction between rational and reasonable. Reasonableness for Rawls lies in the willingness of potential citizens to subject their views to scrutiny, to accept the fair conditions of social organization, and to assess the views of others. He objects to programs, like David Gauthier's or those characteristic of microeconomic rationality, that *derive* reasonableness in this sense from the allegedly more basic structures of rationality (through, e.g., analysis of self-interested bargaining). See Rawls, *Political Liberalism* (New York: Columbia University Press, 1993), Lecture II, esp. pp. 48–54. Cf. David Gauthier, *Morals by Agreement* (Oxford: Clarendon Press, 1986).

12   Stanley Rosen, 'Return to the Origin: Reflections on Plato and Contemporary Philosophy,' *International Philosophical Quarterly* 16 (1976): 169. For a dissenting view on Heidegger, see Lawrence Vogel, *The Fragile 'We': Ethical Implications of Heidegger's 'Being and Time'* (Evanston, IL: Northwestern University Press, 1994), esp. ch. 4.

13   See H.-G. Gadamer, 'The Hermeneutic Relevance of Aristotle,' in *Truth and Method*, trans. Garrett Barden and John Cumming (New York: Crossroad, 1988), pp. 278–89; quotation is at p. 289. (Here-

114   Foundations

after: TM.) Gadamer's decisive encounter with Aristotelian moral and political theory took place, by his own account, during Heidegger's seminars on the *Nicomachean Ethics* in the 1930s. See Gadamer's account in 'Hermeneutics and Historicism,' included as an appendix to TM, at pp. 489–90.

14 Georgia Warnke, 'The Hermeneutic Turn in Recent Political Philosophy,' *Yale Journal of Criticism* 4 (Fall 1990): 207–29, and reprinted in revised form as chapter 1 of Warnke's *Justice and Interpretation* (Cambridge, MA: MIT Press, 1993).

15 TM, p. 283.

16 TM, pp. 286–7.

17 TM, p. 288. Gadamer notes with approval Aristotle's discussion of the *deinos* – the person of practical ability who nevertheless lacks *phronesis* because he lacks orientation to the right ends. It is not enough to possess experience and insight into a situation's possibilities; to be practically wise we must also be oriented to moral ends.

18 TM, p. 289.

19 Richard J. Bernstein, 'From Hermeneutics to Praxis,' in Brice R. Wachterhauser, ed., *Hermeneutics and Modern Philosophy* (Albany, NY: SUNY Press, 1986), p. 95. See also his *Beyond Objectivism and Relativism: Science, Hermeneutics, and Praxis* (Philadelphia: University of Pennsylvania Press, 1983) and 'What Is the Difference That Makes a Difference? Gadamer, Habermas, and Rorty,' in *Hermeneutics and Modern Philosophy*, pp. 343–76.

20 Bernstein, 'From Hermeneutics to Praxis,' p. 95.

21 Stanley Rosen, *Hermeneutics as Politics* (New York: Oxford University Press, 1987), pp. 139, 141. Rosen is one of those who see no salvation in the Habermasian reform of anything-goes hermeneutics. In his view, Habermas's transcendentalism is ultimately empty, provides no basis for any specific political program, and issues only in platitudes: '[W]e do not require theories telling us how to cross the street or that the best way to communicate with people is by speaking to them' (p. 12).

22 Rosen's critical discussion of Strauss (among his targeted gallery of Derrida, Rorty, Kojeve, Foucault, et al.) is particularly illuminating. See ibid., pp. 107–38.

23 Ibid., ch. 5, esp. pp. 191–3. Rosen also has some rather opaque things to say about *phronesis*; see p. 174.

24 Habermas, 'Remarks on Discourse Ethics,' in *Justification and Application*, p. 21; cf. p. 117.

25 Ibid., p. 124. See pp. 120–5 for Habermas's argument that claims of practical know-how are as 'validity-ridden' as scientific claims.

26 Ibid., pp. 124–5.

27 Bernstein, 'From Hermeneutics to Praxis,' p. 95. The thinkers under discussion at this juncture in Bernstein's argument are Arendt, Habermas, Rorty, MacIntyre, and Putnam.

28 Ibid., p. 101.

29 Ibid.

30 Ibid.; emphasis added.

31 See his 'Morality and Ethical Life: Does Hegel's Critique of Kant Apply to Discourse Ethics?' in *Moral Consciousness and Communicative Action*, trans. Christian Lenhardt and Shierry Weber Nicholsen (Cambridge, MA: MIT Press, 1990).

Keeping a Straight Bat: Cricket, Civility, and Post-Colonialism

I Introduction

'What I really hate about cricket,' says Tommy Judd in the film *Another Country*, 'is that it's such a damn good game.' We might be forgiven for thinking the sentiment expresses a feeling deeper than, and ironically at odds with, the Marxist ideology that fuels Tommy's rebellion against his schooling at a thinly masked Eton.[1] 'Judd's Paradox,' his friend Guy Bennett calls it, indulging in a parody of the Marxist analysis that was later, one imagines, to underwrite his own spying and celebrated defection to the Soviet Union. 'Cricket is a fundamental part of the capitalist conspiracy,' mocks Guy. 'There's every reason to suppose that the game ultimately derives from the wholly unjustified right of the medieval lord to the unpaid labour of villeins and serfs at hay-making and harvest.' ('You know,' says Judd, 'you're really beginning to get the idea.')

Then, as the film closes, the tactless American interviewer visiting Guy in his bleak Moscow apartment asks him whether he misses anything English. 'I miss ... the cricket,' whispers Guy pathetically, patrician fop to the last. Which is only to say again what the film (and play) have already said numerous times in a less obvious manner: Guy's Marxist politics flow not from commitment but from resentment – a result of his homosexuality, and the hypocritical reactions it occasions among his schoolfellows as they close him out of their highest echelons. He's not even a fellow-traveller; he's merely a dilettante. For to fancy cricket – to *continue* to fancy cricket, the quintessential upper-class game – is surely evidence of an imperfect conversion, an insufficiently examined consciousness.

The conclusion suggested here is reactionary, to the effect that leftist rallying points, up to and including well-publicized defections, are illusions. The political is the personal – and that's all it is. Guy's unwilling exclusions from school power are held close to Judd's willing ones, but the juxtaposition does both a disservice. Guy is not a pioneer in sexual politics, merely a crybaby; hatred of a class hypocrisy that shuts him out is his only ideological commitment. By contrast, the committed Judd is killed in the Spanish Civil War – which shows what happens to well-meaning parlour pinkos looking for street credibility. ('You're always trying to be different,' a particularly lumpish schoolmate complains at one point.) The fact that Judd is the only character in play or film with any scrap of integrity is not really countervailing here, simply further evidence that he is too good for this world. Finally, it is not an exaggeration to credit the lovingly detailed camera work and exquisite landscapes of Marek Kanievska's film with providing a perfect aesthetic wash for these right-wing sentiments. The scenes of army cadet musters and cricket on Eton's greensward are familiar iconic snapshots that in this context approach self-parody. They're being celebrated, not criticized. Judd's Paradox is not resolved by *Another Country*, only enhanced: class destiny, including a love for cricket, cannot be escaped.

Consider some other examples of Judd's Paradox, these drawn not from conservative pseudo-history but from reportage, and referring not to upper-class Marxists but to working political actors. Ram Manohar Lotha (1910–67), the Indian political theorist and freedom fighter, repeatedly denounced cricket in his writings as a colonial relic keeping the Indian people from their destiny. Yet he eagerly attended Test matches. And journalist Mervyn de Silva, writing of a Sri Lankan cricket victory, noted the 'romantic paradox' of the late N.M. Perera, who felt more pride in being president of the Sri Lanka Board of Control for Cricket than in being a founding father of Sri Lanka's Marxist revolutionary movement.[2]

We have, finally, the greatest exemplar of Judd's Paradox in C.L.R. James, the Trinidadian Marxist whose lifelong association with cricket is, perhaps contrary to expectation, the master key to his political awareness. These are not isolated instances of the ambivalence that exists between politics and sport, even the decisively aristocratic sport of cricket.[3] The game's place at the centre of English imperial attitudes should make it a clearly antithetical element in revolutionary movements, especially in colonial settings: a mark of the old rule that simply must be thrown off. Yet, in view of the pervasive influence of the game in colonial societies[4] – its ineradicable effect on questions of national character and destiny – the matter cannot be viewed so simply.

But what role does cricket play in true revolution? one is tempted to ask. Is love for the game simply a socialized aberration from the party line, a regrettable piece of leftover cultural baggage? Or is there, perhaps, a critical possibility in cricket that marks it as not only not opposed to social restructuring but allied with it? Is there, in other words, a political resolution of Judd's Paradox through a closer examination of cricket itself?

In exploring such a possibility, one is obliged to fend off (at least) two cherished but one-sided interpretations of cricket's political role. These may be called for convenience the *imperial* and the *colonial* versions of cricket, and the similarities suggested by the pairing are not coincidental, for these are in reality two shades of the same colour: the culture of dominance and the culture of subordination, both playing the game for ends that may be teased out with good results. These interpretations do not give us the whole story, however. In what follows I will attempt a joining of these two interpretations which gives us more of that story, if not its entirety – for this is a story whose ending remains by design (and with clamorous approval) forever deferred in the great ellipsis of all sporting events, that there is always next year.

Before beginning, one is likewise obliged, more basically, to deal with the limited but increasingly influential notion that cricket has, as a professional sport, no political role whatsoever. This can be done briskly by invoking the firm voice of James, here discussing his falling away from Trotskyism in the 1950s. 'Trotsky had said that the workers deflected from politics by sports,' James writes in his autobiographical essay *Beyond a Boundary*. 'With my past I simply could not accept that.'[5] Even more firmly, James notes with apparent wonder that a 'professor of political science publicly bewailed that a man of my known political interests should believe that cricket had ethical and social values.' Declining into colloquialism for perhaps the first and only time, he writes, 'I had no wish to answer. I was just sorry for the guy' (BB, p. 241).

That sports and politics link up in numerous and complex ways cannot here be doubted, without anyway misunderstanding the meaning of the words 'politics' and 'sports' – and we may feel sorry for those who do. In cricket especially, we might think, the sports–politics dialectic simply cannot be ignored: James's considered answer to this professor's challenge is his entire life, a life spent reflecting on the destiny of the West Indies, a destiny that simply *makes no sense* without the culture of cricket. Because this is so, because for any West Indian (or Indian, and to a lesser extent Australian) life is not explicable without cricket, James will repeatedly ask the famous question ultimately traceable to the great cricket writer Neville Cardus: 'What do they know of cricket who only cricket know?' To know only the game is not to know the game, and the autobiographical and political details of *Beyond a Boundary* are therefore no more or less indispensable in making it a treatise on cricket, as conversely the details about what makes a great bowler or batsman are indispensable in making it a treatise on radical politics. In what follows, then, we will explore the critic Ashis Nandy's view that 'some arguments about colonial, neo-colonial, anti-colonial and post-colonial

consciousness can be made better in the language of international cricket than that of political economy.'[6]

What I will suggest, circumscribed now in a world where
cricket is any and all of metaphor, battlefield, polling booth,
hustings, editorial column, national mirror, and cultural history, is that the *culture of civility* embedded in cricket provides
it with radical political possibilities missing in other team
sports. The claim may appear counter-intuitive. We are not
used to thinking of civility as a condition of social reform, nor
do we typically consider cricket as anything more than an
expression of, on the one hand, social superiority or, on the
other, colonial inferiority. Nor, for that matter, do we often
push sports to the forefront of political awareness, however
much we might incline to the view defended by James that
they cannot be understood outside a social and political
context.

No one would reasonably deny that football, for example,
expresses a set of 'ethical and social values' that could be codified with relative ease as the dominant ideology of a large
post-industrial nation like the United States: team spirit, ag-
gressiveness, ruthlessness, territorial commitment, a high-tech
reliance on state-of-the-art equipment. It is no mistake that
many of the reigning metaphors in business and government are football-derived. Yet the cultivation of such values in
these wider contexts puts into question the role of football
itself. Is it indoctrination, colourful expression of what is
already dominant, reinforcement of the wavering? Perhaps
none of these?

The peculiar advantage of cricket lies in its having ethical
and social values which are, in the current political atmosphere, reformative in orientation – and this sometimes
despite appearances to the contrary. Which is of course not to
suggest that cricket can, or even should, acquire a wider popularity than it now has; cricket will never catch on in America,
not simply for aesthetic or cultural reasons but for structural
political ones, which contain the others and also go beyond
them. What I have called cricket's culture of civility may indi-

cate, however, political lessons that tell beyond the boundaries not only of the pitch itself – that can no longer be doubted – but of the countries in which the pitch lies.

Though one might choose another focal point, in what follows I will concentrate on the figure of James, and this for at least three compelling reasons. First, the strong element of autobiography that is woven through James's reflections on cricket provides an object lesson in the inextricability of the personal and political in the realm of sport – without cricket we cannot understand James either as a self-described 'Puritan' nor as the author of *Black Jacobins* or *The Case for West Indian Self-Government*. Second, then, the delicious incongruity – an incongruity I will suggest resolves itself, under analysis, into complex shades of meaning – of the committed Marxist who is also committed to the aristocratic game cannot be ignored. No North American sport could provide the same apparently paradoxical juxtaposition.

Third, then, these factors combining, it is no small matter that James's life spans the last days of the Victorian 'golden age' of cricket, with the amateur sportsman foremost and a sense (if not always a reality) that 'It isn't cricket' and 'Keep a straight bat' were phrases with meaning,[7] and the first days of the new professional ethos which, in common with professional sports everywhere, finds such sentiments either simply naive or, worse, cynically useful as platitudes for the sports pages. The turning point between these eras is, famously, the 'bodyline' controversy of 1931–2, and James's reactions to it provide an illustration of the possibilities that might still exist for a culture of civility, now somewhat chastened and worldly but nevertheless vital – in cricket and elsewhere.

II Victoriana: W.G. Grace and Cricket's Golden Age of Imperialism

A good deal has been made of the influence the physician W.G. Grace (1848–1915) had on the game of cricket, not least by James himself, who argues that with Thomas Arnold (of

Rugby School fame) and Thomas Hughes (of Tom Brown fame) Grace completed the Holy Trinity of the Victorian Age. The matter is put succinctly by the philosopher Alasdair MacIntyre. Drawing a distinction between goods 'external' to a practice and ones 'internal' to it, MacIntyre notes that whereas the former must be either won or lost – that is, they are goods by exclusion and can be enjoyed only by the winner – the latter must be considered good for everyone engaged in the practice. 'Internal goods are indeed the outcome of competition to excel, but it is characteristic of them that their achievement is a good for the whole community who participate in the practice,' says MacIntyre. 'So when Turner transformed the seascape in painting or W.G. Grace advanced the art of batting in cricket in a quite new way their achievement enriched the whole relevant community.'[8]

It is in this sense of enriching an entire community that the qualities allowing great exemplars to cultivate internal goods are relevantly called 'the virtues' – those traits of character without which such goods would not be possible. We might even say, in Grace's case anyway, that his achievement *created* the community, for organized first-class cricket was a phenomenon whose popularity and recognition grew with Grace himself through the latter part of the nineteenth century. Though the game was much older than that, dating back in some accounts to the twelfth century, it was Grace's singular achievement to make of cricket the repository of those values of sportsmanship and elegance we at least unreflectively associate with the game.

That he did this with refinements of the art of batting – the details of which do not concern us here, nor would they make widely diverting reading – cannot obscure the fact that it is the *figure* of Grace, the image of the portly bearded doctor with his artful style and crude willow wand, that draws cricket's virtues into a recognizable human shape.[9] The economy of that image is what concerns us here: its iconic roles, its referential stock and charge, possibly its susceptibility to manipulation. There are no obvious parallels in the history of North American sport, though a few images perhaps suggest a cognate power (the mustachioed, ramrod-straight Walter Camp at Yale, for example, or the celebrated photograph of Jackie Robinson stealing home).

In this sense Grace, the father of virtue in cricket, is not merely its Abner Doubleday but also its Odysseus. The comparison is apt in another sense too, for Grace was by all contemporary accounts a crafty and cheerful competitor, given to rapid and brilliant calculations of tactical advantage, moreover fond of deceit and ruthlessness in his quest to win. He was suspected of using an oversize non-regulation bat, frequently intimidated umpires to make favourable calls, and was not above outright cheating. He was, finally, a cricketer who donned the mantle of the gentleman while nevertheless making money at the game. 'W.G. Grace,' says Geoffrey Moorhouse, 'was not only one of the outstanding mercenaries of all time, but one of the most conspicuous offenders against that spirit of cricket which became glorified during his era and which he was supposed to represent.'[10]

There are a number of possible responses to these less immediately desirable traits of Grace's character. We might, like his opponents, seek to undercut his position as the game's exemplar, or at least call attention to its hypocrisy in a damaging fashion. ('It's only cheating. Everybody does it,' says Guy Bennett in *Another Country*. 'Sportsmanship – it's all hypocrisy.') Why, after all, should opposing bowlers feel inclined to see Grace's batting prowess as something that 'enriched their community'? In the short run, of course, it did not: he – and soon his imitators too – knocked them all over the pitch. In the long run, the development and refinement of batting led to advances in bowling as well, for tit-for-tat refinement is the nature of sport as it is of warfare and espionage.

Then again, we might view Grace's peccadilloes as did many contemporary fans, the forgivable foibles of a great man, comparable to the philandering of an inspirational leader or the habitual rudeness of a famed opera singer. But that response, too, leaves the problem of countervailing vices unsolved. Neither of these attitudes to Grace – one negative, one positive – makes any headway in understanding the relationship between aspects of Grace's character, aspects of Victorian cricket more generally, and aspects (let us not forget) of the Victorian mind. The possibility unexplored in such responses is the one willing to accept Grace's hypocrisy as an integral part of his gamesmanship, an aspect of character no more separable from the standard virtues of the amateur cricketer than from the man himself.

This is to suggest that what was peculiar to the emerging Victorian mind was a systematically ambivalent attitude to the very values it was in the process of exporting, through colonial incursions not the least of which was cricket itself, to much of the world.[11] As a repository of values concerning good conduct, civility, sporting fairness and grace, cricket represented the alleged bright side of this exportation, those qualities that were supposed to make the de facto triumph of the British colonizers ultimately a de jure matter. We are naturally suspicious of such legalistic, and prescriptive, sleight of hand; but so, I am suggesting, were the exporters themselves. For cricket had a dark side too, embodied in the concealed drive to win, the aggression and brute desire to crush opponents that lay beneath its surface show of polite elegance. These sides of the game should not be seen as conflicting aspects but rather as complements, indispensable to one another and neither, of itself, all that is cricket. The dialectic between them is instantiated not just by Grace himself, the wily gentleman of the pitch, but also by the division that developed in first-class cricket between 'the Gentlemen' (that is, amateurs of independent means who played for pleasure) and 'the Players' (the professionals, often of lower-class origin, who played for money).

This division, which persisted until quite recently, is only the most obvious institutional illustration of the inner conflict of Victorian or golden-age cricket, an inner conflict that without exaggeration may be said to be typical of the Victorian mind, especially in its colonizing activities. The disappearance of the distinction indicates, not surprisingly, that one side has won out. There are no longer Players versus Gentlemen, merely players – all of whom, in first-class cricket, are paid to play though they still come from a variety of social backgrounds. The triumph of the players in this generic sense may indicate, however, a loss of value charge in the game itself – such that, for reasons I will explore presently, it no longer has the reformative possibilities it retained, however oddly, in its Victorian manifestation.

On the one hand, then, we have the values of the gifted amateur Gentleman – the lover of the game – who is typically a rich man of taste and discrimination who plays cricket mainly for its show of elegance and grace. In the stereotypical version, the Gentleman is concerned more with aesthetic values than competitive ones. He would rather be retired on a stylish stroke caught at the boundary than plod through a workmanlike innings devoted to wicket protection and slow accumulation of runs. He would, in other words, rather go down gloriously than stay in and win without style. He prizes fair play, the show of politeness to opponents, and the willing display of good conduct thought appropriate to the game. On the other hand, the typical Player is interested mainly, or possibly only, in winning – for his livelihood depends on it. He is ruthless because he has to be, and moreover because that is the best possible way to gain victory. He is not prepared to go beyond the rules, unless he is certain he will not be caught, but he is fully prepared to exploit the rules to their fullest extent in the interests of winning. He may not be entirely blind to the aesthetic aspects of the game, but they simply cannot compare in weight to the issue of winning. He will not win 'at any cost' but he will win 'at any *reasonable* cost' – the qualification to be determined precisely by circumstances, available personnel, and the laxity or otherwise of the umpires.

The mythology of cricket is such as to indicate that these stereotypes formed themselves into relatively stable groups with very little value-seepage between them, a mythology reinforced by the Gentlemen versus Players matches popular through the nineteenth century and into the beginning of the twentieth. Though the Gentlemen frequently lost, especially before Grace, their losses reinforced rather than challenged a cherished self-understanding: they did not play the game to win if that meant playing at the cost of good sportsmanship, for this was no longer playing the game. Thus protected, they could win or lose with equal assurance as long as the values of cricket – values expressed in the idea of doing 'what's cricket' – were maintained. The movement of this phrase from the playing field into wider social contexts, however ironically as time went on, was evidence that cricket represented the best a Gentleman could be.

But this narrative of self-protection, the value of the so-called moral victory (i.e., defeat done properly), is more a result of that mythology being the property of writers, journalists, and artists who were often middle-class snobs – the people most likely to feel a yearning for the Gentlemen's values and the culture there represented, a culture of which they were not members. Grace was only the first cricketer who, though technically a Gentleman in the cricket sense, was a canny, aggressive competitor given to, say, sacrificing an elegant but doomed shot for a sneaky deflection for one or two needed runs. It was in this sense of combining the dark and light of cricket that Grace was the representative Victorian, an embodiment both of the best values to be found in the era's notions of fairness and civility and of the blithe hypocrisy that went with flouting those values when the occasion was right. 'Grace was one of those who defined the Victorian period,' says Ashis Nandy, echoing James and MacIntyre, in *The Tao of Cricket*. 'He did so by redefining cricket to make it a representative Victorian game – at one plane a violent battle which by common consent had to be played like a gentle, ritualized garden party; at another, a new profession which had to be practised as if it was a pastime.'[12]

This, then, is what Nandy calls the 'intrinsic schizophrenia of traditional cricket' (TC, p. 97), a kind of inner dynamic that pitted the overtly valued virtues of good sportsmanship against the largely unmentionable, but nevertheless widely

recognized and valued, virtues of aggression and drive to win.
'It was,' says Nandy,

> to keep [working-class] cricketers at bay that the cultural hierar-
> chy between the Gentlemen and the Players evolved in cricket.
> The class discrimination in cricket legitimized the class discrimi-
> nation in society by ranking sportsmanship, individuality and
> flair, reportedly the qualities of the gentlemanly amateur, higher
> than competitiveness (defined as an over-eagerness to win),
> application and consistency, all reportedly the qualities of the
> professional player ... Cricket thereby epitomized the basic prob-
> lem – the fatal flaw of character – in the Victorian personality.
> The Victorian had to see the lower classes as carriers of those
> 'vulgar or 'dirty' modern qualities which allowed the upper
> classes to uphold the traditional virtues and yet enjoy the bene-
> fits of modernity. (TC, p. 19)

With this schizophrenic nature of traditional cricket laid bare
before us, it is harder to make sense of the superficial but now
canonical narrative of cricket's descent from amateur glory
into an era of win-at-all-costs professional pragmatism.

Grace reminds us, as no one else can, that the story is not so
simple – that, even if there has been a discernible sea change, it
is not one of simple light to dark. (The language is not coincidental to this story's typical contours, especially when one
factors in, as we must, the influence of colonial challenges to
the game's practice.) The schizophrenic nature of traditional
cricket, whatever its obvious drawbacks, preserved something
of value that has been lost in the one-sided reaction to it, a
reaction exemplified by the aggression of bodyline bowling
and the modern triumph of the professional. In making such a
claim, it will remain important that Victorian cricket did not
triumph over its inner conflict but instead embraced it. Judd's
Paradox, in other words, will not be resolved by removing
one or the other side of cricket's nature; we must, rather,
understand the conflict as productively dynamic, a sporting
dialectic.

This may be seen more clearly if we reflect on a comment by the Indian prince K.S. Ranjitsinhji, one of cricket's most famous heroes. Grace, according to Ranjitsinhji, was a great cricketer because he had 'made utility the criterion of style' – a judgment that may seem at odds with images of Grace as the great aesthetic stylist of batting. But the remark is acute, for it provides a clue to the line of conflict we have been pursuing. Style, for Grace, was acceptable insofar as it was useful to the object of the game, namely, winning; but it was nevertheless style that lay at the centre of his lifelong study of batting. Ranjitsinhji does not say that Grace made utility the criterion of *playing*, but of *style*. The point may seem small, but it is significant. It was only as a great stylist of batting that Grace could take up his possession as the virtuous exemplar of cricket's internal goods – goods which include, but do not end with, winning. If Grace had merely been adept at winning, he would deserve no place in cricket's pantheon, and would have none. For in cricket, at least of the traditional variety, winning is not (*pace* Vince Lombardi) the only thing – however much it may still be the most important thing.

The internal conflicts of traditional cricket were, I have said, dynamic. In the event, that meant it could not survive the process of exportation unaltered, for its class-based social balance and peculiar brand of hypocrisy were too delicate for overt challenge. That challenge came from the colonies, in a manner that may prove surprising – and may, in the end, give credence to James's claim in *Beyond a Boundary* that colonialism is both oppression and liberation. Or, to put the point in Nandy's provocative formulation, now from an Indian rather than West Indian perspective: 'Cricket is an Indian game accidentally discovered by the English' (TC, p. 1).

Nandy means a great deal by saying this, more than I can reasonably approach here, so I will restrict myself to exploring one meaning only of this proclamation, a meaning shared by James's close study of West Indian cricket. The exportation of cricket contained within it the seeds of its own destruction, Nandy suggests, just as colonialism more generally would lead to the destruction of empire. 'Victorian cricket reversed the process' of exporting aristocratic values, he argues. 'It allowed Indians to assess their colonial rulers by western values reflected in the official philosophy of cricket, *and to find the rulers wanting*. The assessment assumed that cricket was not the whole of Englishness but was the moral underside of English life which the English at the turn of the century, even with much of the world at their feet, found difficult to live down' (TC, p. 7; emphasis added). And to the extent they could not live down these values, the oppressors gave the oppressed the exact means of their own liberation. Was it, Nandy wonders, for reasons like this that Rudyard Kipling, the arch-imperialist with more insight than most into colonial thinking, appeared to despise cricketers as 'flanelled fools at the wicket'?

III Colonial Responses: Beating the Masters, Changing the Game

The contours of Victorian cricket are the contours of imperial cricket. Nandy's analysis suggests there are two levels at which the game must be viewed in order to understand the product that was being exported by the Empire, and the transformative reception of that product by the colonies; we can call these, with him, the levels of 'rule' and 'norm.' We can likewise agree that the dual valence of cricket's principles is a response to the nature of the game, 'its culture of anarchic individualism [and] the peculiar, non-repressive collectivism based on that anarchy' (TC, p. 4).

For it is only in such a context of barely controlled individual effort that there arises the need for, and culture to support, non-stated norms of sporting behavior. The game by its nature gives individual players inordinate responsibility when representing the team, in particular with batting. And it is also in the nature of the game that tiny slips can result in dismissal while batting, a tricky reminder of fate's proximity that is unlike almost any other sport.[13] As a result of these and many other similar features of the game, it is never clear whether the best team – that is, the team with the best players – will succeed in winning. 'When a game permits such anarchy, plurality and randomness, how does one judge quality and defy fate while conforming to the norms of the game? Even more important, how does one define transgressions or determine culpability?' (TC, p. 27).

The rules/norms distinction provides an answer, for it specifies not just two ways in which one can 'play cricket' but also specifies a number of possible relationships between the two levels of principle, relationships put into play by the acts of cricketers themselves. The *rules* are, as Nandy says, the 'lower-order rules or laws of cricket: they are the rules in the rule book of the game and the only officially recognized norms of cricket' and '[o]vertly, the world of cricket believes that there is no other rule except these and that these rules, combined with adequate sportsmanship, can guarantee good cricket. In this respect, the game is no different from other games in which the good player must learn to push the rules to their limit or to exploit them fully.' But the *norms* of cricket are a different matter, being 'a set of higher-order or overarching rules which control the culture of the game and which underlie the slogan of sportsmanship' (TC, p. 27).

These norms are not rules in the strict sense, not being part of the rule book (which, incidentally, calls the first-order rules Laws, as though they were unto eternity unchangeable), but instead consist of the values, both articulable and not, that go into such phrases as 'Keep a straight bat' and 'It isn't cricket.' The norms need not be articulated so long as the culture of sportsmanship is vital, and indeed articulation is dangerous for it suggests they could be codified and by doing so makes them weaker.[14] It is for reasons like this that

> for the makers of the first set of rules these [second-order norms] are mere conventions or traditions. These are not even mentioned in the rule book, except in the form of occasional exhortations to good, sporting cricket. Yet, the complexity and subtlety

of the second set is what gives cricket its uniqueness. Most games are predominantly controlled by the lower-order rules; some like chess entirely by them. In cricket, *if one follows every lower-order rule one still may not be playing cricket*, since many of the higher-order norms of cricket, like the constitution of Britain, are not written down but yet constitute standards by which players and teams are constantly judged. (TC, p. 28; emphasis added)

The implications of such a distinction are wide, and not merely for cricket. The force of 'It isn't cricket' is that certain styles of play or pitch behaviour may, while not being actively unlawful, flout the conventional norms of playing the game 'properly.' This opens up the possibility, explored briefly in the example of the Gentleman, of what C.B. Fry called cricket's 'aesthetic morality' – what matters is not who wins or loses, but how one plays the game. How one plays the game is a function of style, and since style cannot be learned by rote but only cultivated, the less cultivated remain at a disadvantage so long as the norms of cricket are lexically prior to its rules.

This lexical priority cannot be doubted, for the rules/norms distinction is not value neutral. And given the social charge of golden-age cricket, the cricket in which this ordering remained largely unchallenged, there should be doubt as to what underlies the ordering. 'Traditionally,' says Nandy, 'the amateur cricketer, the gentleman, was supposed to be specially well-versed in the intricacies of the crucial unwritten laws of cricket, in addition to being well acquainted with the written laws of the game.' By contrast, 'the professional was not trusted in the matter of his knowledge of and allegiance to the unwritten norms. That is why for many years the captaincy of national teams was reserved for only the gentleman-cricketer, openly in England and less blatantly in other countries' (TC, p. 28).

This association of the familiar class division with the rules/norms distinction contributes, in some cases quite openly, to a gradual devaluing of the norms of cricket, for they 'sound moralistic, old-fashioned and slightly comic to the professional, modern cricketer' (TC, p. 28). On the other hand, the function of the norms as governing conventions in situations where rules cannot be specified or as a background of style against which all use of the rules is carried out, indicates that loss of the norms through social challenge may actually weaken the game. Thus the paradox of colonial and professional challenges to cricket, challenges that arise coincidentally with and reinforce a general shift from amateur to professional in the game. The ruthless competitiveness of colonial challenger and professional alike undermine cricket's uniqueness and, more importantly, its integrity as a game. Unwittingly, such challenges have the ultimate effect of removing cricket's capacity for social critique.

The point is clearer if we specify the role of the norms in cricket's practice. Cricket, says Nandy, 'is almost unique in providing ample scope for unjust play as well as having strong taboos against such play and yet, at the same time, not having much concrete protection against unjust play or against someone trying to take full advantage of the loopholes in the laws.' Moreover, 'the culture of cricket also emphasizes that whatever else it might be, it will not be cricket if the game tries to build into its laws total protection against all transgressions' (TC, p. 30). The norms play the crucial role of providing nonlegalistic, unwritten (and often unspoken, except in generalities) principles by reference to which the scope for unjust play is minimized.

If that reference is no longer available, there is no restriction on the full exploitation of the rules' many loopholes; and if, moreover, the key value of the game shifts from playing well to winning, there is no way to curb that exploitation. Without sportsmanship, the game is no more than a brute contest of canniness and ruthlessness. Sportsmanship is, for cricket, 'the over-arching value, which gives structure to many of the higher-order norms, including conventions or folk-ways, of cricket, and connects the two kinds of norms which face the cricketer – the traditional and the rational-legal' (TC, p. 37).[15] Sportsmanship does not mean that winning is unimportant, but it maintains its hold on exploiters of the rules by valuing a sporting defeat more than an unsporting victory, as in this priority chain:

| Sporting victory | > | Sporting defeat | > | Unsporting victory | > | Unsporting defeat |

'It is as if the culture of cricket was ambivalent towards competition and performance,' says Nandy, 'and sought to contain the ambivalence by maintaining the illusion that success was not the goal of cricket; sportsmanship was.' Therefore '[c]ricket in its purest forms can be seen as either a display of sportsmanship through the instrumentality of competition and performance, or as a display of playful competition and playful performance in which the playfulness of the exercise is made clear through sportsmanship' (TC, p. 38).

The ambivalence mentioned here is clearly class-connected to the extent that the gentleman-cricketer was thought to embody the sporting values while the professional player sought victory at any cost.[16] This is why it was acceptable to have players on a national side, but not in the captaincy. The class connection is also maintained in what I called earlier the descent from light to dark in cricket. With the disappearance of the gentleman-amateur as a viable social type, a disappearance dating to the first part of the twentieth century, the triumph of the player and the player's values was complete. The modern trend in cricket is that the rules

> instead of being part of a framework within which the conventions or traditions dominated, have now become supreme. The rules now rule by themselves. The goal is no longer to display one's superior conformity to the rules by showing one's superior conformity to the higher-order conventions or to the idea of sportsmanship. The goal is to display success as a sportsman or

as a sports-team within the confines of the rules by making the best *use* of the rules. Such use rejects all traditions as guides to action and it rejects the idea that there could be norms not specified in the rules. Mechanical conformity to the rules is still looked down upon but superior conformity has now come to mean superior exploitation of the rules. (TC, pp. 39–40)

This modern triumph of use-values in cricket represents one kind of resolution of the inner conflicts of the Victorian game explored earlier, but it is a resolution without progressive possibility. Cricket is no longer a delicate combination of two notions of success: successful participation in the game (shown by winning) and successful show of sportsmanship (shown by playing well).

The modern game emphasizes only the value of entertaining with success, not succeeding with entertainment. Nandy illustrates this trend with the following schematic, which shows the competing hierarchies of success in cricket.

Victory > Draw > Defeat (professional)
Victory > 'Grand' Defeat > 'Tame' Draw (transitional)
'Grand' Defeat > 'Inglorious' Victory > 'Tame' Draw
(amateur)

'The interplay of these orders,' he says, 'gave cricket its charm, even though the allegiance to the second and third orders was often hypocritical ... The game has acquired its new hardness by virtually eliminating the second and third orders' (TC, p. 42). And it is that 'new hardness' that is associated with the social triumph of the professional.

What role did colonial responses to cricket play in this? The accepted interpretation of the colonial appropriation of cricket is one that sees it reinforcing the professional's victory. That is, to the extent that colonial cricketers were less bound by the strictures of norm-behaviour in cricket, they were more fully able to exploit the rules to their advantage. The desire to beat

the masters at their own game, a celebrated colonial enter-
prise, succeeded in changing the game because it made it
impossible to win in any fashion other than the aggressive,
exploitative style adopted by, say, the Australian sides of the
1920s. Even committed gentlemen cannot sustain themselves
on a pure diet of sporting defeats, and anyway the English
teams of this period were not gentlemen all through. On this
view, the colonial competitiveness, a competitiveness not sufficiently fettered by the culture of sportsmanship, transformed
cricket by chipping away the patina of hypocrisy the Victorian
game had given itself. And, like all demonstrations of hypocrisy, this transformation has access to a certain cynical piece of
high ground, for our moral culture is such that any exposé
of hypocrisy, no matter how self-serving, provides an illusion
of ethical bona fides.[17]

But the colonial reception of cricket is not so simple, as
James's tale of West Indian cricket makes clear. The long opening sections of *Beyond a Boundary*, which detail James's rather
old-fashioned education into a simulacrum of an English gentleman, are crucial in this regard. Though he describes himself
as, by the age of ten, 'already an alien in my own environment,
among my own people,' James's ultimate contention is that
this education was peculiarly West Indian in a less superficial
sense than his egregious preference for Thackeray might indicate. 'I began to study Latin and French, then Greek, and much
else,' he says at one point,

> But particularly we learnt, I learnt and obeyed and taught as
> code, the English public-school code. Britain and her colonies
> and the colonial people. What do the British people know of
> what they have done there? Precious little. The colonial peoples,
> particularly the West Indians, scarcely know themselves as yet. It
> has taken me a long time to begin to understand. (BB, p. 33)

In time, James became that peculiar colonial product, the
English gentleman more gentlemanly than his objects of imita-

tion. All the dicta of sportsmanship were internalized effortlessly, joyfully, by him and his fellows. Socially they were a
diverse group. 'Yet rapidly we learned,' says James,

> to obey the umpire's decision without question, however irratio-
> nal it was. We learned to play with the team, which meant subor-
> dinating your personal inclinations, and even interests, to the
> good of the whole. We kept a stiff upper lip in that we did not
> complain about ill fortune ... We were generous to opponents
> and congratulated them on victories, even when we knew they
> did not deserve it. We lived in two worlds ... [whatever went on
> elsewhere] on the playing field we did what ought to be done.
> (BB, p. 34).

'Eton and Harrow,' James concludes, 'had nothing on us.' And
we cannot doubt him, for there is no more perfect sportsman
than the displaced sportsman.

This is, of course, colonial behaviour at its most obvious.
What better way – indeed, what *other* way? – to challenge the
masters than to illustrate their own ideals more perfectly than
they themselves? What more serious challenge to domination
than to beat the masters at their own chosen game, whether
that is cricket itself or the civil norms lying beneath cricket?
That this response to domination is in fact a structural defeat,
result of a double bind on colonials, seems rarely to occur to
agents exhibiting the behaviour. The double bind resides in
there being no really effective response within the constraints
of imperial domination: difference is proof of subordination
(the natives aren't even civilized), while simulation is proof of
submission (the natives have no identity of their own).

Both strategies are defeatist, in fact, because the parameters
of the situation allow no other possibility. 'It was only long
years after,' James notes,

> that I understood the limitation on spirit, vision and self-respect
> which was imposed on us by the fact that our masters, our cur-
> riculum, our code of morals, *everything*, began from the basis

that Britain was the source of all light and learning, and our business was to admire, wonder, imitate, learn; our criterion of success was to have succeeded in approaching that distant ideal – *to attain it was, of course, impossible.* Both masters and boys accepted it as in the very nature of things. (BB, p. 38; emphasis added)

The triumph of imperialism is that such structural domination gives the masters an ability to interpret any and all behavioural responses in terms that reinforce, and never challenge, the contours of the domination. But with this gloomy awareness comes no respite from the response's attractions.

James is a master at defending this paradoxical aspect of his colonial character. 'I never appealed for a decision unless I thought the batsman was out,' he says of his playing days. 'I never argued with the umpire, I never jeered at a defeated opponent ... From the eight years of school life this [public-school] code became the moral framework of my existence. It has never left me. I learnt it as a boy, I have obeyed it as a man, and now I can no longer laugh at it' (BB, p. 35). But more rarely, James is also adept at turning this feature of colonial character to political advantage. The concatenation is, on reflection, a natural one: 'My Puritan soul burst with indignation at injustice in the sphere of sport,' he confesses. 'Cricket had plunged me into politics long before I was aware of it. When I did turn to politics I did not have too much to learn' (BB, p. 71).

But this public-school ethos, which James had to take seriously, was also a focus of political challenge. 'The British tradition soaked deep into me was that when you entered the sporting arena you left behind you the sordid compromises of everyday existence,' he says, emphasizing the imported game's most sacred tenet. 'Yet for us to do that we would have had to divest ourselves of our skins ... Thus the cricket field was a stage on which selected individuals played representative roles which were charged with social significance' (BB, p. 72). The peculiar grandeur of cricket in this era was that it could allow expression of so much political value without losing its integrity as a sport. This, according to James, was as good for the West Indies as it was for cricket. 'I haven't the slightest doubt that the clash of race, caste and class did not retard but stimulated West Indian cricket. I am equally certain that in these years social and political passions, denied normal outlets, expressed themselves fiercely in cricket (and other games) precisely because they were games' (BB, p. 72). Which is to say, ultimately, that cricket's glory lay in being 'a game which, in lands far from that which gave it birth, could encompass so much of social reality and still remain a game' (BB, p. 97). Remain, that is, not society itself but the most effective critique of society available.[18]

It is this advantage that makes of colonial cricket more than a matter of beating the masters at their own game. The danger in such a view of the game is that it will change the game in a way that destroys its critical possibilities: the colonial killer instinct, which achieves the ultimate goal of winning – beating the masters – will triumph only at the price of making cricket a game like all other professional, commoditized sports, one without the culture of civility that can become (or become again) a focus of social critique. What looks simultaneously like a valuable expression of national achievement and a salutary exposure of hypocrisy in the code of which James speaks turns out, on reflection, to be a capitulation not only to domination but also the worst imperatives of hypercompetitive modern sport. Colonialism's unique possibilities, whatever they may be, are here sacrificed for a false goal.

James lays the foundation of this argument, though he does not explicitly make it, by recounting two events which were central to his enmeshed political and sporting development. The first concerns his first visit to the United States in 1938, the first time he allows contempt for the schoolboy values to enter his consciousness. But not for long: the stimulus of reaction is a baseball game, attended with friends. Between raucous shouts and denunciations of opposing players, he says, 'they asked me if I were enjoying the game. I was enjoying the game; it was they who were disturbing me. And not only they. Managers and players protested against adverse decisions as a matter of course, and sometimes, after bitter quarrels, were ordered off the field, fined and punished in other ways' (BB, p. 52). James even attempts to play cricket with some of his American associates, but the results are predictably disastrous: they argue calls, shout abuse, and generally import the cheerful incivility of baseball into the sphere of cricket, where it could only be incongruous. James's bewilderment at American sporting culture is increased by news of a college basketball scandal, in which players were implicated for taking bets to influence games. James's well-bred shock meets no reception in his friends, whose responses consist of shrugs: why shouldn't they cheat? The college, after all, does nothing but exploit them anyway.

Apart from reinforcing James's own regard for his public-school ethos, the incident has two implications. It underlines, first, the importance of civility in cricket even when it is the game, as James has said, most fully charged with political significance. In fact, that civility, made especially visible by its absence in other sports, may prove essential in allowing cricket its extraordinary political possibilities. And it shows, second, that the absence of a culture of civility in sport is a necessary condition (if not also a sufficient one) for opening the door to pure self-interest in sport. I will explore the implications of these issues in the next section of this paper, but the immediate question is whether cricket retains the civility that, for James, set it apart from baseball and the cheating basketball players. (One can only imagine, incidentally, how appalled he would be by current norms in American college football and basketball.) Is cricket, in other words, still cricket?

James is forced, like many others, to conclude in the negative: the midnight of cricket's culture of civility has been passed. 'The blow from which "It isn't cricket" has never recovered came from within and it came in 1932. This was bodyline' (BB, p. 185). In the England–Australia Test of that year, the English captain Douglas Jardine, fearing defeat from a more powerful Australian side that included legendary bats-man Donald Bradman, counselled his bowlers to bowl a short length and bounce the ball into batsmen's bodies. Since cricket bowling properly aims at the wicket, which the batsman is defending with his bat, not his body,[19] the effect of this strat-egy is roughly equivalent to throwing a succession of brush-back high inside fastballs. If some of the bodyline balls hit the batsmen, so much the better: the obvious intent of this strategy was to intimidate the free-swinging Bradman and his col-leagues, and a little rib bruise might go a long way in achiev-ing that goal, a goal justified by the desire to win.

That we may find such tactics more or less acceptable, or at least understandable, is evidence that the culture of sports has changed. There were many reasons for Jardine's strategy – some have suggested he was furious at Bradman's own well-known lack of chivalry, while Nandy engages in a long psy-chological profile – but the simplest explanation is probably also the most accurate. Jardine was not prepared to allow another colonial victory. That his strategy undermined the val-ues he was ostensibly trying to protect in bringing home a vic-tory is the incident's deep irony; that it changed the face of cricket possibly forever is its political legacy. It is of course true that 'It isn't cricket' had already come under sustained attack, from athletes and others, and was no longer a phrase with real meaning. 'Bodyline,' says James, 'was only a link in a chain. Modern society took a downturn in 1929 and "It isn't cricket" is one of the casualties' (BB, p. 190). One might place the date even earlier: the First World War's destruction of Edwardian values, the late Industrial Age revision of Victorian values, or even Victorianism itself, with its culture of utility. Here it is useful to revert to the earlier discussion and note only that Jar-dine exposed what was ever-present in cricket, the competitive urge, but exposed it in a way that made impossible its return to control by cricket's strictures and norms of civility. Thus the game was spiritually halved, and the triumph of having uncovered hypocrisy is ultimately a small reward for the loss of the game's dynamic critical possibilities.

James's own attitude to 'It isn't cricket' is ambivalent, as we have seen, but he mourns its loss, not because of nostalgia for schoolboy days but because the possibility of turning the values of cricket back on themselves was retreating. 'Cricketers try to preserve the external decencies,' he says carefully. 'The tradition is still strong. But instead of "It isn't cricket", now one hears more frequently the cynical "Why isn't it cricket?"' (BB, p. 189). That sentiment is merely a defence of hypercompetitiveness, the drive to win at all costs. At the same time, it surrenders a standard of value that can be used to challenge the hegemony of imperial dominance in the only way that is effective: from within, by indicating an internal contradiction. If, in other words, 'It isn't cricket' has no meaning, everything is justified; and in such an atmosphere, the subordinate are lost forever.

James illustrates the critical possibilities of cricket's traditional values in his account of the 1960 campaign to make Frank Worrell, a black man, captain of the West Indies team. It is by pointing out that there was no possible *cricket-based* justification for this exclusion that Worrell's case is won. '"The Case for West Indian Self-Government" and "It isn't cricket" had come together at last and had won a signal victory,' James notes with some satisfaction, referring to his influential book. 'When I confessed I was angry' at Worrell's treatment, James says, 'even sympathizers balked at this ... According to the colonial version of the code, you were to show yourself a "true sport" by not making a fuss about the most barefaced discrimination because it wasn't cricket. Not me any longer. To that I had said, was saying, a final goodbye' (BB, p. 232). And I think that goodbye is not, significantly, to the entire culture of 'It isn't cricket' but rather to its *submissive* colonial interpretation.

James's triumph here is to reinvigorate the values of cricket with new political energy, to see how they can contain and direct anger in a manner that is truly liberating – that is, quite possibly, the one and only truly liberating strategy for the colonized. Not simply by beating the masters at their own game, not by changing the game by destroying its values, but by reinterpreting those very values as vehicles of political change.

IV Post-Colonial Civility

I suggested earlier that cricket's reformative possibilities reside, if anywhere, in its culture of civility. But civility may seem an unlikely place to look for political critique, for reasons that should be obvious. Polite behaviour (to take the most overt display of civility) has long been a means of social control, a way of constraining discourse such that those in inferior positions, or simply those thought to be, were denied a proper voice in which to articulate their claims. This dominating strategy of politeness is therefore a key feature of colonial control. Politeness reinforces the structural domination that characterizes colonialism by (a) allowing the superordinate to condescend to those not versed in proprieties and (b) forcing the subordinate to capitulate to those proprieties in response to condescension. The double bind of politeness, from the colonial point of view, is that I can neither fail to observe its dicta, nor observe them, without underlining my status as dominated. It is useful to think of this along the lines of Marx's analysis of ideology: politeness operates by making my interests and claims phraseable only in the terms of a dominant ideology, terms which will make those interests and claims ultimately redound to the benefit of that ideology. I can neither speak nor be silent without reinforcing my own subordinate position.

So much for one standard view of politeness. In concluding this examination, I want to suggest a different interpretation of politeness, an interpretation which turns on points Nandy and James bring to our attention within the game of cricket. My thought here is the following: if civility is an expression of values that a ruling class considers desirable, or at least thinks it ought to, it is possible civility may be turned to political advantage through colonial use – not by imitation, which gives the game away, but by selective internal application. The most effective colonial strategy will therefore not be a kind of glee-ful surrender to hypercompetitiveness, the value that ignores civility, for this will only reinforce the colonial position; the most effective response will be an ironic maintenance of just those values which the ruling classes profess to admire, a maintenance that, as suggested earlier, will ultimately indicate how little in fact they live up to them. This is beating the mas-ters at their own game, but not by winning – or anyway not by winning at any cost.

The strategy may seem defective both politically and in terms of sports strategy. The culture of sport, in North America especially, is such that a commitment to civility would now be considered evidence of poor commitment to the game as a whole. Athletes now consider it more appropriate to say how much they hate losing, how ungraceful they will be in defeat, and this is evidence of their laudable desire to win. The shift of values is obvious and blatant – classic poor sportsmanship is here assessed a virtue, perhaps the only articulable virtue of the modern sportsman. A rearguard action for civility might seem, from this vantage, a naive venture. Politically even more so: the kind of internal change apparently advocated by James in the Worrell case is feeble compared to a frontal assault that might have changed things earlier, or more definitively. But is this really so? If James's account of the social dominance of the West Indies is accurate, no change of a definite kind could have been achieved earlier, nor would it have succeeded so well done by other means. The colonial position is defined in just this way, that frontal assault short of revolution cannot succeed – and revolution is a dangerous business.

Just so in sport. We are so used to the values of the profes-sional dominating our sporting consciousness that we may forget a time when good conduct and politeness counted for something in games. The winner-take-all approach to contem-porary sport diminishes the significance of games because it robs them of value dimensions they possessed earlier. No sin-gle competitor, or team, can hold out against the modern drive to victory at any cost – he, or they, would be obliterated – but it is possible an entire game can. Traditional cricket's culture of civility is not to be ignored, not even by today's players. What use would its maintenance be? There would be, first, the consciousness that violence and aggression, however omnipresent in human conflict, are controllable: not merely through rules, the avoidance of punishment, but by reference to a set of shared values that make up morality in its widest sense.[20] Such control would not deny the presence of drive and the urge to win, nor would it always succeed in controlling them, but the dynamic of civility is that restraint posts its value even when it succeeds only partially. It reminds us of the possibility of shared values, in other words, even when it is not yet clear what they are. Civility, like cricket itself, is more than a set of rules, for politeness is not simply the sum of dicta unearthed in etiquette books. The culture that supports such books rests on a firmer foundation: the willingness to consider the interests and claims of others, the willingness to restrain myself in countless subtle ways in the service of a common project.

But this is also, it should be noted, a project with liberating possibilities. Nandy embraces the apparent contradiction of using aristocratic values to reformative purpose when he notes that '[c]ricket is aristocratic by virtue of being a great leveller ... It shows – in fact, this is the only thing about which cricket provides certitude – that there is not only the survival of the fittest but also that of the weakest ... cricket reaffirms, against the better judgement of the modern world, that the meek can inherit the earth' (TC, p. 120). In a game where fate plays such a large role, the permutations of possible meaning are endless and crucial; the only permutation of meaning that is not warmly accommodated is the one in which victory is everything. 'It is pointless,' Nandy says,

> to waste time, energy and money on a five-day, thirty-hour game which refuses to be fully responsive to human effort and skills. This is the special, realistic meaning of sportsmanship which the Victorians, defying their own rational self, tried to capture in the tradition-bound, rules-scarce culture of cricket. That is why it is not enough only to say that rules are not crucial in cricket; one

must also affirm, however strange it may sound to modern ears, that the cricket in which rules are crucial is a negation of cricket itself. (TC, p. 121)

This is the sense in which cricket 'is a Victorian negation of Victorianism'; it is, moreover, the sense in which traditional cricket is hostile to the values of modern sport. In understanding the bodyline controversy, Nandy argues, we should see that Jardine 'expected to win by fully and most ruthlessly exploiting the existing rules' of cricket; yet, by so expecting, he had in a crucial sense ceased to play cricket. Of course this point holds only insofar as cricket can be understood as something more than its rules, that is, a game with a culture of civility underlying the rules. If the game itself is so changed by the financial and managerial pressures of modernity it may, by bending to its imperatives, cease to be the game any longer – a prospect already underway in the shift from test matches to limited-overs matches.[21]

The presence of civility in a sport like cricket may also remind us that, in MacIntyre's usage, it is a practice with goods internal to itself. Excelling at the game in its widest sense is a contribution to the entire culture of the game; virtue is possible only here, where the practice is grounded in common interests and not simply a matter of who can win. Paying attention to civility means paying attention to the fact that the sum of the game is not victory. Valuing civility may appear anachronistic because it appeals to a version of the game no longer supportable by the realities of modern life – the realities, as it is frequently expressed, of the marketplace. But this is just what the game is meant to do, to show up those values as not omnipotent and, perhaps, not very desirable.

If cricket, says Nandy, 'survives the vicissitudes of our time – and many hope against hope that it does so – it will perhaps survive as a defiance and critique of modernity in a world moving towards post-modernity' (TC, p. x). If games cannot do this, if they capitulate to the perverse imperatives of the marketplace, they will have surrendered utterly their role as critical reflections on the social order. It will no longer be possible to view national struggles and imperial-colonial dynamics through the lens of cricket or football, no longer possible to observe the clash of fate and character in baseball. They will be not reflections of life, but simply more life, their artificial constraints contributing to nothing except a definite and time-bound outcome. That will make them – already has made them, in some cases – lesser games; it will also make us lesser citizens, for it will rob us of critical political possibilities.

Judd's Paradox is finally resolved, then, by in some sense ceasing to look for a resolution. One hates the game (as a repository of aristocratic values) *because* it is a good game (compelling in its own terms, able to reflect on those values). Judd's Paradox is really the nature of cricket itself, the aristocratic game with so many revolutionary possibilities, the colonial symbol that undermines empire, the internal dynamic of sportsmanship and aggression. It is because cricket possesses this unique interplay of values and charges that it has sustained so much political interest, and succeeded as the vehicle of national self-consciousness in so many different contexts. It is for these reasons, finally, that cricket succeeds as a complex ironic critique of social and political life – succeeds at realizing a possibility that can reside in any organized sport insofar as it is a repository of values.

I am aware that this is a great burden to place on our games. In the case of cricket, at least, it is a burden that was formerly borne without demur. Nevertheless, it is possible we have now passed the time when it was possible to reinvest our games, even cricket, with such social weight. The question of whether cricket is still cricket, or can be again, cannot be decided here. We can only conclude with the hope that it may be so.

Notes

1 The play and screenplay of *Another Country*, written by Julian Mitchell, mixes facts and character traits associated with all of the four celebrated patrician spies recruited at Cambridge in the

1930s: Guy Burgess, Kim Philby, Anthony Blunt, and Donald Maclean. The film (1982) was directed by Marek Kanievska and starred Rupert Everett as Guy and Colin Firth as Tommy.

2 Both instances are mentioned in Ashis Nandy, *The Tao of Cricket: On Games of Destiny and the Destiny of Games* (New York: Viking, 1989), pp. 43, 134. These expressions of the paradoxes are instances of what Nandy calls the 'divided hero' presence in cricket. I will have more to say on this below.

3 That this aristocratic patina was acquired relatively recently – in the last century and a half, perhaps – does not obscure the point. Andrew Lang makes a good case, in his popular history of cricket (*English Illustrated Magazine*, 1884), that cricket, as opposed to tennis, 'is the game of the people' – it developed from natural bat-and-ball amusements of a variety of classes. And working-class Yorkshiremen have long been among the best cricketers going. Yet the idyllic, elegant character of the game, its association with English public schools and leisured amusements, cannot be shaken off. It is also, in contour, a game of refined beauty: the white flannels, the linear action, the lack of body contact. Iconically, cricket remains aristocratic.

4 I am naturally restricting myself to the colonial societies formed by the British Empire. It is an obvious point that some former British colonies, notably Canada, have not maintained a culture of cricket. The standard, and still plausible, explanation for this is the cultural influence of the United States. Cricket is played in Canada – and there is a national team – but enthusiasm for the game has gradually shifted from a small group of expatriate English people and Anglophiles to a growing but still small West Indian and Indian immigrant population. To the extent that cricket remains a game incomprehensible to the North American sports mind, cricket will never flourish in the Canadian context.

5 C.L.R. James, *Beyond a Boundary* (London: Fontana, 1963), p. 151. This meditation on colonialism and cricket's role in the West Indian experience will be a central part of the thesis outlined in this paper. All further citations are given in the main text, abbreviated BB.

6 Ashis Nandy, *The Tao of Cricket*, p. ix. Nandy's view of the issues,

with which I substantially agree, is summarized in the following rather complex passage: 'I view cricket as [a] medium of self-expression on four planes: traditional English cricket (which is in many ways a reflection of earlier social hierarchies but is also unwittingly a criticism of the values associated with modern industrialism), modern cricket (increasingly an endorsement of the hegemonic, urban-industrial managerial culture and a criticism of the pre-industrial values now associated with defeated ways of life), imported cricket (the cricket which was exported to non-western societies as a criticism of native life-styles from the point of view of the industrializing West but which, as reconstructed by the natives, brought out the latent function of the game in the West and became a criticism of the common cultural principles of capitalism, colonialism and modernity) and new cricket (the cricket which by its close identification with the industrial-managerial ethos is becoming increasingly an endorsement of the ruling culture of the world and a criticism of the victims of history)' (p. xi). These points will be clarified in what follows.

7   The first phrase is a catch-all expression of rightness or fittingness in behaviour, transported from the playing field to the wider field of life; the second is originally a technical requirement of the game, part of taking up the batsman's position, which metaphorically expresses a sense of integrity or propriety. It is the metaphorical or symbolic weight of these phrases that I am concerned to address here.

8   Alasdair MacIntyre, *After Virtue: A Study in Moral Theory* (London: Duckworth, 1982), pp 190–1.

9   The influence of Grace simply cannot be underestimated here. In an 1895 *Strand Magazine* interview with Grace, Fred W. Ward notes that the Doctor had probably scored more than 70,000 runs in his thirty years of competitive cricket – an incredible total. 'Well, indeed,' enthuses Ward, 'may one of the verses of an earlier song be repeated:

There's a name which will live for ever and aye,
In the true-born cricketer's mind –
A name which is loudly re-echoed to-day,

And borne on the wings of the wind.
Britannia may gladly be proud of her sons,
Since who is more famous than he,
The stalwart compiler of thousands of runs,
"Leviathan" W.G.?'

10 Geoffrey Moorhouse, *Lord's* (London: Hodder and Stoughton, 1983), p. 43.
11 Historical accounts of cricket's spread around the world turn on the presence of the British military in colonial regions. This was instantiated most obviously in India, where it is possible the game was played as early as 1743. There was certainly a Calcutta Cricket Club by 1792. In other countries, for example, Samoa, cricket developed in odd ways on the native soil: 'Matches of 200 a-side took place, with four or five umpires and three batsman at each end, the contests lasting for weeks,' *Cricketer Annual* reported in 1922/3. 'Work was neglected, and steps had to be taken to compel the natives to return to reason. Men who played were expelled from Church, and the King had to issue a special decree.'
12 Ashis Nandy, *The Tao of Cricket*, p. 8. Despite its rather unfortunate title, and though occasionally marred by sociological jargon, Nandy's book is the best available full-length treatment of cricket's political implications. All further citations will be given in the main text, abbreviated TC.
13 One might be inclined to offer baseball as a counterexample here, but Nandy is convincing on the significant differences: a baseball batter has three strikes to work with, and moreover represents his team only once every nine at-bats – he may get three or four chances to succeed. But the comparison is fruitful, for baseball surely shares the 'culture of anarchic individualism' in a way that non-linear, territorial team sports like football cannot. You are never alone on a football field – unless your teammates have failed you in fairly obvious ways.
14 I explore this danger in the larger context of a culture of civility in a later section of this paper.
15 Sportsmanship should not be confused with gamesmanship, the canny exploitation of the rules for tactical advantage. Gamesman-

ship taken too far is a danger to sporting values. 'At its worst,' says Nandy, 'traditional gamesmanship takes advantage of the sporting spirit and allegiance to norms in others – and one's own partial commitment to the norms – to advance the cause of individual or team success' (TC, p. 38). This cannot occur in a game whose culture of sporting values is vital. There are games, however, where no culture of sportsmanship can be presumed. An attempt to specify with rules the contours of sportsmanship is almost always an indication that this culture has broken down, or never been present. In American football, for example, the presence of a penalty called 'unsportsmanlike conduct' – which includes fighting and late hits – is strong prima facie evidence that there is no real sportsmanship in the game: a player will be sportsmanlike only because, and to the extent that, he cannot get away with doing otherwise without damaging his team. It is significant that transgressions in this game are not, except in extreme cases, punished with ejection from the game but rather by loss of territorial advantage – in the case of unsportsmanlike conduct, fifteen yards.

16 It is thinking such as this that led Neville Cardus, in his 'Tribute to P.G.H. Fender' (*Illustrated Sporting and Dramatic News*, 1928), to praise a captain – understood to be a Gentleman – who 'is a hard fighter. [Fender] does not belong to the soft school of captaincy. Too many contemporary captains apparently imagine that cricket is honoured by the policy of "Give your opponents *every* chance". This is not chivalry; it is weakness which really does indignity to the greatest of games. A brave opponent is worthy of the most killing steel: he expects no quarter.' This enjoinder is only necessary because of a discernible gap in attitudes between Players (who made up most national sides) and Gentlemen (still the choice set for captain).

17 Judith Shklar explores our love of exposing hypocrisy in her book *Ordinary Vices* (Cambridge, MA: Harvard/Belknap, 1984), especially ch. 2. Shklar's suggestion is that 'putting hypocrisy first' – considering it the most serious vice, more serious than cruelty, say – leads to misanthropy and a cacophony of accusing and counteraccusing voices.

18 This possibility of remaining a game – a possibility increasingly minor as cricket approaches the degree of professional dominance typical in other major sports – is what underwrites its critical abilities. If big sport becomes professional sport in the way, for example, pro football and basketball have in the United States, the lines between game and life are obscured. Thoroughly professional sport, in other words, is just life continued by other means: its only difference lies in posting winners and losers, which in itself may constitute a danger.

Professional dominance may, of course, be ambivalent. In the pro football satire *North Dallas Forty* (1979), a character attacks a coach in a scene that has become famous for expressing the professional athlete's peculiar frustration: 'When *we* call it a game, *you* call it a business,' he yells at the coach. 'When *we* call it a business, *you* call it a game.'

19 One of the several ways a batsman can be got out – and the one least immediately understood by casual observers – is by stepping in front of the wicket and touching the ball with anything but his bat. This 'leg before wicket' or 'lbw' decision is the umpire's, who cannot intervene unless appealed to, hence the many shouts bowlers and defenders give after a bowl: they are asking the umpire for an out, believing (or merely claiming) that the batsman has blocked the ball with his leg.

20 Nandy reminds us that the 'crucial behavioural trait demanded by the dominant culture of cricket – for that matter, by all professionalized modern sport – is hypercompetitiveness. As opposed to the normal competitiveness of sport, hypercompetitiveness is the behaviour which ignores all the conventions of sport, including all limits on competition, once the limits stand between success and failure. Hypercompetitiveness abides by the laws limiting competitiveness *only when success is guaranteed or when the penalties prescribed by the laws of the game make transgressions overly expensive.* In other words, there is no moral check against transgression; the only check is the fear of punishment' (TC, p. 93; emphasis added). He compares this attitude to one of the early Kohlbergian stages of moral development, in which moral standards have yet to be internalized.

21 A cricket match is traditionally played until each team's entire
    side of batters have been dismissed twice, in successive innings.
    Even with variations of strategy – declaring, following on – this
    may take three or four days. Limited-overs or 'one-day' cricket
    creates a fast result by limiting the number of bowls a team can
    make. Limiting run production, rather than dismissing batters,
    becomes the main object of the game. Anyone familiar with the
    two games knows how different the dynamics are. The look of the
    game is also different in some cases: rather than the traditional
    whites, Australian and New Zealand cricketers play in leagues
    with coloured uniforms and stadium floodlights.

PART II
REACTIONS

Two Concepts of Pluralism

Discussed in this essay:

Philosophy in an Age of Pluralism: The Philosophy of Charles Taylor in Question, edited by James Tully (Cambridge University Press, 1994).

There are many strands in the thought of Charles Taylor, a gathering of philosophical interests diverse enough to embrace both political theory and philosophy of science, epistemology and practical ethics, Nietzsche and Davidson. If he has not succeeded in generating any supreme synthesis out of this diversity (sometimes, to be sure, conflict); if, indeed, he has sometimes finessed the material to fit a bigger picture, as in the controversial details of his grand intellectual history of modern consciousness, *Sources of the Self*,[1] Taylor has nevertheless created, within his own work, a lively conversation – a dialogue at least as expressive and interesting as the one he has repeatedly advocated as the centre of any vibrant intellectual and political life. In Taylor's philosophical works plurality is met, not with the fractured incommensurability now so often in vogue, but rather with a compelling – if necessarily endless – attempt at deep reconciliation.

In making that attempt his life's work, indeed, Taylor may just have shown us a new way of conceiving our position as late-modern thinkers, ever forced to size up our role. 'It is possible to recast the philosophical task of a "reflection on modernity" as an invitation to a philosophical conversation with the diverse voices of modernity and their respective sources and traditions,' James Tully writes in his preface to this Festschrift volume (p. xiv). Taylor's aim, Tully suggests, is not to reach an articulation of Hegelian 'objective spirit' or agreement on universal rational principles in the manner of Kantian transcendentalism. It is, instead, to find a more comprehensive account, a better articulation, a richer history of sources, a conceptual fusion of horizons – in other words, to achieve the goals now recognizable as characteristic of Taylor's philosophizing, the things that hold his diversity of interests together.

The goals of this pluralistic conversation have extended to Taylor's many commentators, who have ranged over the wide expanse of his work and, as in this collection, provoked useful responses and revisions.[2] If they too have failed to generate a unified theory out of this extensive philosophical give and take, that is perhaps to be expected. As a critic, one must necessarily enter this conversation at a particular point, thereby doing some injustice to its scope. Yet this is a form of injustice from which justice may come. In what follows I want to focus on a distinction central to Taylor's political philosophy, but which surfaces explicitly only in his replies to criticisms offered here by Richard Tuck, Daniel Weinstock, and Guy Laforest.[3] In that sense this essay does not constitute a survey of the book under discussion – which, given the many significant contributions, anyway could not be done except at much greater length than is available (or maybe desirable) – but rather a teasing out of one strand of debate I think especially significant, and one somewhat neglected in this otherwise comprehensive volume. The distinction in question illuminates an enduring feature of both the philosophical conversation Taylor exemplifies and the sort of liberal political dialogue he supports. It concerns the notion of pluralism, the framing idea of this collection and, it could be argued, of all Taylor's work.

It has become a commonplace in contemporary political philosophy to speak of 'ethical pluralism' as the starting point of meaningful reflection about the state of society. That is, we begin with a recognition that citizens of modern states have (to use Rawlsian language) various *conceptions of the good* that they wish to maintain and foster. These conceptions are various because we no longer believe that there is one, and only one, answer to Socrates' basic ethical question, What is the life worth living? and so we are no longer content to have one vision of the good human life elevated to the status of a political destiny.

It follows that political organizations should surrender the attempt to create, for example, a uniform state religion or to legislate on the basis of some 'general will' which is on this view necessarily repressive, and should instead concentrate on basic social structures that will allow this variety of ethical outlooks to cohabit in relative peace and with a measure of justice – whether that means fairness in distribution schemes, market regulation of contract and exchange, neutrality in adjudication, principled non-cognitivism in systems of conversational justification, or whatever.[4] (I do not mean to suggest that these are all equivalent, or indeed that there are no significant differences between the contemporary liberals who advocate them, only that the conceptual commonality with respect to pluralism holds.) The great saving insight of classical liberalism, that persons might choose different paths to Christian salvation without endangering their immortal souls, is thus transformed into the base-level enabling condition of late-modern liberalism. Diversity is now no longer simply religious but broadly ethical. Seeing that we have different ideas of what is good, we live and let live. Pluralism therefore leads to toleration – where, at least, it does not lead to war.

It is unnecessary, here, to reiterate the problems that the

resulting 'neutralist' version of liberalism has encountered just in the last two decades or so. Suffice to say what everyone knows: that what looks to some like liberation from the inevitable conflicts of ethical pluralism seems to others just a new form of repression, arguably worse because advanced under cover of well-meaning toleration. Either the neutralist program leaves out of account many things which some of us consider essential to our lives, or it advances the interests of one dominant social group over those of less powerful groups. Or, most often, both. In a different sort of criticism, this form of neutralist liberalism is held up to rational ridicule, not political disapprobation. Neutralism, the criticism goes, cannot even defend itself against itself. It has no means of ruling out conceptions of the good, say anarchism or genocidal racism, which are actively hostile to the social order it claims to defend.

Once again, I need not supply the details of the resulting debates, which have become familiar, if not tedious, to students of contemporary political philosophy. The charge of incoherence can be dealt with fairly briskly, though. Defending neutrality does not entail defending it neutrally, even or especially if the neutrality in question is procedural; nor does it entail a prior commitment to value scepticism or relativism – we are not faced with a polity where nothing is good any more, simply one in which goods must be balanced with other goods. Also, because we may conceive liberal values as ones chosen from within various conceptions of the good, without exhausting those conceptions, it is not necessary to suppose that diverse groups will always find them oppressive. Rawls's overlapping consensus provides a model of such a choice, as does the resulting picture of a social union of social unions. It is folly to pretend that liberalism is immune from challenge, but rearticulations of its basic tenets in the light of recent criticisms has resulted in more substantive, balanced and compelling versions of the theory.

Taylor has of course been a central figure in this rearticulation, in some large measure because he has refused the easy 'liberal-communitarian' oppositions that have dogged too much recent debate.[5] In doing so, he has shed light on a different sense of pluralism that becomes more and more important for contemporary political thinking: a pluralism not *between* ethical views, but *within* them. This is the sort of inward pluralism that Taylor inherits in part from his teacher and friend Isaiah Berlin, but which extends back, in intellectual lineage, at least to Aristotle's subtle account of the inner conflicts of the ethical life. It is also fair to say, I think, that emphasis on the first concept of ethical pluralism – what we might call 'extramural' pluralism – as against this 'intramural' sort has obscured from many political theorists some of the important limitations of their craft.[6]

For Berlin, ethical pluralism is intimately related to, and part of the defence of, what he famously called negative liberty – a defence with which Taylor would later cavil, in an early 'liberal-communitarian' skirmish, arguing that it was too thin.[7] But if they disagreed about liberty, they agreed about pluralism, because Berlin does not mean by pluralism what most political theorists do, namely the diversity in life plans and conceptions of the good that sets the stage of contemporary political debate. Rather, he is in search of a deeper insight: that value is always, even within a given world view or substantive theory of the good, plural in nature. 'Pluralism,' Berlin writes in 'Two Concepts of Liberty,'

> with the measure of 'negative' liberty that it entails, seems to me a truer and more humane ideal than the goals of those who seek in the great, disciplined, authoritarian structures the ideal of 'positive' self-mastery by classes, peoples, or the whole of mankind. It is truer, because it does, at least, recognize the fact that human goods are many, not all of them commensurable, and in perpetual rivalry with one another. To assume that all values can be graded on one scale ... seems to me to falsify our knowledge that men are free agents, to represent moral decision as an operation which a slide-rule could, in principle, perform.[8]

It follows that we need to give up 'the conviction that all

the positive values in which men have believed must, in the end, be compatible, and perhaps even entail each other.'[9] To demand this form of value entailment is, Berlin comments, 'perhaps a deep and incurable metaphysical need; but to allow it to determine one's practice is a symptom of an equally deep, and more dangerous, moral and political immaturity.'[10]

We do not, in other words, inhabit a moral universe in which only one kind of meaningful normative reason has pull with us: happiness, say, or duty. Instead the moral world is full of various *and often contradictory* normative concerns. Charles Larmore, a thinker deeply influenced by Berlin, calls this 'the heterogeneity of morality' and defends it this way:

> we have an allegiance to several different moral principles that urge independent claims upon us (we cannot plausibly see the one as a means for promoting the other) and so can draw us in irreconcilable ways. The ultimate sources of moral value are not one, but many. This heterogeneity holds, whatever our situation.[11]

Hence, in any given moral situation I might face an irreconcilable desire to satisfy duty, positive consequences, *and* partiality to those close to me. All three are moral values we approve; but no one of them consistently trumps the others, nor is there any acceptable means by which we can translate them into some common-yardstick language like Bentham's felicific calculus where conflicts can be adjudicated.

Berlin's pluralistic moral world is psychologically more compelling than any monistic one. It is also politically more salutary, for on its basis we can decisively reject the 'Ionian fallacy': the idea, enshrined by ancient Ionian physicists, that there is a determinate answer to the question 'What is everything made of?' (Their answer: earth, air, fire, and water.) Rejection of the Ionian view is in the first instance methodological, but it is also substantive. No unitary account of human life – moral or political – can suffice. It is not merely, then, that we meet with a fact of extramural ethical pluralism in diverse societies; it is also that intramural ethical pluralism is part of being human. And that chastens the desires of monistic political theorists even more, for they can no longer seek refuge in the dangerous idea that divergent views should simply be eliminated. Divergence is an ineluctable feature of being human, not simply of being in a late-modern Western democracy.

Now compare Taylor on the point. He calls this awareness of pluralism an Aristotelian insight 'which has tended to get lost in modern philosophy.' 'There are always a plurality of goods, vying for our allegiance,' he writes in response to a challenge from Daniel Weinstock concerning the language of 'strong evaluation' deployed in *Sources of the Self*,

> and one of the most difficult issues is how to combine them, how to adjudicate at the places they come into conflict, or mutually restrict each other. I have no difficulty with the idea that offering the greatest scope for different modes of life and conceptions of the good is *an* important goal. I cavil at the idea that it can be *the* important goal; that is, that it doesn't have at a certain point to compose with other ends, which will require its limitation. (p. 250)

One of those ends, as Taylor makes clear in his reply here to Guy Laforest, may be ethnic nationalism – or rather, to be more precise, historically based group nationalism of the Québécois kind: *la survivance*. And if that end must compose with the strict right-over-good ends of neutralist liberalism – if, that is, it *can* so compose – then the resulting state is going to look quite different from that association of citizens treasured in the liberal imagination, especially as worked out in the American context as what Michael Sandel has called 'the procedural republic.'[12]

But it is also clear, as Taylor has often said, that his views on neutralist liberalism do not place him in some rival camp of communitarian apologists – however often he might be so placed by commentators. He is a critic of liberalism's monomania, we might say, but not of its entirety; and so he joins a long line of liberals who would resist the emptying out of ethical meaning they see as a consequence of procedural or neutral versions of liberalism. '[O]ne of the many reasons why I'm unhappy with the term "communitarianism,"' Taylor says in this volume, is that

> [i]t sounds as though the critics of [neutralist] liberalism wanted to substitute some other all-embracing principle, which would in some equal and opposite way exalt the life of the community over everything. Really the aim (as far as I'm concerned) is more modest: I just want to say that single-principle neutral liberalism can't suffice. That it has to allow for other goods with which it will have to compose, and put some water in its wine, on pain of our forgoing other very important things. (p. 250)

This insight, and the goal it grounds, may appear simple, but together they have far-reaching political consequences. For example, we can begin to see more clearly the lines of defence Taylor had in mind with the celebrated (if controversial) 'Liberalism 2' language in his contribution to Amy Gutmann's *Multiculturalism* collection.

In the view of Quebeckers and other goal collectivists, Taylor argues there, 'a society can be organized around a definition of the good life, without this being seen as a depreciation of those who do not personally share this definition.'[13] Such a definition cannot be captured by a revamped version of procedural liberalism, Taylor says, despite the efforts of nuanced liberals.[14] Instead it models a different, and incompatible, version of the liberal story (largely the modern story) of equal respect and authenticity. In this version of liberalism, a society's liberalism consists mainly in its treatment of minorities who diverge from the shared conception of the good, in particular in drawing a distinction between 'fundamental liberties, those that should never be infringed and therefore ought to be unassailably entrenched, on one hand' and 'privileges and immunities that are important, but that can be revoked or restricted for reasons of public policy – although one would need a strong reason to do this – on the other.'[15] While recognizing the conflicts likely to arise when the two versions of liberalism confront one another within a single polity, as obviously in Canada, Taylor has consistently been quite sanguine about the possibilities that a Liberalism-2 society will actually be liberal: 'the problems are not in principle greater than those encountered by any liberal society that has to combine, for example, liberty and equality, or prosperity and justice.'[16]

The difficulty, of course, is that this distinction between the basket of fundamental liberties, which are safe from challenge, and the basket of privileges and immunities, which are not, is highly contestable. So, indeed, is the scale of reasons that might count as strong enough to justify an infringement of the latter. This is certainly true between individuals, and may be true within them as well: we do not always agree, even with ourselves, on what counts as a fundamental right – or how far, and how long, something so counts. As a liberal more or less of type 1, I get nervous when philosophers talk of respect for minorities and justified infringement in the same breath. Taylor has chosen to argue that Liberalism 2 is still liberalism, but recent experience in Quebec politics does not offer much reassurance on the point. Some of the recent anger and prejudice can be rationalized as bitterness following the failed referendum of October 1995, but not all of the misgivings we Liberalism-1 liberals feel at these events can be explained away as an inability to expand our imaginations. Assurances that Quebec is and will remain a liberal society ring hollow when combined with the ethnic hatred sometimes evident in Quebec.

Still, Taylor's point is an important one for political philosophers to consider, especially in light of the difficulty we in Canada have so far encountered in our attempts at reconciliation. Taylor's insistence upon intramural pluralism leads to an apparently powerful argument against adopting a single principle, even one as important as the priority of right, at the centre of a society. Here we transfer Berlin's (and Aristotle's) insight about the heterogeneity of value within persons to the centre of our political philosophy, accepting that no society can be ruled by a single value either. 'Neutral liberalism as a total principle seems to me here a formula for paralysis,' Taylor says, 'or else for hypocrisy, if one tried to occlude the real reasons. It is at this point that it begins to appear more than costly; in truth, inapplicable' (p. 253). Or, with particular reference to the Canadian situation and its apparently endless disagreements:

> Why go on trying to squeeze blood from a stone, trying to torture everything we hold dear out of a single canonical principle? It is very reminiscent of utilitarians trying to find ways of proving that the felicific calculus would never justify torture or gladiatorial combat on late-night TV. Why don't they just relax and admit that goods are plural, and save themselves from all these strained arguments? (p. 251)

We should instead seek a polity that is pluralistic along two dimensions, then: *between* groups and their sometimes divided interests, as liberals have long maintained; but also *within* the governing ideas of the society itself, reflecting in this way the same potential conflict of values that exists within each one of us. Why should we expect a society to succumb to a single interpretation of itself when a person cannot – indeed, perhaps would not even if he or she could?

To be sure, this kind of 'just relax and accept it' language can seem a little cavalier. To some ears, it may be uncomfortably reminiscent of Rorty's repeated admonitions that we stop scratching where it does not itch, surrender useless locutions, slough off false problems, and the like. Taylor himself has identified the danger inherent in this sort of casualness: 'It might be tempting to follow Rorty in just abandoning a host of troubling expressions,' he writes in response to Rorty's essay in this collection. 'But not if one becomes incapable of saying important things, or is forced to banalise important distinctions' (p. 222). It may also sound a little odd to proponents of neutral liberalism to have their very refusal to take sides in ethical disputes derided as a social perfectionism on the order of Rousseau's general will, which Taylor calls 'unity as unanimity' (p. 255).

More pragmatically, can we expect a workable social union to emerge from this kind of pluralism at the centre of society? Not many Liberalism-1 liberals argue that neutrality is the most important or highest value in a world of value; most argue, more conservatively, that it is simply the value most likely to produce the sort of society that, on the whole, we would like to inhabit. Looking at Taylor's idealized version of the Liberalism-2 nation, indeed, I cannot find much to say against such an open-ended and compromise-happy view of politics, and plenty to say for it. And yet some basic worries about Liberalism 2 persist, old and simple ones from the dawn of liberal thinking; and ones that are not obviously or decisively laid to rest by this late-century updating of liberalism: What if I did not happen to share the conception of the good at the centre of that nation? What if something the nation regarded as a privilege was something I regarded as a fundamental right?

Can the two types of liberalism cohabit a single social space? Can the two concepts of pluralism be combined at the level of social organization, perhaps even make for a more just arrangement than any possible under one or the other separately? More pressingly, can we in Canada forge the kind of value reconciliation, the fusion of conceptual horizons, necessary to continue our existence as 'an experiment in diversity,' as Taylor calls it here? As always, it remains to be seen. But I believe Taylor is right that Canada represents a key staging area in the evolution of liberal political theory. I also think he is right that ethically richer and more interpretive versions of liberalism must emerge to meet the demands of our deep diversity – indeed, the interesting work in political philosophy during the last decade has addressed precisely that issue.

Yet I also agree with Isaiah Berlin, who says in his introduction to this volume that '[t]he chief difference between my outlook and that of Charles Taylor is that he is basically a teleologist – both as a Christian and as a Hegelian ... I think that Taylor believes in essences, whereas I do not' (pp. 1–2). What worries Berlin here is that Taylor's version of intramural pluralism still seems to leave room for a strongly end-directed conception of human life, indeed one which, like Aristotle's, could have unpleasant consequences for those who diverge in basic value commitment, say, on the question of religious belief.

Because we cannot assume that every one of us, or even a majority of us, does believe in essences, or in the essences that move Charles Taylor, I suspect that pragmatic arguments – arguments geared not to realizing metaphysical ends but to settling real-world disputes – are going to count more highly than teleological ones in the process of working out answers to our political questions. Certainly we want *sittlich* accounts of political life because we want our theorizing to be rooted in real ethical experience and commitment; yet we also know that too much ethical substance has the effect of defeating the original ambition, namely, of accommodating conflicts between people as well as within them. That means that type-1 liberalism will look more, not less, convincing as time goes on. Convincing not because wholly right, or exhaustive of the truth, or right to the exclusion of everything else; but because more useful, better suited to our difficult tasks, more flexible.

Of course we may find, as I have suggested elsewhere, that in order to continue to command the assent of diverse citizens, right-over-good liberalism will have to become more interpretive and less foundational, more detailed and less rationalistic, than hitherto dominant models.[17] We may find too, as recent work indicates, that republican ideas of virtue and obligation will have to be folded into liberal theorizing to make it more compelling to actual social actors than the stripped-down rights language and self-interested economic bargaining of the classical models.[18] Nevertheless the need for some version of a neutral theory will continue. Though liberalism is importantly, as Taylor has said himself, 'a fighting creed'[19] – it is and must be always based on human values, if not necessarily on strong theories of human nature or rationality – its supporters have consistently embraced the need for compromise in political life.

And this need for compromise not only gives point to the defence of neutrality in political theory, it sketches the limits of the only justifiable version of that neutrality in society where ethical pluralism runs along two dimensions. Taylor's own work, in one of its voices anyway, supports this goal: when he speaks in Gadamerian tones of horizon-fusion rather than the Hegelian tones of final settlement that give Berlin, and me, cause for worry. This, indeed, is the idea of non-transcendental reconciliation that is the most compelling feature of Taylor's philosophizing.

A sophisticated form of neutralist liberalism gives us what any too-substantive version of collectivist liberalism cannot, namely, the resources necessary to reach political agreements even when we remain in conflict with our fellow citizens, and indeed with ourselves. It gives us, in other words, the kind of self-interpretation we need to conduct, and continue, the sometimes fractious conversation of politics. Neutrality is by no means the only value here, and Taylor is right that it would be folly to think so. Nor is it even, for many people, the most important value. It may nevertheless be, when understood correctly, politically the most useful value.

Notes

1 The essays in *Philosophy in an Age of Pluralism* demonstrate the range of objection to *Sources of the Self* (Cambridge, MA: Harvard University Press, 1989). Quentin Skinner begins his sharply critical essay by saying, 'The historian Alexander Kinglake wanted the following inscription to be placed on all churches: *Important if true.* The same motto could equally well be inscribed in Charles Taylor's masterly new survey, *Sources of the Self*' (p. 37). Susan James

is critical of Taylor's reading of Descartes's foundationalism as a
'turning inward.' In addition, Michael Morgan attacks his easy
theism, Jean Bethke Elshtain his rather blithe celebration of ordinariness, Mette Hjort his Romantic (and elitist) idea of artistic creation, and Clifford Geertz his apparent hostility to the methods
and goals of the natural sciences – a strained relationship that
Geertz labels 'the strange estrangement.'

2 Sometimes, indeed, the exchanges exhibit a certain dry humour.
Richard Rorty's essay, in particular, is a model of baffled condescension. 'I shall confine myself to a parochial topic,' he says, 'one
about which only philosophy professors find it profitable to
reflect: truth' (p. 21). 'Taylor and I both pride ourselves on having
escaped from the collapsed circus tent of epistemology – those
acres of canvas under which many of our colleagues are still
thrashing aimlessly about,' he continues later. 'But each of us
thinks that the other is still, so to speak, stumbling about among
the tangled guy-ropes, rather than having escaped altogether'
(p. 29). Taylor returns the favour with as much wit, if less colour:
'It seems so hard to get a final, clear fix on just what is at stake
between us,' he writes of Rorty's essay. 'There are passages where
I find myself nodding in agreement, but then suddenly the text
veers off on to a terrain where I can't follow' (p. 219).

3 See Richard Tuck, 'Rights and Pluralism,' pp. 159–70; Daniel Weinstock, 'The Political Theory of Strong Evaluation,' pp. 171–93; and
Guy Laforest, 'Philosophy and Political Judgment in a Multina-
tional Federation,' pp. 194–209. Taylor's replies to their criticisms
are at pp. 246–57.

4 To name the leading theories of contemporary American liberal
justice. See John Rawls, *A Theory of Justice* (Cambridge, MA:
Belknap Press, 1971) and *Political Liberalism* (New York: Columbia
University Press, 1991); Robert Nozick, *Anarchy, State, and Utopia*
(New York: Basic Books, 1974); Ronald Dworkin, *Taking Rights
Seriously* (Cambridge, MA: Harvard University Press, 1984); and
Bruce Ackerman, *Social Justice in the Liberal State* (New Haven, CT:
Yale University Press, 1980).

5 There are many places to sample this opposition. See, variously,
Shlomo Avineri and Avner de-Dahlit, eds., *Communitarianism and*

Individualism (Oxford: Oxford University Press, 1992); Stephen Mulhall and Adam Swift, *Liberals and Communitarians* (Oxford: Basil Blackwell, 1992); Bruce Douglass, Gerald Mara, and Henry Richardson, eds., *Liberalism and the Good* (New York: Routledge, 1990); Nancy Rosenblum, ed., *Liberalism and the Moral Life* (Cambridge, MA: Harvard University Press, 1989); David Rasmussen, ed., *Universalism vs. Communitarianism* (Cambridge, MA: MIT Press, 1990); and Michael Sandel, ed., *Liberalism and Its Critics* (New York: New York University Press, 1984).

6 I do not except myself from that judgment. In *A Civil Tongue: Justice, Dialogue, and the Politics of Pluralism* (University Park, PA: Penn State University Press, 1995), I focused on revising liberal ideas of right in the light of hermeneutical insights gleaned from Taylor, among others. But I did so exclusively in an attempt to deal with *extramural* pluralism, the ethical conflicts or disagreements between groups of citizens – as if ethical interests within groups, or individuals, were always reconcilable, if not actually fixed. In more recent work concerning the political virtues I have tried to address this shortcoming.

7 See his 'What's Wrong with Negative Liberty?' in Alan Ryan, ed., *The Idea of Freedom* (Oxford: Oxford University Press, 1979).

8 Isaiah Berlin, 'Two Concepts of Liberty,' in Sandel, ed., *Liberalism and Its Critics*, p. 33. This essay has of course been extensively reprinted; it was originally delivered as Berlin's inaugural professorial lecture in Oxford in 1957.

9 Ibid.

10 Ibid., p. 34.

11 Charles Larmore, *Patterns of Moral Complexity* (New York: Cambridge University Press, 1987), p. 138.

12 See Michael Sandel, 'The Procedural Republic and the Unencumbered Self,' *Political Theory* 12 (1984): 81–96.

13 Charles Taylor, 'The Politics of Recognition,' in Amy Gutmann, ed., *Multiculturalism* (Princeton, NJ: Princeton University Press, 1994), p. 59. While Taylor drew the initial contrast, it was Michael Walzer who labelled the two visions, one procedural and neutralist, the other substantive and good-driven, Liberalism 1 and Liberalism 2; see ibid. at p. 99 ff.

14 That, indeed, is the thrust of his reply in this volume to Daniel
   Weinstock, who in a manner somewhat analogous to recent work
   by Will Kymlicka (see his *Liberalism, Community, and Culture*
   [Oxford: Oxford University Press, 1991]) urges a possible Rawlsian accommodation of rights to cultural survival. But '[s]urviv-
   ance is just another matter,' Taylor bluntly says here. It is not just
   an extension of Rawlsian liberal goods, but 'another good.' 'I don't
   think any useful goal is served trying to pretend that we aren't
   dealing with two independent goods which have to be combined,'
   he concludes (p. 251). The same point arises, and is dispatched as
   summarily, in 'The Politics of Recognition' at p. 58: 'It might be
   argued that one could after all capture a goal like *survivance* for a
   proceduralist liberal society,' say, by treating language as a
   resource analogous to clean air or green spaces. 'But this can't
   capture the full thrust of policies designed for cultural survival.'
15 Taylor, 'The Politics of Recognition,' p. 59.
16 Ibid., pp. 59–60.
17 See Kingwell, *A Civil Tongue*, especially chs. 1, 2, 6, and 7. I argue
   there that the dialogic virtue of civility must be at the centre of any
   just liberal society, and that a rich characterization of that virtue
   gives us a superior interpretive version of dialogic liberalism, as
   against (for example) the strictly enforced conversational neutrality of Bruce Ackerman, which builds a determinate outcome into
   the defended decision procedure.
18 The new 'liberal virtue' theorists include, prominently, William
   Galston and Benjamin Barber. See Galston, *Liberal Purposes: Goods,
   Virtues, and Duties in the Liberal State* (Cambridge: Cambridge University Press, 1991) and Barber, *Strong Democracy: Participatory Politics for a New Age* (Berkeley: University of California Press, 1984).
   For a survey of the place of the virtues in recent political theory,
   see Will Kymlicka and Wayne Norman, 'Return of the Citizen: A
   Survey of Recent Work on Citizenship Theory,' *Ethics* 104 (1994):
   352–81, especially pp. 365–9 on liberal virtues. I address the issue
   with some historical context in Kingwell, 'Defending Political Virtue,' *Philosophical Forum* 27 (1996): 244–68.
19 Taylor, 'The Politics of Recognition,' p. 62.

Critical Theory and Its Discontents

Discussed in this essay:

Critical Theory, by David Couzens Hoy and Thomas McCarthy (Blackwell, 1994).

Of Critical Theory and Its Theorists, by Stephen Eric Bronner (Blackwell, 1994).

On the evidence of these two very different but equally excellent books, one might conclude that the growing influence of critical theory, the school of post-Marxist political and aesthetic thought inspired by the Frankfurt School and its inheritors, is largely owing to a basic uncertainty at the heart of rationality. The point is nicely captured by McCarthy and Hoy in the introduction to their *Critical Theory.* Referring to Francisco Goya's well-known etching *El sueño de la razon produce monstruos* (1799) – a scene of a prostrate man, presumably Goya himself, afflicted by a host of bat-like demons – they note the image's 'notorious ambiguity.' That is: 'The title can be read as either "The *sleep* of reason produces monsters" or "The *dream* of reason produces monsters"'(p. 1). It is hardly an idle choice. Do the demons arrive when reason lets down its guard – or when reason runs amok?

The question is central to understanding the legacy of the

Frankfurt School, with its challenges to the Enlightenment project and its attempt to supersede the grand narrative of 'traditional theory' with historicist, contextual analyses of power and social construction. But it also resonates more widely. A distrust of reason, particularly in its instrumental forms, is characteristic not only of many political movements of our day but of dominant schools of thought in the disciplines of sociology, politics, comparative literature, legal studies, and philosophy. The most extreme versions of this distrust – those of the 'against theory' school of literary and legal criticism – take their cue, and derive their cachet, from insights mapped out decades ago by the German thinkers associated with the Frankfurt School. The intellectual stock of the School has risen steadily, if not unbrokenly, since the first English translations of its major works began appearing on this continent in the early 1970s. The interest in the legacy of the Institute for Social Research shows no signs of lessening.

But that legacy is itself ambiguous. The greatest exemplar of the Frankfurt influence in contemporary philosophical circles, Jürgen Habermas, is, as Stephen Bronner says in *Of Critical Theory and Its Theorists*, 'everywhere legitimately recognized as a giant of social theory' (p. 1). Yet his own work has described an arc of apparent divergence from his early critical forays and, even more so, the thought of his teachers Max Horkheimer and Theodor Adorno. Habermas's theories of communicative action and discourse ethics, with the well-known (perhaps infamous) 'ideal speech situation,' are so apparently transcendental and rationalistic in scope as to render any distinction between traditional theory and critical theory meaningless. In famous disputes with Gadamer and Foucault, and in his collection *The Philosophical Discourse of Modernity*, Habermas has made it amply clear that for him the *sleep* of reason represents the true danger – not to mention more particular dangers such as 'levelling the genre distinction between philosophy and literature,' to name an influential excursus from that collection. Yet all the while Habermas has maintained his conviction that his is the true inheritance of both Kant's project of critical philosophy and the social-democratic politics of the critical left.

McCarthy and Hoy focus their attention on the figure of Habermas, in that their discussion of critical theory is really a multilayered and nuanced argument about what role 'the rational pivot' must play in the 'perennial problems' of philosophy: subjectivity, truth, knowledge, legitimation, action, and so on. Theirs is a wide-ranging discussion, given this scope of concern, but yet focused enough on the issue of how critical theory speaks to these problems that the book walks a nice line between eclecticism and anarchy.

This is in large part a success of form. *Critical Theory* is structured as a debate, with each thinker given the opportunity to contribute a long original essay and then, the exchange effected, offer a short reply to his opposite number. This makes for a very lively book, and one that turns a useful double play in functioning both as an original contribution to contemporary debates in social and political philosophy and as an effective introduction to the thought of leading figures in Continental philosophy, particularly Habermas, Gadamer, and Foucault. Though each contributor begins his essay with some thoughts on Horkheimer and Adorno – and thus provides interestingly different versions of these thinkers, consistent with their own positions – the focus of debate is really elsewhere. The book is not concerned with exegesis.

McCarthy speaks first, and reprises the basically Habermasian position familiar to readers of his *Ideals and Illusions: On Reconstruction and Deconstruction in Contemporary Critical Theory* (MIT, 1991). Reading Horkheimer's anti-rationalism as nuanced rather than sweeping, and passing by 'the more Nietzschean' versions of critical theory found in, e.g., *Dialectic of Enlightenment*, McCarthy notes that while 'critical theory is concerned precisely with the historical and social genesis of the facts it examines' (p. 16), 'cultural criticism is not the self-sufficient, self-enclosed undertaking its more textualistically inclined practitioners sometimes make it appear to be' (p. 18).

Criticism is instead motivated by some of the very 'idealizing presuppositions' characteristic of Enlightenment rationality. If it were not, the critical project would make no sense, for the attempt to call out implications of a social or political kind would be mired in self-contradiction: using the tools of reason to deny reason. 'There must, then, be a reconstructive as well as deconstructive side to any critique of reason,' McCarthy says, 'for it will be important to identify and analyze those presuppositions to which participants in the discourse of modernity either have no alternative at all, or none they would want to defend' (p. 22).

McCarthy finds the 'reconstructive side' most usefully presented in Habermas, and echoes Habermas's standard charge of 'performative contradiction' to demolish Rorty, Foucault, and other thinkers too much seduced by the critical-theoretic dream of a thoroughgoing critique of reason (pp. 32–8). Reason, for McCarthy, is not simply reducible to ideology in the sense of false consciousness; it is not mere superstructural accretion of dominant social interests. The laudable Frankfurt School focus on concreteness does not entail a refusal to transcend the given state of social affairs. ('"Our" culture,' he notes, 'is permeated by transcultural notions of validity' [p. 40].) Indeed, McCarthy goes further and suggests that there is a whiff of negative metaphysics in the postmetaphysical thinkers who have traded in one set of hypostatizations for another: 'the one for the many, the universal for the particular, identity for difference, reason for the other of reason, the structures of thought for the infrastructures of thought, the logical essence of language for the heterological essence of language, and so on' (p. 36).

The only way to avoid this contradiction is to take seriously what McCarthy calls 'the pervasive normativity of social life' and, by focusing on ethnomethodological insights, 'plot an approach to communicative reason that steers a middle course between the inflationary aims of classical rationalism and the deflationary spirit of contemporary poststructuralism' (pp. 63–4). This focus gives us a Habermas who is, like the one Richard

Bernstein favours, pragmatic and interpretive rather than transcendental and universalistic. Nevertheless, because normativity is so pervasive, there is both generality and particularity here. We reject a God's-eye viewpoint, because it is impossible, but we retain the important ability to move between the viewpoint of the concrete and specific and that of the general and critical.

Following Harold Garfinkel and other sociologists of action, McCarthy thus rejects the picture of citizens as 'cultural dopes' moved by material and ideological forces beyond their understanding and control. Instead he reads the social situation as one in which shared understandings both constitute *and regulate* the sphere of interaction. We find meaning in our socialization, but that very meaning retains a critical-reflective ability to call us to account. It follows that scorched-earth policies of rational critique are flawed because they obliterate the fact that, paradoxically, transcendence is immanent in the social. The act of understanding, though it must begin in a given context, is itself always a request to go beyond that context.

This is perhaps the most persuasive available reading of Habermas's attempt to articulate the idealizing presuppositions of discourse, and McCarthy's use of the sociological and ethnomethodological material is quite illuminating. It parallels Habermas's debts to Mead, Piaget, and Kohlberg in his account of 'rational reconstruction,' but has the advantage of persuasive detail culled from, e.g., sociolinguistic accounts of turn-taking in conversation. It adds a new dimension to North American reception of Habermas's ideas, and in this sense is an important original contribution to the debate. Yet the reading may nevertheless fall short of convincing, for familiar reasons.

Hoy articulates these, beginning, in parallel with McCarthy, with a reading of some early Frankfurt School texts, particularly Horkheimer's 'Traditional and Critical Theory' (1937). Here he asks an important question: 'Is critical activity *necessarily* totalizing and utopian (and thus "theoretical"), or can it succeed even if it is piecemeal and pragmatic?' (p. 107; italics added). That is, can the critical element of the Frankfurt School be excised from its longing for the authority of theory, precisely the longing that led it into the thickets of self-contradiction? Hoy's aversion to theory is here, by his own estimation, reminiscent of and influenced by the work of Gadamer and Foucault. He thus calls the approach – critical theory without the theory – 'genealogical hermeneutics': an interpretive-historical examination of the forces that go into creating, for example, the Enlightenment notion of reason. Since what was made can be unmade, this has liberating potential without insisting on change for its own sake; a ruthless critique of everything existing does not, in other words, necessarily entail an equally ruthless *destruction* of everything standing.

Gadamer's emphasis on tradition is thus usefully read by Hoy as opening up into a plurality of understandings, a 'hermeneutic conversation' (to use Georgia Warnke's phrase). This conversation is not, crucially, grounded by presuppositions of an ideal kind: 'Hermeneutics is not forced to go beyond its pluralistic account of understanding and interpretation by adding the additional, much stronger requirements of ideal consensus and evolutionary reason posited in Habermas's theory of communicative action' (p. 200). Yet this pluralism is not relativistic, Hoy claims, because the immanent possibilities of critique are not lost in an insistence on contingency. On *this* reading of the true promise of critical theory, then, it is Gadamer and Foucault, not Habermas, who truly inherit (albeit anachronistically) the Frankfurt School mantle.

Hoy's claim cannot be substantiated without defeating McCarthy's version of Habermas, however, and this Hoy conspicuously fails to do. He offers versions of the standard objections to Habermas, including the charges of emptiness and abstraction, the unlikeliness of agreement as a political goal, and the weakness of proceduralism in real life (pp. 160–3). But the version of Habermas that succumbs to such objections can only be found in an uncharitable – and unnuanced – reading of his work. Among other shortcomings, such a reading bypasses with apparent equanimity the crucial status of rational presuppositions as regulative ideals, not goals; to say that agreement will never be achieved (p. 161) is not yet to say anything about what role the goal of agreement might play in our actual discussions. Hoy's quick negative response also ignores the subtlety of Habermas's responses to Gadamer in an early debate, the political engagement of his responses to Foucault in a later, and the now copious material offered on the issues of application, compromise, practical politics, and law.

At the same time as his critique fails to convince, Hoy opens himself up to the charge of performative contradiction. Indeed, Hoy's attempt to evade the charge becomes the central issue of the rebuttals offered in the book's latter third. 'Hoy sets dialogue in opposition to the regulative ideas of universality and consensus,' McCarthy says in his rebuttal;

> in reality, those ideas are often its driving force. Dialogue in the form of discourse lives from the effort to persuade interlocutors of the validity of one's claims [...] So Hoy has to argue that we could do without practices, like the one in which are presently engaged, in which claims are advanced on grounds meant to persuade any competent and reasonable judge. I will leave the very considerable burden of that proof to him. (pp. 244–5)

Not surprisingly, Hoy does not meet that burden. And given that Habermas is not, as Hoy charges, against pluralism but only against the 'anything goes' pluralism that leaves social actors without a critical frame of reference (p. 238), can Hoy cling to his opposition? On the evidence presented here, no.

I have suggested that McCarthy gets the better of Hoy in this debate, but in the end the differences between them are less significant than the convergences. Hoy is in fact a reconstructionist too, and he objects mainly to what he calls Habermas's 'whiggism': the devotion to a strong notion of 'rational progress.' Hoy's genealogy, by contrast, 'is reconstruction without the assumption of the necessity of progress' (p. 164). Though this assumption may reside more in Hoy's mind than in Habermas's work, he nevertheless has a point about reason's arrogance. '[S]ocial actors,' he says (p. 253), 'are neither simply social zombies nor fully self-transparent rational agents'; thus the suggestion that rational presuppositions should regulate discourse will frequently come up against its own limitations. He notes (pp. 257–9) that the 'hermeneutic turn in political philosophy' (another Warnke phrase) has clarified the problem of community limits in social claims. To put it crudely, universalism seems to demand too much of justice. Thus we should lower the gaze of dialogue, make it local and contingent – without making it irrational and relative. Conversation, not consensus, is the goal we seek; but that is not tantamount to parochialism.

Hoy and McCarthy converge, then, on a position that we might call 'weak universalism,' or perhaps 'contingent universalism.' Claims certainly extend past given contextual boundaries, but they originate within those boundaries and do not acquire their validity against a background of strong all-rational-agents universality. The ideals of rational discursive agreement can, and do, regulate our actual discourse, but not because of some presumed metaphysical background – they do so because this is what we, as actual speakers and in actual social situations, mean them to do. We realize that we may not convince others, for all sorts of common reasons; we also realize, consistent with the tenets of *Ideologiekritik*, that we may be deluded in our desires. We nevertheless make (some) claims intending for them to strike others as compelling agreement.

I have of necessity passed over much of the nuance and detail of this dispute. This is a very enjoyable book, thought provoking and written with verve. Though occasionally difficult, it provides a first-class introduction to the topics under discussion, and resonates widely with debates in theory of action, relativism, the status of contemporary pragmatism, and postmodernity.

An introduction of a more conventional kind is provided in Stephen Bronner's series of essays *Of Critical Theory and Its Theorists*. Bronner begins with readings of leftist thinkers who influenced the Frankfurt School – Karl Korsch, Georg Lukács – and then offers thoughtful, sometimes surprising, assessments of the central figures: Horkheimer, Adorno, Bloch, Fromm, Marcuse, and Habermas. The collection is not as unified as its title suggests, for Bronner takes the opportunity to reprint some essays of his that lie on the periphery of the topic. These efforts – a rather blithe reading of Heidegger, a discussion of expressionism in aesthetic theory, and a critique of rational-choice Marxism – are out of place. They detract from the overall coherence of the remaining, closely linked essays on each of the main figures in the critical-theory movement.

Those essays, ten in all, are detailed and nuanced in pursuit of their subjects, from Lukács's 'reification' thesis to Habermas's 'linguistic turn.' They are largely driven by the particularities of the subject matter, but some common themes emerge, and these are collected as sustained argument in Bronner's last essay, 'Points of Departure: Sketches for a Critical Theory with Public Aims.' Bronner is consistently drawn more to the utopian and hopeful elements of critical theory than to the cultural pessimism evident especially in the later work of Horkheimer and Adorno, when the former declined into an almost bitter conservatism and the latter surrendered political engagement for aesthetic theorizing. Bronner finds more inspiration in Bloch, whose magisterial *Principle of Hope* is only now gaining a wide North American audience; in Marcuse, who, far more than the then-untranslated Horkheimer and Adorno, fuelled cultural unrest in 1960s America; and in Fromm, who popularized and disseminated critical ideas decades before more 'respectable' members of the School. Of the last he notes, bucking received wisdom: '[p]opularity does not preclude political commitments any more than clarity of style precludes clarity of thought' (p. 210).

There is some nostalgia in these assessments, but Bronner's voice is a vibrant one and he makes a worthy guide through the reefs and shoals of critical theory. I found it refreshing to see Bloch and Marcuse elevated to a stronger position than Horkheimer and Adorno, whose later developments do seem

unduly negative. (Bronner also complains of 'the cult embrac-
ing Adorno, identifying his ideas with those of critical theory
per se' [p. 194].) By the same token, the emphasis on utopia
and hope is invigorating, and manages to avoid any suggestion of political naiveté.

Bronner is not uncritical. For example, Bloch's utopia – the
teleology contained in his 'left Aristotelianism' – is clearly seen
as insufficient (however necessary) to all the contingencies of
political life. And Habermas and Apel were right, Bronner
says, to argue that the temptation of what Lukacs called (after
Kierkegaard) the 'teleological suspension of the ethical' no
longer meets the political case (p. 54). In addition to hope we
need the regulative ideal of justice; and hope itself must be
severed from strong teleology or ontology in order to avoid
controversial metaphysical commitments (p. 295). Yet Bloch's
work teaches us, Bronner says in a statement that might have
been directed at Hoy, that 'radical analysis is not just a matter
of sociological analysis or explaining the "immanent" historical roots of ideas. It is a matter of unearthing their "transcen-
dent" potential as well' (p. 68).

On the other hand, Bronner would agree with Hoy that
Habermas's 'point[ing] ... critical theory in a new direction'
(p. 284) has lessened the critical impact of the original program, making it more a defence of liberal democracy than a
critical deepening of it. Like many others, Bronner aims his
criticisms of Habermas at the political inefficacy of discourse
ethics, raising genuine problems of application and detail
(pp. 303–10) and concluding that '[t]he discourse ethic is useless where democratic institutions and values are not already
extant' (p. 311). On this basis he plots his own, more radical
version of critical theory, which takes on the philosophical
sophistication of Habermas but directs it toward more obviously social-democratic political ends. He argues that transcendence and grand narrative are not inimical to critical
theory, and, more familiarly, suggests that class analysis and
emphasis on solidarity need to be brought back into view. He
concludes with an attempt to fuse the Blochian and Haberma-

sian streams of critical theory. If Bloch's teleology is a utopia of content devoid of form, then the universalization at the heart of discourse ethics is a utopia of form devoid of content. The dialectical option is to sublate these options in what he calls 'a critical theory with public aims' (p. 348).

This theory is no more than sketched, and that leaves Bronner's argument incompletely defended. But his forward-looking assessment of critical theory in a North American political context is timely. He worries that 'critical theory began to lose much of its allure' over the last decade; he also argues that 'critical theory has become increasingly domesticated' (p. 321) as a result of its exposure. But both assessments seem to me unduly pessimistic, if not simply false. The 'domestication' – which probably just means wider dissemination – has provided, on present evidence, much food for thought. And the allure is, if anything, still growing. It is the success of these two books to make that clear.

Nietzsche's Styles

Discussed in this essay:

What Nietzsche Really Said, by Robert C. Solomon and Kathleen M. Higgins (Schocken, 2000).

Why Nietzsche Still? Reflections on Drama, Culture, and Politics, edited by Alan D. Schrift (University of California Press, 2000).

'Where Is the Anti-Nietzsche?' by Malcolm Bull, *New Left Review* 3 (May/June 2000): 121–45.

Nietzsche Contra Democracy, by Fredrick Appel (Cornell University Press, 1999).

The Good European: Nietzsche's Work Sites in Word and Image, by David Farrell Krell and Donald L. Bates (University of Chicago Press, 1997).

Why We Are Not Nietzscheans, edited by Luc Ferry and Alain Renaut (University of Chicago Press, 1997).

Nietzsche's Corps/e: Aesthetics, Politics, Prophecy, or, The Spectacular Technology of Everyday Life, by Geoff Waite (Duke University Press, 1996).

'The whole art of Kafka,' said Albert Camus, 'consists in forcing the reader to reread.' So true. The hanging storylines, the vague not-quite-endings, the dreamy unfulfilled narrative logic – all these features of Kafka's style turn the reader back to the story, and so back upon the experience of reading itself. Kafka's works are not metafiction in the recently conventional sense of the term: there are no Foster Wallace–style footnotes, no extended Barthian flourishes, no Cooveresque direct address. But his fiction is nevertheless about the fact of fiction itself.

The whole art of Nietzsche consists, it seems, in forcing the reader, at least a certain sort of reader, to write. Usually to write a lot. Indeed, this is so much the case that it has become customary for commentators and preface writers, reviewers and round-up multitaskers, of any book to do with Nietzsche to note the fecundity of the current Nietzsche industry, the astonishing productivity of those who write to wring the significance out of the unfortunate man's brilliant work. And that convention won't be flouted here.

So here's the news, which is not news if you haven't been living under a rock these past few years: there is a booming trade in Nietzsche scholarship, with more books and articles published each year than even a dedicated acolyte could possibly hope to master. More than that, his name is bandied about not only at high-end dinner parties but in pop songs, first-class comic books, and second-class movies. He is ubiquitous and misunderstood, his familiar image glowering insanely in every corner of the cultural landscape from behind his post-breakdown moustache, the one grown, as Walter Kaufmann once said, 'beyond all reasonable proportion.'

The second custom, then, is to wonder why this should be so – using that gesture of wonder, in almost every case, to offer a trite argument about Nietzsche's continuing relevance to the world of mass culture, economic globalization, and ceaseless consumer frenzy. Nietzsche, these writers say, is the philosopher of our times, dead proof of his own claim that he was before his time, a prophet and harbinger denied glory in his own era. Lately these familiar arguments have an additional, usually banal, millennial tone that too often smacks of striving for a resonance that is not really present. Sometimes this is said to link the nineteenth-century fin de siècle, and Nietzsche's version of its crisis, with our own era, as when Alan Schrift chooses this quotation from Nietzsche's *The Gay Science* to serve as the frontispiece of his edited volume of essays, *Why Nietzsche Still?*:

> Even now one is ashamed of resting, and prolonged reflection almost gives people a bad conscience. One thinks with a watch in one's hand, even as one eats one's midday meal while reading the latest news of the stock market; one lives as if one always 'might miss out on something' ... Living in a constant chase after gain compels people to expend their spirit to the point of exhaustion in continual pretense and overreaching and antici- pating others. Virtue has come to consist of doing something in less time than someone else.

Certainly that is a chunk of Nietzsche worth knowing about, and reading, in these multitasking, cellphone, dial-up days. Other times, though, the millennial gesture is a lot more pro forma and a lot less illuminating. For example: 'Here at the end of the twentieth century, Friedrich Nietzsche has become one of the most talked about philosophers in history,' write Robert C. Solomon and Kathleen M. Higgins in their recent, baldly titled rehabilitation primer, *What Nietzsche Really Said.* 'Unfortunately, he has not also become one of the best under- stood.'

In the present context of ever-greater sophistication and nuance in Nietzsche scholarship, where more and more arcane differences can anger interlocutors to the point of derangement (and/or very bad prose), Solomon and Higgins are not only old-fashioned Nietzscheans but also old-fash- ioned paint-by-numbers teachers, the kind who want every single student, even the disaffected ones at the back of the room, to get the point. They want to save Nietzsche from a looming crisis of crude, undergraduate-style misunderstand- ing. To that end they offer, after the style of David Letterman, top ten lists of Nietzsche's most and least favourite thinkers. They also enumerate a catalogue of ugly rumours about him that need to be laid to rest, running from #1, 'Nietzsche Was Crazy,' to #30, 'Nietzsche, Who Insisted That the Philosopher Should Be an Example, Was Himself a Pathetic Example.' Whether that last is properly styled a 'rumour' – it sounds to me more like a potentially important argument expressed as a cheap shot – is really beside the point. Solomon and Higgins are very, very keen, as they make very, very clear, to rescue what they call Nietzsche's 'affirmative philosophy' from the depredations of dumb interpretation. That such interpretation exists I have no doubt; that this book, with its toy-time style and gee-whiz enthusiasm, will do anything to counter it is another question.

Which illustrates the first pitfall for those who must engage, like it or not, with Nietzsche's style. However difficult, no doubt it is possible to *reduce* Nietzsche, to even out his contradictions and wackiness in pursuit of a clearer line of argument and a cleaner personal profile, one where the elitism and irrational prejudices are moulded into an apparently coherent philosophy of individual development. Possible, but not advisable. Sometimes the project of rehabilitation should be left to individual encounters with the author and text, and sometimes rehabilitation is not what a great thinker's legacy demands. The mystery of *What Nietzsche Really Said* is this: What happened to Nietzsche? He does not emerge from these pages clarified so much as neutered, rendered without style and, therefore, without substance.

Alan Schrift, in his introduction to *Why Nietzsche Still?*, does not make such a rookie mistake, but he does play a jazzy variation on the rehab rhetoric by contrasting his volume with one from 1985 called *Why Nietzsche Now*. The issue is not so much, Schrift argues, Nietzsche's continuing relevance for the post-modern world as his *renewed* relevance for the post-post-modern world. Because, somewhere between 1985 and 1995, Nietzsche fell out of favour with intellectuals in Germany, France, and the United States, who decided his anti-democratic politics and wobbly interpretive theory were not what they wanted after all. Hence a new rescue project, but one no less millennial and salvational in tone. 'The essays collected here,' Schrift says, 'will, I hope, answer definitively this charge of Nietzsche's critical irrelevance. For as they demonstrate, whether at the aesthetic, cultural, psychological, or political level, there are important perspectives to be drawn from Nietzsche as we struggle to frame these critical issues for a new millennium.'

The two volumes are of course very different, one intended for a general (read: almost entirely unschooled) audience and the other a more typical example of contemporary scholarship, with various (and variously successful) papers solicited for a conference session gathered into a university-press volume. Together, however, they illustrate the range of what we might call the Problem of Nietzsche's Style. This most reckless and influential of writers is constantly put in peril by those who would claim credit for rescuing him. He is never left to his own devices, and the booming industry is the most obvious manifestation of that fact.

To be sure, many writers are picked over by the genteel grave robbers of the scholarly world. But few are as bent, folded, and spindled as Nietzsche, few used to such bizarre and disparate purposes. This is surely in part because Nietzsche is, as Tracy Strong and Michael Gillespie put it in the introduction to their 1988 volume of Nietzsche essays, *Nietzsche's New Seas*, 'the most protean of protean thinkers.' Liberal or fascist, elitist or higher-order populist, spiritualist or debunker, philosopher of happiness or of despair – Nietzsche has been rendered into all these shapes and more, indeed seems to beg for this shape-shifting treatment on the part of his readers and inter- preters.

But why should this be so? What is it in Nietzsche's oeuvre that allows, even demands, the creation of multiple and suc- cessive masks, each apparently coexisting without violence in a single body of work? One proximate cause, perhaps the main one, is that Nietzsche's writing, so diverse and elusive, so invigorating and poetic, offers itself up time and time again for interpretive picking. Like lines drawn from scripture, its very compression and nuance begs for extended commentary. In one fairly straightforward sense, Nietzsche's problem is that he is *too good a writer*: his German sentences, so exquisitely well formed and energetic, seem to invite at least a page of unpacking. And each time, the eager interpreter is likely to claim that he or she has, finally, got the matter right.

Nietzsche's style has thus taken him through successive generations of leading-edge scholarship in English, from the early American Kaufmann years, when he was simply a brilliant marvel fighting off misplaced charges of Nazi flirtation, to the poststructuralist appropriation of the 1970s and 80s, when American scholars caught up to Heidegger, Derrida, and Foucault and their respectively different Nietzsches. Now, with his reputation suffering in Europe once more (Heidegger, a real Nazi flirter, leaned so hard on Nietzsche's idea of the will to power that his version of the thinker grew intolerable), Nietzsche is being propped up and maintained on these shores even as smart Continental critics cut him loose because of his unpleasant politics.

All of that would be merely diverting, if largely intramural, if it did not indicate something else important about the work itself. It is not unusual, after all, for a rich and provocative body of work to generate a massive posthumous scholarship. Nietzsche's case is different, in large measure because of his own rhetorical strategy. There is a reason so many commentators want, so consistently, to save Nietzsche, to perform rescue missions, whether from crude misunderstanding or from threatened (imagined?) irrelevance. It is that Nietzsche's own style of superior collusion, where every remark is in effect an invitation to join him in the ranks of the clear-eyed and the strong, produces a weirdly irresistible desire to prove oneself a good disciple.

It is not merely that Nietzsche is a good writer, in other words. He is a good writer who writes almost exclusively in the peremptory, imperative tones of the charismatic cult leader or dictator. He makes you want to believe – even if it's not always clear what believing entails, or will cost. And that desire to be the good disciple leads, by a paradoxical but familiar turn, to a desire to be the good protector. For how is devotion better measured than by fending off the various misguided attempts by others to be devoted?

Even the recent gestures in anti-Nietzschean scholarship succumb to his influence, as Malcolm Bull points out in a clever recent article, 'Where Is the Anti-Nietzsche?' (There is probably an essay in the specific question of why so many of Nietzsche's probing critics favour titles phrased in the interrogative – it's as if questions are the natural response to the perplexity of his interpretation.) The fiercest denouncers of Nietzsche, Bull says, are the ones who succeed in making him immortal 'as their eschatological nemesis, the limit-philosopher of a modernity that never ends, waiting to be born the day after tomorrow.'

In particular, the recent crop of anti-Nietzscheans – Bull cites the French liberals like Luc Ferry and Alain Renaut, editors of a provocative recent collection called *Why We Are Not Nietzscheans*; the literary critic Geoff Waite, author of a jargon-heavy screed called *Nietzsche's Corps/e*; and Fredrick Appel, author of the more straightforward *Nietzsche Contra Democracy* – still labour under the bewitching spell of Nietzsche's rhetoric. They cannot get away from his deep psychological influence even as they repudiate his anti-humanism and intolerance – thus leaving the field more cluttered but not less dominated by the man himself.

Waite, Appel, Ferry, Renaut, and other opponents of Nietzsche are reacting to what they see as an uncritical acceptance of Nietzsche as, with Marx and Freud, part of critical theory's Holy Trinity. These figures gave twentieth-century theory its most powerful weapons, the combination of class analysis with an understanding of hidden motives and creative resentment. But now this orthodoxy must be challenged and Nietzsche's apparently liberating tendencies re-examined in the light of his more basic illiberalism, his long-standing spell on otherwise suspicious readers finally broken.

All to the good. And yet, as Bull shrewdly points out, this is, in effect, merely second-order interpretive ownership. Now the critics, not the disciples, are the ones who understand Nietzsche correctly. Hence a new move in the dance of influence. 'Postmodernity has spawned plenty of post-Nietzscheans anxious to appropriate Nietzsche for their own agendas,' Bull writes, 'but there appear to be no post-Nietzschean anti-Nietzscheans, no critics whose response is designed not to prevent us from getting to Nietzsche, but to enable us to get over him.'

This happens, Bull argues, because even when the critic is seen to be opposing Nietzsche against his readers, he or she reuses Nietzsche's rhetorical strategy in the act of uncovering it. Stanley Rosen, for example, wrote of Nietzsche's pernicious influence this way: 'An appeal to the highest, most gifted human individuals to create a radically new society of artist-warriors expressed with rhetorical power and a unique mixture of frankness and ambiguity in such a way as to allow the mediocre, the foolish, and the mad to regard themselves as the divine prototypes of the highest men of the future.' Especially as applied to the mediocre, the process will be familiar to everyone who has taught Nietzsche in a freshman classroom, where a room of a hundred eighteen-year-olds is, if you can believe their own reports, revealed in the act of reading *Thus Spoke Zarathustra* as harbingers of the new world. (University students may be harbingers of a new world, but it is probably more Nike's than Nietzsche's.)

Nietzsche's whole point is, by both personal inclination and authorial design, to make *you*, the individual reader, believe that you are a superior being. That is the effect his style is deployed to achieve, and Nietzsche's own obvious sincerity in its deployment does not make it any less a matter of rhetoric: Nietzsche knows, and moreover frequently acknowledges as part of his strategy, that he needs sympathetic readers. This is true of many if not most writers, of course, but few have managed with such success to thematize that need as the point of the writing itself – that, after all, is one of the things which makes Nietzsche so effective as a bringer of devotees, a master of disciples. The irony coiled at the heart of Nietzsche as a thinker, and as a person, is this evident need for mastery – and the weakness that need in turn makes evident.

Such a point is always worth making against Nietzsche, and against the usual run of minute-bake Nietzscheans, who are indeed among the more annoying of recent collegiate spores. But Bull's argument runs even deeper than this. The critical point against Nietzsche's style (and resulting easy reception) is itself a new form of Nietzschean style, a way of suggesting higher-order forms of higher-order existence. Reading Nietzsche critically becomes, almost despite itself, an apparently inescapable kind of superiority vortex. 'Is there no way,' Bull asks rather wildly, articulating a desperation many readers must feel now and then, 'to reject Nietzsche without at the same time demonstrating one's masterly superiority to the herd of slavish Nietzscheans from whom one is distinguishing oneself?' Apparently not. We can't live with him, and we can't live without him.

Well, consider the available options. Reading Nietzsche as if he were some sort of feel-good philosopher of life-as-art is certainly one way of coping – or appearing to. Solomon and Higgins succeed in doing something I heretofore thought impossible, namely, to make Nietzsche sound like a rather dull virtue theorist, far duller than Alasdair MacIntyre or Martha Nussbaum, with his sprawling, incendiary, contradictory mass of writing reduced to the Pindaric injunction to 'become who you are.' That may be good advice, but it is the least of Nietzsche's contributions to philosophy and literature, and if it were all that Nietzsche had to offer us he would hardly be worth all this attention, madness and moustache or not.

Taking Nietzsche piecemeal on the subjects of drama, culture, and politics, as the academic contributors to Alan Schrift's volume do, is another way of coping. Reading Nietzsche on 'the problem of the actor,' 'miscegenation and the master race,' or 'Shakespearean figures' is, in a sense, to avoid reading Nietzsche in general, and that may be both productive and diverting, though I suspect (in the usual way) only for a very few: the true route to having just a small number of disciples is never to write as well as Nietzsche, but rather to write like, or indeed to be, an academic.

A still more interesting strategy is the one adopted by David Farrell Krell and Donald L. Bates in their beautiful coffee-table book, *The Good European: Nietzsche's Work Sites in Word and Image*, which juxtaposes biographical material and vintage photographs with Bates's nicely realized images of Nietzsche's Europeans haunts, the isolated mountain retreats and *Mitteleuropäische* drawing rooms alike. If the very idea of a Nietzschean coffee-table book strikes you as bizarre, then make an extra effort to seek out this one. It is both beautiful and, in the context of the ever-present problem of Nietzsche's style, wise. Eschewing textual commentary, and therefore neatly sidestepping the paradoxes of superiority, it nevertheless gives us a Nietzsche who is brilliant but also human, all too human; and so succeeds in illuminating his body of work where many more obviously critical efforts fail.

Are there any other options? Bull, by contrast to all these, does not flinch from the challenge he poses himself and us, the challenge to be anti-Nietzschean. He tries to counter the vortex tendency in reading Nietzsche by offering a different approach, what he calls 'reading like a loser' (an unfortunate, if apt, phrase). This involves surrendering the need to master material as one reads it, the deeply ingrained narrative-response tendency we have to find and identify with protagonists, even in non-fiction. 'Reading to one's own overthrow, to convict oneself from the text is an unusual strategy,' Bull concedes. 'It differs equally from rejection of a text as mistaken or immoral and from the assimilation of a text as compatible with one's own being. Reading like a loser means assimilating a text in such a way that it is incompatible with one's self.'

That sounds intriguing, but the reality is a little vague. Bull asks us to consider, for a moment, how we respond to the famous passage in *The Genealogy of Morals* in which the birds of prey express their regard for lambs: 'Of course we admire the lambs. Lambs are tasty.' Reading that, do we adopt the position of the hawk or the lamb? Do we find it funny or terrifying? Or consider Nietzsche's famous claim in *Ecce Homo* that he is dynamite. 'Rather than thinking of ourselves as dynamite, or questioning Nietzsche's extravagant claim,' Bull says, 'we will immediately think (as we might if someone said this to us in real life) that there may be an explosion; that we might get hurt; that we are too close to someone who could harm us. Reading like losers will make us feel powerless and vulnerable.'

It might also make us feel a bit silly. Bull's arguments are not made without irony. He concludes his article, for example, with a suggestion that we extend society to non-human species, and divert the resources of now-redundant cultural undertakings to the needs of these new citizens. ('Perhaps the Louvre, and its collections, could be put at the disposal of apes freed from zoos and research laboratories: the long galleries could be used for sleeping and recreation, the Jardin des Tuileries for foraging.') But there is a more insistent difficulty with this last possibility of reading Nietzsche, namely that the idea of reading like a loser seems to recapitulate the original problem anyway, only now at an even higher level. It is still presented – as it must be – as a *superior* way of reading Nietzsche; still offered as a way of getting the better of Nietzsche, and of ourselves reading Nietzsche. In advancing his loser's cause, Bull is no less peremptory than Rosen (or Nietzsche himself). In a twelve-line paragraph on how to read like a loser, the phrase 'we have to' is repeated three times.

Of course, in making that point against Bull I may be caught in a similar position. I am trying to get the better of him even as I assess his arguments sympathetically. Indeed, the difficulty is general, and therefore insuperable: isn't all criticism, after all, even when subtle and elevated, a way of getting the better of someone else? Isn't all reading of text a simultaneous abjection before, and inevitable transcendence of, its argument? Sometimes, perversely, we are most critical of the text that moved us most, that gripped us with conviction, that got under our skin. Then, returning to the world beyond the text, we want to reassert our superiority over it. It is merely a text, and I am a man! Here is a form of *ressentiment* become creative that is insufficiently remarked. We all know (some of us at first hand) the bitterness of the graduate student, the severe criticism of the acolyte. As readers, we are always threatening to tumble into it, for that, in the end, is what reading does.

Because of his exceptional rhetorical honesty, his bareheaded need to force understanding even while decrying its impossibility, Nietzsche is not an exception to this rule, instead an unusually clear illustration of it. He writes against the tyranny of reason only to replace it with a tyranny of style and emotion. Some succumb to that new tyranny without too much resistance, others (often, it is worth noting, the older and putatively wiser versions of these early devotees) repudiate it. Yet the repudiation is as much bound to its intricacies as the straightforward approval: Nietzscheans and anti-Nietzscheans are locked in a dance of mutual need. But even attempts to transcend this dialectic find themselves, willy-nilly, pulled back in. As do, finally, attempts to rise above the entire fray – attempts like this one right here.

Every writer, finally, even when he or she is no stylist in Nietzsche's league, is caught in the web of style's paradoxes. To write is to insist, to crave agreement, whether in commentary, or commentary on commentary, or review of commentary on commentary. Nietzsche's continuing relevance – for that is something that is hardly in doubt, even if (as we have seen) pretending to doubt it, even while insisting upon it, is itself an enduring rhetorical gambit – in some ways has little to do with anything he said about life, strength, morality, or the future. It has far more to do with the fact that he said it the way he did, that he said anything at all, that he made its saying his deepest and most ineluctable philosophical subject – and therefore ours.

Viral Culture

Discussed in this essay:

Cultural Software, by J.M. Balkin (Yale University Press, 1999).

Ecstasy Club, by Douglas Rushkoff (HarperCollins, 1998).

Consciousness Explained, by Daniel Dennett (Little, Brown, 1991).

The Selfish Gene, by Richard Dawkins (Oxford University Press, 1989).

A man, let's say a quarterback or a hockey centre, does something extraordinary and erupts into celebration. Randall Cunningham points both index fingers at the sky; Wayne Gretzky goes into a sliding crouch while pumping his fist. It's spontaneous, it's unthinking. The next thing you know, everyone from college athletes to the kid down the street is doing it. Somebody turns his baseball cap around, who knows why. Overnight, as if by divine fiat, every cap in the land is backwards. Paula Abdul or Scary Spice or Snoop Doggy Dog comes up with a new dance move. Soon we're all moving that way, swivelling our hips, pointing flathanded, raising imaginary rooftops.

It happens all the time. But why does it?

Theories come and theories go, from the innovation-diffusion research that compares cultural spread to hydrodynamic trickle-down, to epidemiological models that posit analogies between cultural influence and influenza. Depending on their nuances, such theories can become very good at predicting how, and how fast, a fashion will make its way from New York to Spokane, from MTV to your neighbourhood. All models of this spread face one basic problem, however, whatever their variation on the viral or irrigational pictures, and it is this: what, exactly, is being spread when human behaviour shifts in these apparently trivial ways? What are the relevant units of cultural infection, and how do they work their insidious way with us? More importantly, do the same dynamics that shift fashions and trends work with more important things like civility and toleration?

The latest candidate for this role is an unlikely one, an offshoot of evolutionary biology known as memes. According to the theory, memes are self-replicating bits of cultural material – 'cultural software,' to use the title of one prominent book on the subject, by the Yale law professor J.M. Balkin – that take up residence in the material world by colonizing the imitative, fertile brains of language-using creatures like us. Like the genetic theory that spawned it, meme theory is metaphysically reductive: it makes of culture what genes make of human life more generally, namely, a play of blind forces of reproduction. And like genetic theory, which sucks the romance out of life with the relentless energy of a great explainer, making of every emotion an evolutionary impulse and every stroke of genius a random mutation, meme theory ultimately plots a reduction of ourselves to our software. Memes are the DNA of our taste.

Which might be one reason the theory has lately moved out of the small circle of Netheads, fringe thinkers, and cutting-edge artists who first embraced it to catch the imagination of advertisers, marketers, image consultants, and even some media-savvy political parties. In an age of pervasive computer technology and inescapable image- and information-driven media like television and the Internet, the idea that our brains are running various kinds of subconscious software, which can be altered and copied and spread by the file transfer protocols we call our experiences, is enormously seductive – even, we might say, natural. What else is a marketer trying to do but plant a unit of cultural meaning in the audience's brain? What else is a politician trying to effect but a change of behaviour? If the athlete can do it without trying, why can't we do it with intent?

Fine. But is meme-talk merely a harmless fad, just the latest cool way to talk about cool? The musician Augie March said 'Thanks for the Memes' in a 1998 CD release, but are the long books and pages of detailed theorizing that now crowd the bookshelves just an intellectual gloss on what shills, brainwashers, and rhetoricians have known for centuries, if not millennia? Or is there something deeper going on? When a friend of mine, a wealthy financier with a web of international business and charity interests, recently sat me down to discuss meme theory, I became convinced that something had indeed changed.

It's not just that the business world is apparently more interested in acquiring intellectual capital now than at any time since the Renaissance – a fact amply demonstrated by the fat consulting fees and kickbacks available to anyone with a cultural studies degree. It's rather that for a man of commerce, even an exceptionally intelligent one, to speak casually of memes shows we are in the midst of a decisive change in self-image. Meme theory is widespread, and that means the world is now truly *materialist* – not in the common sense of acquisitive (though that's true) but in the philosophical sense of believing that only matter exists. When culture is understood as the play of viral agents in the heedless flesh, we have finally completed the deflation of our self-conception that began a century ago with evolutionary theory.

So what are memes, exactly? Well, begin with the obvious, yet mysterious, material facts. You are looking at these black marks of ink on this white page of paper. The light thus varie-

gated is reflecting off the page and hitting, through your sac-
cading eye's lenses, your retinal wall. That sends information,
via the impulses of the optic nerve, to your brain. Your brain is
processing these electrochemical messages. The result? You
hear a kind of voice inside your head, the inward mental appa-
ritions of sound that exactly match the ink-marks on the page –
their rhythm, the slight trickiness of their syntax, the complicated sense they try to make. If the marks on the page are set
down in a certain order and with a certain elegance, new ideas
are entering your mind: you are thinking thoughts you have
not quite thought before, perhaps could not (I flatter myself)
think unaided. What oft was thought, but ne'er so well
express'd? No, not at all. What was not quite thought until
expressed just now.

The term 'meme' was coined by the celebrated Oxford University biologist Richard Dawkins in his influential 1976 book
The Selfish Gene. Dawkins did no more than sketch his idea,
devoting a scant twelve pages of text to what he called 'the
new replicators,' but since his book was published, the manner
of explaining what happened to you just now has changed
decisively. (For his part, Dawkins has been lately sidetracked
into apparently endless popular debates concerning the details
of Darwinian theory.) Memes, Dawkins said, are self-replicating bits of coded information that take up residence in our
brains, like parasites, and pass from organism to organism via
entirely material transfers like the one involved in your reading this page: a matter of ink, paper, light, neural impulses,
and electrochemical changes. Like genes, in other words, they
disseminate and reproduce via material hosts like us, without
particular regard for the individual agents or even for the species as a whole.

Also like genes, they are selfish: they care only about repro-
ducing themselves through time, nothing else. But they are
new, in evolutionary terms, because they are not physical
codes for particular adaptive organisms, as genes are, nor are
they simply ideational means of furthering the survival of
given organisms, as in, say, the developed ability to wield

tools. 'Memes and genes may often reinforce each other,' Dawkins noted, 'but they sometimes come into opposition,' as, for example, in the meme for celibacy, which is genetically doomed but may, under certain conditions – in a theocracy, say – be culturally persistent. A more vivid, if fanciful, example: violent video games or action movies, which seem to demonstrate high memetic success, might prove genetically disadvantageous if they encourage pointless social violence.

While memes need material hosts to live, the information they code is not necessarily to do with the biological organism itself, or its chances of evolutionary success, but instead with various catchy ideas, memorable songs, well-turned phrases, enduring literary themes, and useful mathematical equations – among other cultural programming that realizes itself through us. 'All that is necessary is that the brain should be *capable* of imitation,' Dawkins concluded; 'memes will then evolve that exploit that capability to the full.'

His own tentative list of meme examples, circa 1976, included 'tunes, ideas, catch-phrases, clothes fashions, ways of making pots or of building arches.' He talked of belief in God and the tune 'Auld Lang Syne,' of the stiletto heel and Jewish religious law: memes of varying degrees of short- and long-term success, passed from host to host through material exchanges of sounds waves, paper, light. 'When you plant a fertile meme in my mind you literally parasitize my brain,' the critic N.K. Humphrey writes, 'turning it into a vehicle for the meme's propagation in just the way that a virus may parasitize the genetic mechanism of a host cell.' Memes, Dawkins argued, are highly successful and rapid replicators, compared to genes, and they exhibit a range of benignity with respect to the host, from ones that actually impair our thoughts (belief in God, for him, is one such) to more useful 'symbiont' memes that make life more interesting, and possibly better in other ways too.

'As material structures,' the nanotechnologist B.C. Crandall puts it, 'memes are always on their way, transformationally, from medium to medium: speech vibrates air molecules that, if near an ear, enter the brain through the tuning forks of the inner ear and thus into more or less stable molecular patterns in the brain.' They travel via the mouth in words or lyrics, from the hands in gestures or the use of tools. 'Today,' Crandall continues, 'memes exploit the new media and travel as electronic and electromagnetic pulses and hibernate as magnetic patterns and as microscopic pits on laser-read compact disks.' In all cases of such transfer, what we call culture is really a matter of matter, for, as Dawkins says, '[t]he computers in which memes live are human brains.' When we have an idea or remember a song, there is nothing distinctively mental, nothing superadded, to the chain of exchange in the material world. Nor is there any criterion of value beyond survival: the meme version of the Darwinian tautology that success breeds success. The good scientific (or other) idea is, roughly, the one cited most often.

Now take, as an example of meme success, the familiar sentence from an earlier paragraph in this essay, my allusion to Pope's *Essay on Criticism* and his views on the natural nature of true wit: What oft was thought, etc. What reality does that sentiment have? Well, it has its various token expressions, of course, all the many places where ink actually forms the words on paper in editions of the *Essay*, in your library and mine, in Norton Anthologies and school readers, quoted in undergraduate essays and high-toned annual reports, and who knows where else. It also exists as part of a neural state in our respective brains – as, you might say, a tiny piece of my brain's hardware, and yours.[1] If you didn't have it before, you have it now: your wiring has been very slightly exploited. And if you knew it before, it's been reinforced through my tweaking: the relevant neural pathway is that much more deeply scored.

Of course you and I will someday perish, and this page crumble to brittle flakes, but because the tag is both useful and memorable – it does what it speaks of, in fact, condensing a common thought into rhythmic pithiness – it has a fighting chance of evolutionary survival in the great press of words, sounds, and images that assault us human hosts from day to day. This one has survived for some 290 years and, with a little push right now from you and me, might just hang on for a few more.

The 'meme' meme itself has proved relatively durable. The word, a combination of truncated Greek (*mimesis*) and allusions to *memory* and *même* 'is now quite widely used,' Dawkins proudly wrote in the 1989 edition of *The Selfish Gene*, 'and in 1988 joined the official list of words being considered for future editions of the Oxford English Dictionaries.' More significant than lexicographical success, though, or rather the necessary precondition of it, is acceptance of the word, and the concept, by thinkers who claim to understand the nature of the mind: philosophers, psychologists, neurobiologists, and systems theorists. The study of consciousness, or as it is sometimes styled, cognitive science, is booming in these early days of the new century. The success of the meme meme is a sign of vertiginous changes in self-consciousness among these specialists, changes that have trickled down to the rest of us in the form of a pervasive, unnoticed modelling of our cultural selves as wired.

The Tufts University philosopher Daniel Dennett has been responsible for much of this success. A genial, bear-like man with a voluminous grey beard and gruff, cheerful mien, Dennett is a charismatic and tireless speaker and a writer of exceptional lucidity. Whether lecturing on the nature of the brain as a meme-nest, or writing lively, provocative books like the modestly titled *Consciousness Explained*, Dennett is a one-man crusade to banish the Cartesian orthodoxy from our midst. He is openly contemptuous of those, like the Rutgers University philosopher Colin McGinn, who have suggested the human mind may be beyond its own ken, and more gently dismissive of scientists who cling to vestiges of atavistic belief in a 'central meaner' or 'inner spectator' within the material organism.

The processes of consciousness are perhaps most striking when we give rise to utterances. Much of consciousness, indeed, is a kind of running commentary, linguistic but muddled, on what we call (or choose to heed as) experience: a

Joycean stream of verbiage, or, better, a Nicholson Bakerish spew of asides, cancellations, qualifications, and tangents. Consciousness is like light trapped in the greenhouse of language. And because language must be shared in order to function at all, there is reason to believe that humans were not conscious until they formed quite complex linguistic communities in which individuals could distinguish themselves from one another as I's. We pick up our vocabulary from our culture,' Dennett writes;

> words and phrases are the most salient phenotypic features – the visible bodies – of the memes that invade us, and there could hardly be a more congenial medium in which memes might replicate than a language-production system in which the supervisory bureaucrats had partially abdicated, ceding a large measure of control to the words themselves, who in effect fight it out among themselves for a chance in the limelight of public expression.

Well, maybe. This certainly accounts for things like Freudian slips, malapropisms, and spoonerisms, where semantically incompatible elements press together, reverse themselves without warning, or replace the suitable alternative, invariably with comic results. More commonly, this 'multiple-drafts' account squares with our sense that speaking (and, to a lesser degree, writing) is a kind of fraught-with-danger tightrope-walk from *langue* to *parole*, a constant struggle to find the right word to shape our meaning. This is not easy, even for experienced talkers. We're all Mistress Malaprop sometimes, getting the word just slightly wrong, perhaps not knowing quite why. Sometimes we didn't know what we wanted to say until we said it; sometimes, more deeply, we didn't know *that* we wanted to say until something was said.

So what is going on in our brains that makes of consciousness at every moment a minor cognitive adventure? Well, if this picture, or something like it, is correct, then our consciousness is a very recent feature of a brain well colonized by various memes that have taken up residence in the accommodating electrified flesh. The self as we experience it is like the graphic user interface developed by those proto-Macintosh visionaries at Xerox's Palo Alto Research Center, a comforting and simplistic piece of make-believe that presents a friendly visage, the familiar illusion of the desktop, masking the intricacies of machine code buzzing away below, all those marching zeros and ones. The conscious self is no more the whole organism than the GUI is the whole computational system.

In some ways, indeed, the self is the least element of the organism, because it captures only the final feed, the ever-elaborating story-stream that retroactively, we might even say delusionally, tries to make sense of the massive processing power behind it. The human brain is no simple I/O machine: there is no CPU, no von Neumann bottleneck through which all output must pass, no simple algorithm for storage and retrieval. The brain's parallel distributive processing, its radical decentralization of computation, is one of the things that make modelling android intelligence so persistently vexing. How do you build a computer complex enough to make its 'owner' little more than a merely superficial aspect of the whole operation, when you are only such an aspect yourself?

Meme theory thus jibes nicely with the general sense many people now have, that their minds are usefully analogous to the workings of the computers they employ virtually every day. Moreover, the meme theory is cool in an icky sci-fi way: it all smacks gratifyingly of Ridley Scott or William Gibson, the fashionably gloomy depictions of wetware mergers of human and machine, or the neo-religiosity of Neal Stephenson's cult best-seller *Snow Crash*, with its sly conflation of the categories of virus, drug, language, program, and religion – all of them now understood as different ways of describing the same meme invasion, the same alteration of post-Babel consciousness. 'To the extent that we participate in language, economics, history, or aesthetics, we inhabit a memetic realm,' says B.C. Crandall. 'Using the energy of our living flesh to maintain, mutate, and express themselves, memes live in and through us. Their viral activity generates our hallucinated identities as "individuals."'

The real postmodern condition is therefore nothing to do with 'incredulity towards meta-narratives,' or any other fashionable emergent property of recent French theorizing. It is, instead, captured by this stealthy triumph of hard-core materialism – a triumph which is, ironically, itself a form of metanarrative. For, as Dennett's insistent optimism makes abundantly clear, science is the only solution to problems of self-understanding, everything else reduced to more or less graceful ways of being irrational. The notion that there is something non-material going on in the world is revealed, from this perspective, as little better than a form of illicit mysticism, a kind of wishful thinking or cop-out from the irrefutable material world that science alone vindicates as real.

But what is surprising is how accommodating the meme theory is to newer forms of mysticism, not to mention anarchistic politics, conspiracy theories, and weird scientistic forms of Nietzschean *Übermensch* thinking. Dawkins worried about this at the beginning: 'The analogy between cultural and genetic evolution has frequently been pointed out,' he said, 'sometimes in the context of quite unnecessary mystical overtones.' Dennett stops short of any *Celestine Prophecy* quivering-wavelength hoo-ha, but he goes Borgesian at the end of his book, talking of the self as a *narrative centre of gravity*, accepting the labyrinthine self-mirrorings of our world-constructing language, and cautiously endorsing the views of those trendy literary critics who taught us to speak of 'multiple subject positions' and 'culturally manufactured singularities' rather than selves. Perhaps more surprisingly, Dennett speaks seriously of immortality, a state he claims we can achieve through our memetic progeny.

Once you believe that human culture is entirely material, and thus the possibility of mediated viral infection of people's brains, immortality is only the beginning. Memetic engineering, to use Crandall's term, or memetic revolution, as advocated by culture jammers or the rave warriors of Douglas Rushkoff's novel *Ecstasy Club*, also become plausible. Because memes actually are what people think, installing them in brains is the equivalent of rewriting their cultural programming. This can either be haphazard or directed; and if directed, it can be for good or ill. ('Memetic engineering,' says Crandall, 'can be found at the core of contemporary techno-corporate communication apparatuses.') In *Cultural Software*, Balkin argues ingeniously that meme theory replaces more familiar critical theories of ideology, because it alone explains how people come to believe the things they believe, without reference to dubious assumptions about 'false consciousness' or 'hegemony.' Once we understand this, we can act to change cultural beliefs for the better.

Because memes are selfish, though, their success is not always our success – or anyway the success of all of us. We might have to face up to the possibility that the currently dominant memes, while briefly rewarding for some, ultimately will destroy us through reduced biodiversity, the creation of lethal waste, and potentially destructive computer viruses. Balkin, who writes with careful balance of this old problem in critical theory, is convinced that this is an opportunity, not a dire statement of entrapment: we create memes as much as they create us, for they are the tools we use to make tools. Culture evolves not towards some divinely sanctioned end, but in an unpredictable direction that responds to our desires as well as shapes them.

Most people would stop short of direct meme-insertion into the brain, at least for now, but theoretically there are other ways to reprogram the meme-nest, just as there are various ways to dive into the gene pool. Some meme-heads now talk hopefully of an 'emergent politics' that might seep from the complex play of human consciousness and make the ecosystem more sustainable. Balkin speaks of the 'transcendental value of justice' which, guiding our software efforts, will make of memes not 'just a metaphor' but rather 'a just metaphor.' The editors of the Vancouver-based journal *Adbusters* – where, incidentally, I used to write a regular column – recently declared what they call 'the meme wars,' issuing a 'blueprint for revolution' more or less in the spirit of Guy Debord and the Situationist International of 1968 Paris.

'We must build our own meme factory, put out a better product and beat the corporations at their own game,' they say. 'We identify the macromemes and the metamemes – the core ideas without which a sustainable future is unthinkable – and deploy them.' There follows a list of five such metamemes, including 'True Cost' ('In the global marketplace of the future, the price of every product will tell the ecological truth') and 'The Doomsday Meme' ('The global economy is a doomsday machine that must be stopped and reprogrammed').

Unfortunately, it is easy for all this higher-order meme talk to fall into self-parody or self-indulgence. The Internet acts as a fertile new breeding ground for memes, a huge throbbing brain that hastens the process of memetic infection – but usually for ill, or at least for banality. There is no mounting challenge there to the power of the political status quo; on the contrary. Balkin's confidence in just memes, while laudable, cannot be squared with global cultural software that is more and more in favour of profit taking, resource depletion, and blithe acceptance of yawning gaps between a prosperous few and an immiserated many. It is also difficult to imagine what lasting influence an eco-friendly memetic revolution, say, could have against the massive power of the world's most successful cultural ideas, like consumerism or short-term self-interest. Spreading new memes is a harder business than it seems, because the other aspects of materialism, like who collects the profits on consumption, are much harder to change than a dance move.

The memetic warriors of my own acquaintance – media critics and culture jammers and techno-anarchists of various kinds – spend an awful lot of time writing elaborate e-mails but not much actually changing the world. Rushkoff's novel, which begins with much bold, if mushy, philosophizing about a meme-driven revolution – 'A declaration of independence from status quo reality. We are attempting to intensify the overall level of novelty in the extant cultural organism, in order to change it. Mutate it.' – ends, many misadventures and hits of ecstasy later, with its protagonist forsaking the drug-and-dance craziness of San Francisco's warehouse raves in favour of fatherhood, domesticity, and good old romantic love. So much for memetic revolution.[2]

From one critical vantage, then, meme theory is little more than a slight recasting, in apparently hard-edged scientific terms, of ideas long familiar to those versed in social constructivism and textual analysis: the self as story, the world as interpretation. Memetic revolution is merely a fancy way of describing what we used to call cultural criticism – just as 'meme' itself might be just a tarted-up way of speaking of ideas and allusions. All the meme talk among hipster intellectuals is just a geeky, 1990s version of the 1950s jargon of authenticity or the 1980s deconstructo-speak. What, if anything, has been gained here, apart from a certain form of cultural cachet for the early adopters of this new way of talking about talking?

To repeat: the baseline is that, whatever its appeal to ravers and shamans and leftist critics who fear conspiracy, meme theory is a type of hard-core materialism, and hence reductivist, even eliminativist, in intent. What it eliminates is our ability to speak meaningfully of an existing mind as something other than a feature of a body. What is reductive about reductionism isn't that it reduces the mind to matter – something no mere theory could do if the facts of the case were otherwise. What is reductive about reductionism is its impoverishment of our vocabularies of self-knowledge. What becomes of individuality when what is 'really' going on is a complex neurobiological imperative unrelated to 'my' identity or desires?

Our attitude to such reductions remains confused. Some of us react to the suggestion that we are mere meme-nests with incomprehension, anger, or even horror. At the same time, we are implicitly reinforcing the material picture whenever we, for example, participate in the medicalization of everyday life. Mental states like sadness, badness, or lack of attention are

now regarded by most people as exclusively organic deficiencies – that is, as diseases of the body – which can be treated
most effectively by altering the chemistry of the brain. Dissent-
ers from this position are regarded as unsympathetic, misguided, maybe even evil.[3] Some form of sociobiology,
meanwhile, influences most people's view of what they are up
to in love, marriage, and work – even if they tend to resist giving up a residual sense of themselves as more than drops in
the gene pool.

A good deal of the appeal of these new materialistic models
of consciousness and the self is owing to the highly contingent
social fact of computer ubiquity, of course. In brains softened
up by computer metaphors, the meme meme finds a ready
host. We are very much taken with the idea that we resemble
the cool machines that dominate our lives from their position
on your desk and mine. Much of our growing inclination to
accept the user illusion or the meme-nest as valid models for
our souls is also a matter of currently dominant scientific
vocabulary, rather than some fact of the matter about the
world. Indeed, this point would seem to follow naturally from
memetic evolution itself, and is embraced by some, including
Balkin. The meme meme emerges, on cue, as the latest successful idea in the ongoing process of human self-reflection.

And yet, if all vocabulary, including itself, is just part of a
larger tale of cultural evolution, the theory of memes risks a
quagmire of incoherent self-contradiction.[4] Seen as a grand
explanation of What It All Means, meme theory paradoxically
proves that such grand explanations are impossible. If, on the
other hand, that impasse is resisted, and all objections to the
tale are pre-explained as simply further proof of the tale's
validity – 'Of course you object to memes! That's what your
current memes demand of you!' – then the position is revealed
as triumphantly ideological. To use a different Borgesian
image, it becomes a kind of illicit master key to the library of
reality. Despite the proponents' avowed hatred of metaphysics, and their refusal to endorse the existence of *mentalese*, or a
pure metalanguage of thought, memes emerge as little more

than Plato's Ideal Forms in another guise: a means of fitting all reality into one overarching conceptual scheme which brooks no contradiction, a sort of displaced egotism.

Apart from a certain modishness of vocabulary, then, is there any *real* gain in that reduction? Balkin's account is the most nuanced and convincing on this question, but even he fails to make a good case. He accepts the metaphorical status of meme talk, and he comes closest to acknowledging the potential for self-contradiction when what purports to be a theory of ideology is itself an ideology – the old rap against Marx. But he waves off the objection because, he says, self-reference is inevitable in cultural theory and, anyway, he is 'ambivalent' in his stance on ideology. Meanwhile, his insistence that justice is the governing value of human societies – a value he is forced to water down to the phrase 'normative order' to cope with drastic changes in the idea of justice across distances in time and space – is one of those philosophical arguments that are unhelpful just to the extent that they are valid. It may be meaningful to talk about a universal value of justice; but, at the level of abstraction necessary to do so, the value does no work in solving day-to-day problems of conflict.

And, despite what Balkin claims about the new language of cultural software, recasting the conflicts as battles between competing memes helps us not one whit. It's a bit like explaining to the thuggish hockey players in my local bar that the reason they want to beat me up when I quote Proust is because they have surrendered to the memes of the male competency cluster. As an explanation, it simply fails to meet the case – even if true in some strained sense.

Suppose one day a woman gives a man a postcard of a Scottish beach with these words written on the back: 'My love is strength'ned, though more weak in seeming; / I love not less, though less the show appear: / That love is merchandized whose rich esteeming / The owner's tongue doth publish everywhere.' The man, recalling a sadness at what had seemed a waning passion, feels a new joy, and sadness, at the woman's deft explanation. At the same time, he experiences a swelling of his love for her that is nevertheless already tempered with the harder edges of compromise. Further back, he allows to creep into view certain ironic reflections and literary-critical jetsam – nearly forgotten tales of Dear John letters, the rhyme and syllable structure of sonnets, some lewdness concerning beach-image postcards. Or perhaps 'allows' is not quite right, because they are just sort of *there* without a sense of decision one way or another. Anyway, his eyes fill. And we say: he is moved.

Is the best explanation of this scene that a memetic replicator of relatively high durability has been transferred into his brain? Does the biocomputational theory of reductive materialism change our minds about what has just been described? Does it make any headway, even as a metaphor?

The problem with the memetic engineers is not that they are Borgesian; it's that they are not Borgesian enough. The language of memes, even when understood as a metaphor, is no more than intermittently useful: it is no improvement on the metaphor of the collective unconscious, for example, and it is arguably more dangerous because it has an aura of scientific sanction. But when elevated to the status of a scientific theory, meme theory self-destructs. That self-destruction disappears just as soon as we surrender the need decisively to plant the materialist flag in the current slag heap of belief about ourselves. The need to vindicate materialism is quickly taking deeper root in us in these late wired days, even coming to dominate our thinking, as meme talk shows; but it is a need that can be satisfied only at the cost of drastic diminution of the rich, textured story concerning what it is to be human.

In the end, any attempt to explain consciousness by getting *outside* consciousness, and hence to write the story of the world as if we were not already conditioned by that world in the labyrinthine, hypertextual way Borges so adroitly brings to our attention, is both doomed and dangerous. 'Borges,' says Umberto Eco in a recent essay on the madness of metaphysical ambition, 'comes to the conclusion that no classification in the universe is not arbitrary and conjectural.' As so should we. The psychologist Julian Jaynes once compared consciousness to a flashlight that could only ever illuminate what came within its limited, highly mobile beam: the rest of what was real remained in darkness – including the structure of the flashlight itself.

Balkin, Dennett, and other explain-it-all thinkers would probably call that giving up. I call it *facing* up, to the infinite task of acknowledging our limits. Memes or no memes, when it comes to consciousness, we're all forever on *parole*.

Notes

1 I use 'hardware' advisedly here, since my sense, admittedly unscientific, is that people find the idea of memes easier to accept if they are made analogous to software, or programming. Hardware is nevertheless what Dawkins says. It may be that the now-prevalent distinction between soft-wiring and hard-wiring may be useful here: a computer's operating system is not hard-wired, but it is a necessary precondition of, and de facto limitation on, adding any new applications. Some memes will be OS-based, others will install as apps, but all need hospitable hardware in order to exist.

2 Rushkoff, who is a friend of mine, went so far as to found a software company he called Memes Inc., but has lately moved away from the meme language in his work. 'It's Dawkins's idea,' he said in a recent e-mail, suggesting perhaps that the evolutionary biology did not, finally, sit well with the social and cultural theory he is engaged in.

3 Of course, it is only by classifying these afflictions as diseases that they become eligible for scientific authority, social approval, and, eventually, insurance coverage. Hence, perhaps, the hostility reserved for those who question this particular reduction of mental to physical.

4 Even if we were inclined to buy this kind of explanation in spite of its logical difficulties, it leaves a wholly empirical problem unresolved: why is the meme for the Cartesian mind, the purely mental

self trapped inside a meat cage, so persistent in the cultural sphere? To say it serves some evolutionary purpose does not meet the case, as Dawkins noted, and it's uncertain what such a purpose might be, except perhaps in personalizing child rearing. No, the ghostly-self meme must be self-replicating and fertile, otherwise it would have died off by now.

Interior Decoration

Discussed in this essay:

Life Style, by Bruce Mau (Phaidon, 2000).

The book *Life Style*, like the concept it names, is something you may not realize you already know a lot about. The Canadian graphic designer Bruce Mau, whose work is documented in this heavy, lush volume, is by no means yet a household name, unless perhaps the household is a garden flat in Chelsea, a loft conversion in Amsterdam, or a Lloyd Wright knock-off in the Berkeley Hills. But Mau's work has become stealthily ubiquitous, from early book design for the cult-success Zone imprint to recent advertising campaigns for mainstream bookstores and museums. His type designs, which artfully combine old-fashioned serif faces with clean modern sans-serif ones, are much imitated: countless exhibition guides and gallery pamphlets show his influence, and when he began using a sans-serif typeface called Interstate a few years ago, derived from familiar highway signage, it was suddenly everywhere in leading-edge books and design magazines.

Mau has collaborated with contemporary visual artists on gallery installations in Europe and North America, and with global-celebrity architects like Rem Koolhaas and fellow Canadian Frank Gehry on books, buildings, and parks. He travels the world making design presentations, not all of them successful, to corporations (Universal Studios), magazines (*I.D.*, the *New York Times Magazine*), and museums (New York's Gagosian Gallery, the Deutsche Guggenheim in Berlin, the Getty Research Institute in Los Angeles). More lately he has attempted to reposition himself as an artist in his own right, building multimedia installations in Vienna and Toronto that claim to interpret the stress of contemporary life. If you haven't seen a Bruce Mau design already, in a bookshop or gallery store or magazine layout, if you haven't (a little more probably) heard someone drop his name, you probably soon will.

Life Style is structured as a chronological account of Mau's career as a graphic designer, from humble beginnings with the three-person firm Public Good, which operated out of a small Toronto apartment and had 'business meetings' each afternoon that were really television breaks, to the international collaborations of recent years with Koolhaas, Gehry, and other stars of the global design-and-architecture universe. It includes compressed descriptions of the major projects of his studio – designs for the Andy Warhol Musuem in Pittsburgh, the Seattle Public Library, the Walt Disney Concert Hall in Los Angeles, and the Schmidt Coca-Cola Museum in Kentucky, among others – as well as snippets of personal reflection, lists of bland and often self-contradictory imperatives, miniature essays, and scattered aphorisms. There are scraps of rather mawkish memoir, accounts of meetings with the famous (John Cage, Philip Johnson), a much-reproduced 'incomplete manifesto for growth,' even a copy of the notoriously difficult design-knowledge quiz Mau used as a job ad in a Toronto newspaper.

The principle of selection seems to have been more inclusive than critical: on the evidence, Mau is deeply enamoured of even his least impressive creations. He is also blessed with a rare degree of belief in himself. According to the copy on the beautiful deep purple cover, these accumulated ephemera, taken together, will be 'more manifesto than monograph ... a singular album of playful and critical statements about the visual and cultural trends that influence today's image-driven context.' (Purple is just one cover option: the book comes in an array of eight accessory-friendly colours, like the iMac computer, including hot pink, golden yellow, deep blue, and maroon.)

Each element of this international success story – which it undoubtedly is – is accompanied by visual elements drawn from the project itself or the wider mediascape. There are gorgeous photographs and computer images, charts and drawings, bits of type and pictures morphing across the page. Any number of the resulting spreads are eye-catching, sometimes stunning, essays in the visual presentation of information. The early sections on the Zone books, in particular, make them even more beautiful and interesting than they were in life. And the thick, creamy paper, bound together in the chunky, not-quite-square format, is a pleasure to caress: this is a book you want to take to bed with you (except that it's so heavy it would end up putting your arms to sleep and smothering you until you died an aesthetically exquisite death). The London and New York firm Phaidon Books, who published it, are responsible for making some of the most beautiful codex objects in the world today: not even Rizzoli does nicer work when it comes to stitching paper into covers.

A book like *Life Style* is not, circa the turn of the new millennium, content to be merely beautiful, however. What sets the book apart from others of its type, what elevates it from obscure niche effort to a flag of the Zeitgeist, is its intellectual pretensions. Mau wants to do more than document his practice as a successful graphic designer; he wants, like just about everyone today from advertising copywriters to chartered-bank CEOs, to show himself a sophisticated intellectual, the savviest of savvy cultural critics. In this he shares the signal pretensions of others in the stratosphere of contemporary architecture and design, including his former collaborator, Koolhaas.

Last year Koolhaas was awarded the prestigious Pritzker Prize by the American Institute of Architects, and was lauded by architecture critics everywhere, including the otherwise tart Herbert Muschamp in the *New York Times* (though Muschamp did suggest that Koolhaas had a thing or two to learn from the anti-globalization activists of Seattle and Prague). The critical enthusiasm was mainly for Koolhaas's ideas about culture, especially as found in a 1978 book-length essay called *Delirious New York*, which argues persuasively that we see a city best in its breakdowns and gridlocks rather than its successes, and the 1,300-page doorstop studio document and alphabetical reflection on the nature of scale called *S,M,L,XL*. Mau served as graphic designer for the latter book, which has suffered the odd (but interesting) fate of becoming a sort of household prop, a signifier of cool displayed nonchalantly in hip offices and photo shoots. Indeed, an image of a model reclining her head on the book, taken from a Dutch newspaper supplement, appears twice in *Life Style*.

At 625 pages, *Life Style* is only about half the size of Koolhaas's effort, but it is on the surface at least twice as ambitious. Whereas Koolhaas took two basic ideas – size and the alphabet – and spun them into a thousand uncontrolled but somehow interlocked directions, Mau and his design studio have constructed a vast self-congratulatory scrapbook of their work over the past two decades, from the original typography of the Zone books to the recent art installations and park designs. But greater ambition, and greater evident need for intellectual credibility, has not altered the fundamental economy of appropriation that governs books of this type.

Indeed, the resulting object is a thick slab of free-floating beauty that is already finding its proper place on the brushed-steel coffee-tables and Meccano-set bookshelves of the continent's smarter homes and design firms (which are increasingly indistinguishable). *Life Style* was truly on the road to success when it began appearing a few months ago in the display windows of fashionable Manhattan and London boutiques, built into staggered, multicoloured stacks, beautiful pillars to support silver objets d'art or overpriced wristwatches. And its cultural appropriation was complete when, not long after, it turned up in an episode of the witty, prime-time NBC sitcom *Will and Grace*, prominently displayed on the coffee table of the show's interior designer.

These appearances, the design-world equivalent of celebrity cameos, vault *Life Style* into a strange economy of empty reference. This is, after all, the reduction of critique to mere decorative effect, the analysis of image culture offered within the delicious covers suborned immediately to that culture. It is not even a question of old-fashioned assimilation of style via commodification – the sort of thing the sociologist Dick Hebdige worried about two decades ago in his still-relevant book *Subculture: The Meaning of Style*. No, here style is (as they say) *always already assimilated*, happily taking its place within the relentless industry of lifestyle pornography, which now includes everything from *Wallpaper* magazine and *Martha Stewart Living* to ostensibly critical efforts such as David Brooks's unintentionally helpful guide to interior decoration, *Bobos in Paradise*.

The resulting collision of fragments (and desires) is therefore more than just the latest example of what people will linger over in art-gallery bookshops. It is as good an illustration as we are likely to find of the problems coiled in that overused phrase, the globalization of culture. *Life Style* ends up being part of the problem rather than part of the solution, but the reasons why are instructive. At a time when politics is increasingly a topic without a conversation, a formerly vivid aspect of life collapsed down to the pathologies of telegenic personality or electoral practice, it's good to be reminded that identity without justice, style without substance, is precisely what we don't need.

You also can't do away with that problem – which goes more commonly by another name, international capitalism – by polishing the already slick surfaces of material things and calling the result cultural criticism. It is nevertheless a booming industry, with everyone from software engineers to advertising executives styling themselves (at least for the purposes of marketing and self-aggrandizement) after McLuhan, Deleuze, Chomsky, or Barthes. The result is a special form of virtually costless intellectual capital: the patina of scholarly credibility without any of the effort of actual thought. It's easy to spot these people, because they are usually the very same ones who argue that there is no difference between art and advertising, or between public discourse and self-promotion.

It may not always be obvious, but architects and designers occupy a special position in this regard, not only because their efforts are the ubiquitous materials of urban lifestyle construction, but also because, at their best, buildings and signage and logos, too often simply the eye-catching servants of profit, can and sometimes do perform a critical function within our cultural experience. Design is a concrete form of thought, just as personal style is the outward expression of intelligence, the complex coded message of self-presentation. ('I speak through my clothes,' Umberto Eco said.) And we are surrounded by design as never before, swimming through every day in an ocean of text and image. The individual both versed in this discourse and critical of it is the modern world's new shaman, a compelling guru of the visual culture.

That is surely why there is such a thing as the contemporary celebrity graphic designer, such as the late Tibor Kalman, whose work was recently the subject of a fawning retrospective at New York's New Museum of Contemporary Art. Kalman, a gifted autodidact with a full quiver of bright but often contradictory ideas, worked on everything from Talking Heads album covers to *Colors* magazine. He was socially conscious, angry, and subversive. It also accounts for the superstar status of Koolhaas, an architect who never seems to build anything. (Even casual culture-watchers now know that Frank Gehry designed the Guggenheim Museum in Bilbao; many architecture students cannot name a single Koolhaas edifice.) Kalman and Koolhaas are new creatures, the designer and architect primarily as urban philosophers, not shapers of type or craftsmen of edifices.

Architects and designers have not always seen their work as

possessing a potential political element – the Palladian norms of classical proportion or Inigo Jones's notions of a well-planned public space, for instance, were about otherworldly perfection, not mundane reform – but the twentieth century was given over to more explicit and even aggressive welding of the built environment to political aspiration. (And if anyone doubts the implicit political dimensions of a classical house or garden, a viewing of Peter Greenaway's *The Draughtsman's Contract* is in order.) Designers of the Bauhaus, their Art Deco contemporaries in America, the purveyors of the International Style – all of them knew, and often enough pointed out, the close associations between the shape of daily objects, including the walls around us, and the possibilities of progress, speed, justice, innovation, democracy, and a host of other sometimes self-negating goals. One doesn't have to agree with Ayn Rand's libertarian wet dream of the architect as philosophical superhero to appreciate the fast-forward associations of a Deco teapot or locomotive, the vaulting ambition of the Chrysler Building, the clean logical positivism of Wittgenstein's Vienna house, or the democratic utopianism of Le Corbusier's Brazilian and French housing projects.

So much is perhaps obvious, especially in the ever-more-tortured post-Heideggerian intellectual discourse that tends to dominate architecture and design schools the world over. What is less obvious is how this natural project of wedding design to politics has been debased precisely by the ubiquity of well-designed things. The Bauhaus idea was to have nothing that was not useful, and to find beauty in use; therefore, designed objects should be made inexpensive and accessible to everyone, no longer the preserve of an elite few. That was the way a revolution in thought could be fashioned by a revolution in the material base, at the most mundane level of what objects stood in our rooms and on our tables, what clothed our bodies.

Such objects are no longer hard to come by. Instead, they are all too accessible, reducing the political dimension of the style project to a vestigial whisper. As teenagers everywhere sooner or later sense – it is one of the special hells of adolescence –

style most of the time declines into mere fashion, and the critical possibilities of its expression are lost or assimilated or commodified. Style – the word comes from the Latin *stylus*, and originally indicated one's manner of wielding a pen – is the new narrative of identity formation, the successor to traditions and virtues and life-scripts of a more traditional culture. That's liberating as well as unsettling, but unless we appreciate the true political dimensions of this shift, the way the first wave of Modernists for example did, we risk the same reductions, the same empty imperatives of modishness, that the fashion pages claim. When the style-reader is also a style-maker, deeply immersed in the commercial world of logos and brands, any possibility of critical distance begins to slip away.

We seem never to learn what any sports broadcast proves, namely, that people who can do extraordinary things sometimes have no ability whatsoever to explain how those things are done, or what they mean. Of course, athletes are merely inarticulate or clichéd; architects and designers favour the far more distressing option of warmed-over artspeak.

Without a theory of justice, to use language that rarely gets an airing in this quarter, you cannot simply indulge a taste for picking through the materials of consumerism. Mau senses this, I think, and tries to position his work in a tradition of renegade social-reform typographers that might include Eric Gill, the Vorticists, Jan Tschichold, Edward Johnston and, today, the Web-based font-master, Chank Diesel. Mau has a fondness for Gill's Perpetua typeface, which he used with great subtlety in the Zone books, and he frequently claims an affinity with Marshall McLuhan, who was himself a sort of late-model Vorticist experimenter in his contributions to *Explorations* magazine or the book *Counterblast*. The opening salvo in *Life Style* is, in addition, a reference to the ideas of the Situationist thinker Guy Debord, whose work *The Society of Spectacle* has become a favourite touchstone of art directors and magazine editors (an issue of *Architecture* magazine recently used quotations from it as editorial 'content' in an elaborate spread on the work of Frank Gehry and other 'monumental' architects).

'Life style,' the text begins, ungrammatically. 'There are few terms that have been as savagely commodified and gutted of meaning in recent years. Our first instinct is to leave its empty carcass to the vendors and the merchants. But in the spirit of *détournement* (the diversion of aesthetic artifacts into contexts of one's own device), we are wresting it back. We are interested in recuperating and reinvesting the term "life style" so that it speaks of the designer's role in shaping the lives we lead and the world in which we live ... Style is not superficial. It is a philosophical project of the deepest order.'

True – and yet somehow without any appreciable impact here, just another smooth surface. Twelve pages into *Life Style*, in a sort of opening-trailer section featuring full-page photographs and little chunks of text, one comes across the picture of that beautiful model reclining on a copy of *S,M,L,XL* and the words 'Unless we can come to terms with the global image economy and the way it permeates the things we make and see, we are doomed to a life of decorating and redecorating.' The small-type caption is more honest: '*S,M,L,XL* as a life-style pillow.' No, unless we can come to terms with our own participation in the commodification of design, we are doomed to a life of slick self-delusion.

Mau's rhetoric sometimes echoes the celebrated First Things First manifesto, pioneered by Kalman, which called graphic designers to social account: if ubiquity in the mediascape was acknowledged, so too must be their political responsibility. That Mau did not sign the manifesto is not necessarily an adverse comment on his politics (though it might be), but it does betray a certain arrogance about these issues. It is not enough to say that graphic design must be socially responsible; to cash that out, you need to build bridges to other forms of practice, and you need, most of all, explicit political ideas. This is what earlier design renegades like Gill and Morris possessed in spades – sometimes to the detriment of their careers and lives.

To look at *Life Style*, you might imagine that the world is populated entirely by isolated individuals out shopping, all of whom have the pressing problem of how to dispose of their surplus income in stylish ways. Not an inconsiderable issue, I suppose, especially for those of us it actually describes, but nevertheless a dangerous and misleading focus for global politics. The way to combat the pathologies of the market-based individualism busily colonizing the public spaces of the world is not to make us better consumers but to analyse the collective costs of consumerism – and maybe, along the way, to make us better global citizens.

This might suggest that *Life Style* has no sense of the political, that it is simply a cheerful, apolitical celebration of consumerism, the way Malcolm Gladwell lingers with such delighted, nerdy interest over the mechanics of shop design or ad construction in *The Tipping Point*. But it is instead a more troubling thing: an attempt to claim political awareness that succeeds only in draining everything meaningful from the category of political awareness. By the same token, it is too simple to say, at the level of the object itself, the book is a triumph of beauty over content. It presents as a book which offers to expand the limits of the book, combining image and text in a way that goes beyond both; instead, it wraps itself in an impervious layer of intellectual slickness, making the combinations of text and image somehow less than each alone.

This problem is most obvious in a central section on identity, where there are some nice spreads on the morphing features of various cultural icons – James Bond, Betty Crocker, David Bowie, Madonna – accompanied by some of the sharpest writing in the book. (Whoever is responsible for writing the captions and cutlines of *Life Style* is a more acute cultural critic, and better writer, than Mau himself.) It is of course true that the modern age, the legacy of four hundred years of thought and action, is the Romantic imperative, from Herder and (less comfortably) Nietzsche and Wilde, to make your life a work of art. What we are struggling with now is the paradox entailed by trying to democratize that essentially elitist project: today, *everybody* must be an artist. The buying and selling of style in the global aesthetic marketplace is a key battleground of that struggle, now complicated almost overwhelmingly by the vastness of our options. The very idea of the exotic, for example, once a staple of style, recedes with accelerating velocity: yesterday's cool xenophilic accessories (Japanimation T-shirts, baggy convict wear, kaffiyehs) are today's fashion mistakes.

Constructing a comfortable personal identity has never been harder, and the successful personal artists today are those who surf through the sea of options with a sort of studied casualness, described by Jean-François Lyotard, way back in the uncool year of 1984: 'One listens to reggae, watches a western, eats McDonald's food for lunch and local cuisine for dinner, wears Paris perfume in Tokyo and "retro" clothes in Hong Kong; knowledge is a matter of TV games.' But what we forget, in taking an easy-going line on the contemporary image and experience economies, is the violence that underlies style. Identity is a bulwark against outside contingency, but it is also an act of combined desire and disdain for the other. It is shot through with envy and resentment, and the infinite possibilities of injustice. That is why cultural identity – what is it? does one have a right to it? are there special rights for special cultural groups? – has been such a central focus of recent political thought.

The important conflict here is not really between the image-driven world, dominated (as Mau ri ghtly notes) by competition for your attention and hunger for new and vivid experiences, and you as an individual; it is, rather, between you *and everyone else* who inhabits that world. It is the central failure of *Life Style* that it misses this political dimension of the style project altogether, pushing us each further and further into the existing patterns of individualistic consumption. What is pornographic about most lifestyle design is precisely that it depicts power only to replicate it, not challenge it.

That might sound harsh, especially given the cosy feeling of this book, both inside and out. There is much talk in these pages of how much laughter pervades his studio, how the long days are broken up by impromptu bull sessions and grad-school-quality arguments. There are some illuminating reflections on the nature of work itself. You get the impression that working for Bruce Mau is a matter of round-the-clock happiness. But cosiness is a dangerous property; it hides a multitude of sins. There is no mention at all of the ego-submersion and chaos of the studio model, the long delays and unpaid bills, the disgruntled designers who abandoned ship rather than submit to the anonymity of Mau's Renaissance-master work hierarchy. A studio, according to the incomplete manifesto for growth, should be a place for study. But it is also, less benignly, a site of personal will to power and the persistent influence of money. To glide over those difficulties is to avoid a key element in any genuine understanding of how design functions in our cultural life.

Mau's track record is impressive, of course, especially in his ability to hitch his wagon to fast-moving celebrities. He is a brilliant typographer, and the miniature essay on the art of type design that is nestled in the heart of *Life Style* is a delight – something that might have made the basis for a book of its own. ('Letterform design is the philosopher's stone at the heart of the black art of typography,' the text reads at one point. 'It is the means by which values and emotions are injected directly into information.') Those of us who first heard his name when the Zone books began appearing in the 1980s, presenting difficult theoretical texts in smooth, even seductive form, cannot forget the feeling of liberation from the stolid university-press design norms that had until then imprisoned ideas. But success has its costs, and the ironies of this volume multiply even as its flimsy theoretical underpinnings become more and more nakedly exposed. Point 12 of the manifesto enjoins us to 'Keep moving. The market and its operations have a tendency to reinforce success. Resist it.'

Mau should have taken his own advice more seriously. 'We admit that we are not inhabiting these roles and executing these responsibilities as elegantly or effortlessly as might sometimes be suggested by this volume,' the text tells us. And yet, that blithe caveat invites a series of arguments with the very issue of lifestyle which the text studiously avoids. There is a higher-level contradiction here between rhetoric and reality, and simply noting it offhand, as if that were enough, makes Mau no better than the uncritical 'people' he criticizes earlier in the book when he says (in a different version of the 'we are doomed' speech) that

> people tend only to look at the contradiction and then stop, because they cannot resolve it, cannot get the pieces to fit. Having looked and seen, they prefer to look away, to keep their heads down and get on with their work. Unless we keep our heads up and come to terms with the global image economy and the way it permeates the things we make and see, we are doomed to a life's work of decorating and redecorating. And coming to terms means maintaining the dialogue with the context and facing the contradictions it imposes on our work.

What does facing contradictions really mean? Invoking John Cage, *Life Style* suggests that striving to resolve them is bad practice, the holdover of a binding discursive rationalism that will keep us from 'growing.' Well, okay; I guess nobody wants to be puritanical about logic, especially these days: it won't get you many fans of the younger, basic-black variety. But mere 'playfulness' about contradiction, if that is the alternative, is ultimately just as conservative as rationalism, and maybe more guilty: it leaves everything as it is, even while pretending to the honour of sophistication. Critics of media and culture are always in a paradoxical position, of course. Hebdige puts it this way:

> We must live an uneasy cerebral relation to the bric-a-brac of life – the mundane forms and rituals whose function it is to make us feel at home, to reassure us, to fill up the gap between desire and fulfillment. Instead, they summon up for us the very fears which they alleviate in others. Their arbitrary nature stands revealed: the apparent can no longer be taken for granted. The cord has been cut: we are cast in a marginal role. We are in society but not inside it, producing analyses of popular culture which are themselves anything but popular.

What he could not see, two decades ago, was how popular such analyses would become, and how that popularity would spin the critic's dilemma into new dimensions. It is no longer enough to document the way the image economy functions: that simply fetishizes its products, buffing their attractive surfaces to a high sheen rather than penetrating them to any critical effect. Such an effort is diverting, maybe even reassuring in an odd way. But sooner or later – on recent evidence, mostly sooner – it loses whatever critical bearings it possessed and ends up adding to the already massive stock of smooth consumer objects that need to be demystified, to be thought through. It doesn't help when conclusions are offered in what looks like the spirit of bland banality: 'I increasingly believe,' Mau says, 'that the future of design rests in our ability and willingness to develop new practices and theories of form that are inextricably linked to, and informed by, life and growth.' What?

It might seem minor or finical (or predictable or fogeyish) to say that some pages of this book reproduce text that is nearly impossible to read – including a page that, as far as I can make out, has these critical words to offer: 'These days most "new" design increases noise at the expense of signal: increasing obscurity, decreasing legibility, turning readers into viewers. Often, of course, this is because the signal itself is not as rich as the noise. We are not so quick to abandon the signal.' Does it matter that the design of a book makes it hard to read, makes its ideas virtually opaque? I think it does. *Life Style* is itself an extended noise/signal problem, one that finally descends into a haze of gorgeous but meaningless static. Turning its pages feels like channel-surfing or wandering mutely through a downtown mall.

Partly this is a complaint about what books are for, what they can do. Whatever today's celebrity graphic designers might think as they attempt to make themselves the philosopher-kings of the branded world, there is no substitute for thought conveyed in extended writing, where the beauty of type is precisely its functionality, and where its functionality is invisible. Only then is thought, and politics, possible. The Reverend Sydney Smith once noted that there was 'no furniture so charming as books,' but if books are merely furniture, they are less than themselves. You must open them up and grapple with the extended arguments within. When it comes to lifestyle, what Mau calls 'a philosophical project of the deepest order,' hard thought should not be optional. *Life Style* unfortunately makes it so.

PART III
INTERVENTIONS

Tables, Chairs, and Other Machines for Thinking

It's a curious fact, but one not often remarked, that philosophers have no sense of furniture. Curious because, after all, they spend at least as much time sitting and lying and lounging as the rest of the populace – maybe more so when it comes to lying and lounging, actually. And yet in the vast volumes of Plato and Aristotle, of Kant and Hume, you will not find, to my knowledge, any serious consideration of what they are sitting, lying, or lounging upon. There are many thousands of pages on the nature of knowledge, the question of the meaning of Being, and how to live an examined life. There is scarcely a line on how to know, make, or examine a table or a chair. What of sofas, for example? How many philosophers have wondered about a couch the way they have wondered about relations of logical entailment?

Now, you might think this is to be expected, if not quite forgivable. Philosophers have also largely ignored food, sex, personal grooming, and the common cold. Most of them think, and many of them say, that they have more important things to deal with. But there is, as a result, no philosophy of furniture – a regrettable absence that commands our attention.

Of course there are a few prominent exceptions, though they tend to be among the most amateur of the philosophical ranks, the not-quite-serious members of the tribe whose reputations depend on other achievements and interests. This is not coincidental, for genuine attention to the everyday leads, perhaps necessarily, to a decidedly unprofessional undermining of the philosophical profession's peculiar form of blinkered self-regard. Jean-Paul Sartre, for example, established himself as free-ranging intellectual, not a professional philosopher in the academic sense. He made it his mission to speak to the deepest of human concerns and his works have suffered a regrettable decline in academic reputation as a result. Sartre makes a point of letting us know that the immovable furnishings of existential hell, in the play *Huis Clos*, were of tasteless Second Empire design, as if to underscore the fact that eternal misery is more often banal and tacky than compellingly inventive. And if we consider Freud a philosopher (either a dangerous or an obvious proposition, depending on the company), he is exceptional in fixating on a couch – one which was, as we know, rather unremarkable in dimensions and covered with a layer of Turkish rugs.

True, in Plato's *Republic* Socrates (another principled amateur) introduces the famous figure of a bed to illustrate the theory of the Forms: those timeless essences wherein genuine truth resides. A painting of a bed, he notes, is merely a reflection of an actual bed fashioned by a craftsman. But this three-dimensional bed is itself just as much a reflection, a pale copy, of the ideal bed, the Form of the bed, bedness itself. Each reflection – Form of bed, actual bed, picture of bed, reflection of picture of bed, and so on – represents a declension from Reality, a loss of metaphysical firmness. You can lie on only one of these beds, in short, as Socrates famously does while talking of love in the *Symposium*, but for Plato (here using Socrates as his mouthpiece) the truly real bed is precisely the one you *can't* lie on, namely, the ideal form of bed, or what we might call Bed. And while Bed may be metaphysically interesting, indeed fascinating, it is not what you or I would consider a good option when it comes to supporting the futon or Sealy Posturpedic. However higher up the ladder of reality than physical beds it may be, Plato's Bed will not hold you up when you simply need to lie down.

Socrates sometimes lounged on a couch as well, because the

Greek word for bed can also mean couch. The piece of furniture in question in the *Symposium* was used for both conversation and sleep – not to mention seduction, as when Alcibiades, in an ancient preview of the modern teenage mating ritual, attempted to put the moves on Socrates when the night grew late and the light grew low. Mostly, however, Socrates prowled the Athenian marketplace on foot to pursue his thoughts about justice and virtue. Indeed, philosophers seem to agree with Aristotle, founder of what is actually known as the Peripatetic School, that thinking is something best done while walking.

The philosopher in Iris Murdoch's novel *The Philosopher's Pupil* cannot think unless he is strolling and in conversation, and Nietzsche famously said, 'Only thoughts that come from *walking* have any value.' And yet, no walking thought is anything more than half-formed, and Nietzsche had to sit down somewhere long enough to write that. It is worth remembering that we would not have the benefit of Nietzsche's or anyone else's wisdom were it not for the chairs they sat in and the tables they wrote upon. Ludwig Wittgenstein notoriously placed himself in a canvas deckchair every day in his rooms in King's College, Cambridge, there to think the thoughts that might, on a good day, make it into one of his notebooks. More often, he sat and thought and wrote nothing, or rose the next morning to crumple what he had written the day before. Wittgenstein should have spared some of those thoughts for the deckchair itself. For, despite centuries of effort to make philosophy dead from the neck down, we are still embodied creatures with limbs and frames requiring support.

The question of furniture is thus, in its way, a question about the site of reflection, the scene where thinking happens.[1] Given the importance of time spent in the study, it is therefore remarkable how little of reflection's attention is directed towards its own conditions of possibility.

To be sure, there are once more some oddball exceptions. Kierkegaard spends a good deal of time, some would say too much, considering the nature of his writing table. Among other things, Kierkegaard underwrites a certain romantic interest in the particular table or desk where a work was composed, an interest that is widely accepted but not often investigated critically. Here one might think, for example, of the 1996 collection of photographs by Jill Krementz called *The Writer's Desk*, depicting various twentieth-century authors in their scenes of writing: Joyce Carol Oates's tiny shelf, Saul Bellow's modified altar-contraption, Thomas Wolfe's stand-up desk. The auratic associations of Dickens's plain desk, or Tennessee Williams's sawhorse desk, or Pablo Neruda's bureaucratic Cadillac of a desk, the particular ink stains and carved-in words of the singular article of furniture, point us toward what may make furniture worthy of philosophical consideration.

But ultimately those associations blind us, as auras so often do, to the deeper issue of how the mundane and the profound are related. How, precisely, does a particular article of furniture accommodate certain thoughts and not others? Would Kierkegaard have written differently if he'd had a smaller table? What has the proliferation of the laptop computer done to the act of thinking, especially as transformed into prose? The novelist Richard Ford has said he can write anywhere, in crowded room or airport departure lounge; Raymond Carver allegedly preferred his stationary car for an office. Does that matter to the question of how deeply Ford or Carver (or anyone) can think? For thinking is, after all, the present concern. Interest in the writer's desk focuses more often on writers of fiction than of non-fiction, especially of philosophy – as if the rarefied thoughts of philosophy were necessarily even less embodied than the muddy labours of fiction. This, once more, works paradoxically to squeeze the human life out of reflection as a mode, or act, of being human.

What is it to think? Where can it be done? Well or badly? Furniture takes its place in rooms, and the rooms where thought occurs are likewise a subject worthy of more precise investigation. Montaigne, that most human of the great thinkers, a man willing to examine everything from table manners to his own sexual preferences and bodily functions, goes on at some length about his library and its furnishings. It was a circular room on the third floor of a tower standing at one corner of his property in southwestern France. It had three windows, a desk, a chair, and five tiers of shelves arranged in a semicircle. The shelves held Montaigne's collection of about a thousand books on philosophy, history, religion, and poetry.

'I spend most days of my life there, and most hours of each day,' Montaigne wrote of the room, which had 'splendid and unhampered views' and fifty-seven apposite quotations from his favourite authors painted on the wooden ceiling. Books are naturally the most important objects in a library, and as the novelist Anthony Powell said, they do furnish a room. The Reverend Sydney Smith, a man of great learning and wit ('I never read a book before reviewing it,' he said; 'it prejudices a man so'), famously pointed out that there was 'no furniture so charming as books.' But, important as they are, books are not what we usually mean when we talk of furniture. Books that are merely furniture, perhaps purchased by the yard from remainder stock in order to outfit a pretentious bar or club, do not serve their purpose as books. And books are meant to be opened, one of these days anyway. In seeking a reflective philosophy of furniture we should rather focus on more basic items: tables, chairs, and other machines for thinking.

Lately, of course – especially in the last century and a half – there has been a vast new literature on the theory of design, including the design of furniture. Much of this literature is excellent, some of it is silly, and more than a little of it is incomprehensible. But in any event that is not what I mean by a philosophy of furniture. Design theory mostly involves extending principles of aesthetic evaluation from one realm, the fine arts, to another, the applied arts. It says little about the role that furniture plays in human life, little about the deepest first principles of what we might call the Furniture Idea.

I cannot hope to remedy the situation by myself. But I want to say a few words about what happens when we start thinking about tables and chairs as machines for thinking, essential supports for the essential human undertaking of reflection. This is, in its way, reflection on the act of reflection – and on the places where that reflection occurs. Furniture is a means to that end; it is also, as we shall see, an end in itself.

There is, happily, an essay called 'The Philosophy of Furniture.' It was published in May of 1840 in a periodical called *Burton's Gentleman's Magazine*. But it is not by a philosopher, it is not really a philosophy, and it is not really about furniture.

When Edgar Allan Poe sat down (notably, we don't learn where or on what) to compose some thoughts on furniture, he was mainly interested in decorating taste, not the Furniture Idea. 'The Philosophy of Furniture' begins by noting that different nations have different styles of decoration – the Spanish favouring drapes, but the French too distracted to decorate well, the Chinese too fanciful, and so on. 'The Yankees alone are preposterous,' he says, and proceeds to demolish the excesses of conspicuous consumption in a nation ruled more by money than taste. 'The cost of an article of furniture has at length come to be, with us, nearly the sole test of its merit in a decorative point of view,' Poe complains, 'and this test, once established, has led the way to many analogous errors, readily traceable to the one primitive folly.' There is a basic confusion here of magnificence for beauty, argues Poe, and that leads Americans to what we can only describe today as stupid fashion mistakes. 'Straight lines are too prevalent,' he notes, 'too uninterruptedly continued – or clumsily interrupted at right angles. If curved lines appear, they are repeated into unpleasant uniformity. By undue precision, the appearance of many a fine apartment is utterly spoiled.'

As he goes on in this vein, Poe gradually acquires the definitive, slightly hysterical tones of a commentator on a home-and-garden television show. There is a lot of imperious talk about bad window treatments and unsuitable fabrics, many a harsh judgment of someone's disastrous end tables or ill-chosen colour scheme. 'The soul of the apartment is the carpet,' Poe declares. 'A judge at common law may be an ordinary man; a good judge of a carpet *must be* a genius. Yet we have heard discoursing of carpets ... fellows who should not and who could not be entrusted with the management of their own *moustaches*.' Turkish carpeting, he notes, is 'taste in its dying agonies,' while floral patterns 'should not be endured within the limits of Christendom.' We are forced to wonder: was Poe the first gay interior designer?

Poe describes his own ideal apartment as a counter-example to all the excesses of glitter and mirrors and overdone drapes. He is explicit about the dreaminess of this room, its oneiric allure: 'Even now, there is present to my mind's eye a small and not ostentatious chamber with whose decorations no fault can be found. The proprietor lies asleep upon a sofa ... I will make a sketch of the room ere he awakes.' By our standards this room is still pretty over the top, but Poe's basic message of restraint is timeless. His description is worth quoting at length:

> Two large low sofas of rosewood and crimson silk, gold-flowered, form the only seats, with the exception of two light conversation chairs, also of rose-wood. There is a pianoforte (rose-wood, also), without cover, and thrown open. An octagonal table, formed altogether of the richest gold-threaded marble, is placed near one of the sofas. This is also without cover – the drapery of the curtains has been thought sufficient. Four large and gorgeous Sèvres vases, in which bloom a profusion of sweet and vivid flowers, occupy the slightly rounded angles of the room ... Some light and graceful hanging shelves, with golden edges and crimson silk cords with gold tassels, sustain two or three hundred magnificently bound books. Beyond these things, there is no furniture, if we except an Argand lamp, with a plain crimson-tinted ground-glass shade, which depends from the lofty vaulted ceiling by a single slender gold chain, and throws a tranquil but magical radiance over all.

By any standards, a good room. A room suitable for work but also for conversation, a place where a person might write a book or entertain a friend or carry on a love affair. In short, a place to think and dream and be human.

We may disagree with the details of Poe's taste – I would personally like to see a little less crimson and gold – but we cannot fault his intentions. Yet this is not really philosophy, as I said. There's still something missing, namely, consideration of *the very idea* of the chair or the table. The trouble on the other side is that philosophy seems to miss what Poe knows, namely, that the details matter: that there's a difference between a Sèvres vase and something from Ikea; that rosewood is finer than pine; that too many mirrors spoil a room. Somewhere between *House Beautiful* and Plato's austere *Republic*, in other words, lies the unexplored territory of a true philosophy of furniture. (So far as the metaphysical illustration goes, Socrates' bed could just as easily be a boat or a horse.)

When philosophers of the mainstream sort do write about furniture, in fact, they mostly do so as an act of annihilation. In his book *Meditations on First Philosophy*, for instance, Descartes mentions the study in which he is sitting, including the chair he uses to seat himself comfortably by the fire, and the table on which his writing materials lie. We might be forgiven for thinking that this laudable preoccupation with the conditions of thought is going to lead us to insight about the relation between furniture and reflection. But not really. Descartes is concerned only to give some sense of his immediate surroundings in order to add texture to his thinking – thinking which, indeed, involves immediately demolishing the very existence of those surroundings in a spasm of radical doubt. Descartes is interested in probing the evidence of his senses; he thinks we cannot know anything with certainty. So he starts with the handiest evidence, that of the stuff around him; and then proceeds, by bold steps, to show that he doesn't know what he thinks he knows.

That's how it mostly goes in philosophy, in fact, especially after Descartes: a lot of featureless furniture gets demolished in pursuit of the post-sceptical truth. The modern philosopher is taught to ask, in effect, 'Is this a chair that I see before me?' We observe the chair, but then the existence of the chair is immediately doubted. The chair itself might as easily be any other object of the senses. Even if a chair is the favoured object, it does not matter what kind of chair it is. There is no pause here to distinguish an Eames from a Gehry, or to pick out an original Mission armchair from a mail-order imitation. All of the furniture in this sleight-of-hand exercise is without distinction, a series of generic macro-objects found lying around and pressed unwittingly into service in a desire for certain and complete knowledge of the world.

As the renegade philosopher Stanley Cavell has shrewdly noted, the disappearing table of scepticism is always *just a table*, never a Louis XV gilt escritoire. This should give us pause, Cavell says, because it indicates the weirdness – the manufactured quality – of the philosopher's question about knowledge. The question is too general, too comprehensive, to be real; the certainty and generality it seeks to vouchsafe, the Holy Grail of all modern epistemology, is both misleading and dangerous. We would do better, Cavell suggests, to follow our more pedestrian interests. To most normal people, it matters a lot whether the chair before us is a well-restored vintage Deco or just a piece of cheap pine. But in Cartesian-style philosophy, this sort of issue simply never comes up. Furniture disappears as soon as it is called upon the scene. We learn nothing interesting about it: it is merely a handy, non-specific prop that appears only to be routinely destroyed in acts of epistemological experimentation.

Once more this creates a paradoxical situation, and I want to spend a moment to consider it, for it illuminates both philosophy and furniture. The paradox is that the furniture is annihilated in general but must be present in specific for the act of annihilation to take place. Descartes had to be sitting somewhere in particular, had to be sitting on something in particular, for him to be able to take the bold step of doubting everything in general. What he can't doubt, in the end, is of course his own act of thinking itself: he thinks, therefore he is. But my point is that he couldn't even do that without a chair.

The question in the background here, the unasked philo-sophical question, is really this one: what is furniture for? That may seem so obvious as to be not worth asking, but one of the things you learn as a philosopher is that the obvious-sounding questions are usually the most interesting ones.

Here is one kind of answer: furniture is for sitting on, lying on, sleeping on, and putting things on. We might call this answer *functionalism*, and it emerges as a common enough version of the Furniture Idea when we force the issue somewhat. Func-tionalism views furniture as, in effect, an extension of the human ability to complete physical tasks. Here, for example, is Marshall McLuhan talking about the relationship between fur-niture and the human body in his book *Counterblast*:

> A chair outers the human posterior. The squat position is 'trans-lated' into a new matter, namely wood or stone or steel. The tem-porary tension of squatting is translated and fixed in a new matter. The fixing of the human posture in solid matter is a great saver of toil and tension. This is true of all media and tools and technologies. But chair at once causes something else to happen that would never occur without a chair.

> A table is born. Table is a further outering or extension of body resulting from chair. The new fixed posture of chair calls forth a new inclination of body and new needs for the placing of imple-ments and stirring of food. But table also calls forth new arrangements of people at table. The fixing of a posture of the body in a chair initiates a whole series of consequences.

Or, as Burt Bacharach and Hal David more elegantly put it, 'A chair is still a chair, even when there's no one sitting there.' Notice how McLuhan speaks here of 'chair,' 'table,' and 'body' as if they were proper names or basic essences, categories rather than things. Notice, too, the causality implied in this kind of functionalism: we squat, therefore we need chairs; we have chairs, therefore we need tables; we have tables, therefore we need place settings.

That is not wrong. Once people began eating at tables, whole new vistas of social complexity opened up before them. Table manners became an issue, as did the ability to converse while at table. Carving meat in front of others was alone the subject of numerous Renaissance manuals for gentlemen – and still causes anxiety attacks among certain sons-in-law on their first holiday visit. In our own time, the art of throwing the perfect dinner party has become a bourgeois obsession which shows no signs of diminishing in this, the third decade of Martha Stewart's reign.

So functionalism makes a deep point. Furniture arises as the solution to certain problems, as a way of completing various human tasks – only to create, in the process of so doing, numerous new tasks. It also creates new kinds of aesthetic issues, as Poe reminds us. Any plane surface within a certain range of dimensions, and suspended or supported at a particular height off the floor, may be considered a table. This is the way in which, for example, a philosopher of kinds, natural or non-natural, nominal or real, would speak of tables and chairs. Individual instances are linked together by an articulable essence, consistency with a given design, or certain inductions that can be run, for good reasons, over the class of objects so styled – a good reason being, in this case, something like the combination of cultural and physical factors entailed by 'because you can sit in it.' But to leave the matter there is to fall into a mundane version of the furniture demolition of the Cartesian philosopher. Here all tables are equal because they are all merely extensions of our instrumental tasks and bodily dimensions. This misses a deep point about tables. A 'good' table, a table worth having, isn't just a handy surface or prop; it must also be striking, beautiful, elegant, or witty – or some combination thereof.

These are not functional virtues, they are *aesthetic* ones. But, as is so often the case when it comes to virtue, here aesthetic considerations are not entirely or easily separable from issues of functionality. Any good designer knows that a smooth, highly polished wood surface is both aesthetic and functional; so, depending on your taste, are tapered legs, pediment supports, S-curve lines, high straight backs, and reclining seats. Often enough to be remarkable, the more beautiful thing is also the more useful thing. Functionalism and aestheticism are often thought to be at war, but it would be more accurate to say that they are in creative tension. Rare is the piece of furniture that possesses no aesthetic sense whatsoever, however badly judged. More likely, but still rare, is the piece where aesthetic sense has entirely overwhelmed functionality – though many of us have probably had some near-miss experiences on that score, chairs so beautiful they threaten to pitch you onto the floor at any moment.

That is usually as far as most people get when it comes to thinking about the Furniture Idea, but of course there is much more still to say. Furniture is for doing things, and for being beautiful; but it is also for instantiating, and illuminating, certain kinds of *political* ideas. In *Das Kapital*, for instance, Marx introduces some insights about the nature of commodities by, as it were, putting a few things on the table. 'A commodity appears, at first sight, a very trivial thing and easily understood,' he says. And yet:

> Analysis shows that in reality it is a very queer thing, abounding in metaphysical subtleties and theological niceties. So far as it is a value in use, there is nothing mysterious about it ... The form of wood is altered by making a table out of it; nevertheless, the table remains wood, an ordinary material thing. As soon as it steps forth as commodity, however, it is transformed into a material immaterial thing. It not only stands with its feet on the ground, but, in the face of all other commodities, it stands on its head, and out of its wooden brain it evolves notions more whimsical than if it had suddenly begun to dance.

You might think Marx is evolving notions more whimsical

than dance moves right there, but he means that the material thing is now a bearer of non-material significance, of ideological and social payload.

Commodity is not another word for *thing*, it is another word for *relationship*. That is why functionalism and aestheticism, even taken together, cannot tell us all there is to know about a table or chair. The plainest chair is still a product of someone's labour, and was acquired or made against a background of complex social relations determined in large part by money. Every table, from the humblest do-it-yourself kit to the finest handmade piece from Heidi Earnshaw, tells a tale of who owns what. For centuries, furniture has been, along with clothes, hairstyles, companions, leisure activities, and personal conveyances, a way of signalling one's place in a complex hierarchy of social relationships, key examples of Goffman's 'presentation of self in everyday life.' More specifically, it has functioned as what Veblen first labelled 'invidious comparison' through 'conspicuous consumption.'

In Veblen's jaundiced view, the messages are not always about what they seem to be about. On the surface, the furnishings of the country house or the high-rise apartment purport to send intricately coded messages of personal taste or sophistication or refinement – and indeed these semiotic codes may well be rooted in some degree of reality. But more basically these objects are purchased, placed, and displayed to indicate, sometimes quite precisely, one's average net worth and margin of disposable annual income. As the critic Adam Gopnik notes, 'Veblen is insistent – far more than Marx – on reducing aesthetics to economics.' Here is a typical sentence from the early master of consumerist analysis: 'The superior gratification derived from the use and contemplation of costly and supposedly beautiful products is,' Veblen writes, 'a gratification of our sense of costliness masquerading under the name of beauty.' Whatever bourgeois-bohemian rebels might like to believe, historically taste is most often just another name for status.

Furniture can also bear political messages in less obvious

ways, plotting a new relationship to functionalism. Here, for example, is a passage from Don DeLillo's novel *White Noise*, a scene in which the narrator, a middle-aged Professor of Hitler Studies, catches sight of some undergraduate students scattered in the library of his university, and considers the value of the tuition – $14,000, in 1985 dollars – necessary to attend the elite institution:

> I sense there is a connection between this powerful number and the way the students arrange themselves physically in the reading areas of the library. They sit on broad cushioned seats in various kinds of ungainly posture, clearly calculated to be the identifying signs of some kinship group or secret organization. They are fetal, knock-kneed, arched, square-knotted, sometimes almost upside-down. The positions are so studied they amount to a classical mime. There is an element of overrefinement and inbreeding. Sometimes I feel I've wandered into a Far Eastern dream, too remote to be interpreted. But it is only the language of economic class they are speaking, in one of its allowable forms.

This studied casualness, this topsy-turvy disdain for the standard operating procedures demanded by chairs and tables, is more than youthful awkwardness. In fact, its outwardly awkward aspect actually hides a deep comfort level, a claim on understanding the way things work, a long acquaintance with the inner machinery of entitlement.

Only the truly privileged can lounge so unselfconsciously. Only they can drape themselves over furniture as if furniture has not been fashioned for the human body.

All of these points are part of what I called the Furniture Idea, but there is at least one further level of meaning alive in tables and chairs, and I want to end these reflections by saying something about it. Tables and chairs don't just make us think about function and form and politics. They don't just provide us with the handy platform for our own thoughts. They also make us think about *thinking*.

This happens only where tables and chairs take up their proper places, namely in rooms. And it happens because, as James Agee put it so movingly in *Let Us Now Praise Famous Men*, even the simplest room has the profound grace of human life and everyday aspiration. Writing of the desolate but beautiful homes of Southern sharecroppers that he and photographer Walker Evans examined with such compassion and wisdom, Agee said: 'There can be more beauty and more deep wonder in the standings and spacings of mute furnishings on a bare floor ... than in any music ever made.'

Consider why this is so. Furniture structures space, making what is otherwise undifferentiated into something meaningful. I place a couch in an empty room and it acquires a new significance: the air now shimmers with the possibilities of conversation or napping or seduction. The absent protagonists of the various human stories that room has witnessed and will witness are instantly summoned, necromantically, by the couch's human dimensions, its constant invitation to sit or lie. More than this, though, the couch preserves in its placing the possibility of itself being placed somewhere else: every location of a piece of furniture thus calls attention to all the alternative locations which have, for the moment, been passed over. We are all attuned to this radiant aspect of furniture, though not all of us can tell immediately when or why a chair is placed oddly or suboptimally.

The cliché image of what I am getting at here is probably the fickle matron who, moving into a new space, has the exhausted movers try her massive oak-trim settee in every possible location, only to settle back on the very spot where they first dropped it. That image is outdated and maybe offensive, but I think we all share something of this impulse to rearrange the furniture. In Eugene Ionesco's play *The Chairs*, for example, characters enter the stage in order to add more chairs to the scene, each time rearranging and reordering the possibilities (and crises) of the existential situation. It seems to me that we are always doing this, physically or mentally, because we are looking for new ways to structure our allotted space, to make the most of it. We are, in effect, seeking new forms of meaning to create, new ways to think – and new thoughts to entertain. Naturally we can fail to do this well, and then our movements of furniture will be futile, superficial, merely distracting: as the adage has it, we will be rearranging the deckchairs on the *Titanic*. (A more disturbing contemporary echo of the idea can be found at a web site called www.furniture porn.com, which features photographs of patio and office furniture arranged in various suggestive tableaux. You will never consider swivel chairs the same way again.)

Am I being fanciful? I don't think so. Furniture makes a room what it is, and rooms are where most of us spend most of our time. (Offices, after all, are rooms too.) How these rooms are furnished, what pieces inhabit them and give them shape, determines in large measure what kinds of thoughts are possible there. This is not just a matter of something like feng shui, though clearly that is one rigorous and ancient way of considering the matter. But consider something that is, for most of us, less exotic: rearranging the furniture in our own bedrooms, or even just watching the way the furniture changes as the light does.

In *À la recherche du temps perdu*, Proust speaks of the thoughts that come in hazy early morning, when we indulge, he says, 'the experimental rearrangement of the furniture in matinal half-slumber.' In *The Waves*, Virginia Woolf describes dawn light striking a tree outside her window, 'making one leaf transparent and then another.' At noon, she says, it 'made the hills grey as if shaved and singed in an explosion.' As afternoon fades, tables and chairs 'wavered and bent in uncertainty and ambiguity.' And in the evening, the same articles of furniture regain their solidity, so that they are 'lengthened, swollen and portentous.' Finally, as darkness fell, substance was drained from 'the solidity of the hills,' and the world was annihilated again.

The style of the furniture itself can be dreamy in this way, creating reverie-inducing tables and chairs. In *Le Spleen de*

Paris, Baudelaire describes such a room as the ideal place to think. 'In a prefiguration of Jugendstil,' says Walter Benjamin of this project, 'Baudelaire sketches "a room that is like a dream, a truly *spiritual* room ... Every piece of furniture is of an elongated form, languid and prostrate, and seems to be dreaming – endowed, one would say, with a somnambular existence, like minerals and plants."'

And as with style, so with a particular article of furniture. Gaston Bachelard, in *The Poetics of Space*, focuses on corners and nooks, the parts of a room where, he says, dreams may pool and gather. He likewise favours those items of furniture that enclose space or create inner reaches: 'Does there exist a single dreamer of words who does not respond to the word wardrobe?' he asks. 'Every poet of furniture – even if he be a poet in a garret, and therefore has no furniture – knows that the inner space of an old wardrobe is deep. A wardrobe's inner space is also *intimate space*, space that is not open to just anybody.' Not all intimate spaces are obvious. For instance, I used to take refuge in the improbable inner space of the family clothes hamper, where the dirty laundry was waiting to be taken to the washer. I used to think this strange until I discovered that my best friend also did it, and read Salman Rushdie's account, in *Midnight's Children*, of another child who, with perhaps better reason, sought the asylum of the hamper.

In such a space, with such vistas and dreams alive to our gaze, furniture is no longer something merely to sit upon; no longer the elevated surface where we lay our tools and our mealtime places. Here furniture is instead an invitation to think and to dream, a beckoning of possible ideas and half-formed notions. We all sit somewhere when we think, yes, and chairs hold us up while we work out our thoughts on desks and tables. But more importantly, what we sit upon or write upon are themselves thinking things; not just tools that help us in chosen tasks, but aspects of humanity whose very presence is thought. The attempt of thought to think its own conditions is, as Kant reminds us, infinite and finally impossible: we cannot encompass ourselves within our own reflection. But we can, we must, begin this infinite task anyway, and furniture is one neglected but essential way to do so.

So rearrange the furniture of your ideas by thinking about furniture thinking. The rooms of our existence are throbbing with thoughts waiting to happen, with insights struggling into the ever-changing light. Somewhere right now it is late afternoon, and the midday sun has begun its long fade towards darkness. Or it is early morning and the dawn is slowly, miraculously, illuminating the daily world once more. For a long moment the dim light falls aslant the familiar dimensions of the couch upon which you napped not long ago, or the bedside table that was invisible a moment before, a time impossible to calculate. In the grey light of dawn or dusk, the pieces of furniture appear altered, unfamiliar, slightly threatening – almost alive. The armchair nearby has acquired an air of considered bravado, as if poised for action. The desk stands next to it with an attitude of long-suffering toleration of your many faults. The table glows with boyish anticipation.

Now the light wanes a bit further, and the shapes begin to lose their dimensions – they waver and dissolve. Or the light grows imperceptibly towards its daily intensity, and they take on a new distinctness, an appealing firmness. Stop now, and listen. Listen hard. Listen for the sound of machines for thinking whispering their thoughts to you. They whisper of love and death and honour lost. They sing of good meals and funny friends and art that moves you. They welcome your achievements and ease your pain. They support you when you can no longer support yourself. They croon and warble and hum. They are the undertones of life.

Can you hear them?

Note

1 Since it's germane to the argument, I ought to mention that I wrote this essay in several different rooms using various articles of rather undistinguished furniture, including: a reproduction roll-top desk

in my home office in Toronto, a small pine-and-pillows loveseat in my kitchen, a folded-up futon couch in a loft apartment in lower Manhattan, and a wobbly walnut-veneer table in a minuscule West Village sublet. Also, some revisions were undoubtedly made while sitting in various economy-class airplane seats at thirty-five thousand feet or so.

Being Dandy:
A Sort of Manifesto

'In the figure of the dandy, Baudelaire seeks to find some use for idleness, just as leisure once had a use. The *vita contemplativa* is replaced by something that could be called the *vita contemptiva* ... Dandyism is the last glimmer of the heroic in times of *décadence*.'
– Walter Benjamin, 'Idleness,' *The Arcades Project* (1939)

'In naive, or pure, Camp, the essential element is seriousness, a seriousness that fails ... [C]amp is the modern dandyism. Camp is the answer to the problem: how to be a dandy in the age of mass culture.'
– Susan Sontag, 'Notes on "Camp"' (1964)

My father's mess kit was not what it sounds like, namely, a snapped-together aluminum dinner set, complete with dual-purpose utensils, that you buy to go camping. It was, instead, the formal uniform he wore to attend mess dinners in the Canadian Air Force squadrons – the 404 in Nova Scotia, the 415 in Prince Edward Island – to which he was attached during his twenty-year association with late-century air power. The mess kit was impressive and extravagant, like all military dress uniforms a combination of evening wear and martial regalia.

The black bow tie, white shirt, and cummerbund were standard-issue tuxedo, but the blue-grey melton jacket was cut short and scalloped in the back, with trousers that were high, tight and stirrupped, a gold stripe down each side, ending in gleaming Wellington boots with elastic sides and a leather loop on the heel. The jacket had gold buttons on the cuffs, silk facing on the lapels, a pair of gold navigator's wings, small epaulettes with his captain's insignia, and the miniature versions of his two decorations – British and Commonwealth armed forces being, at least as compared to American and especially in peacetime, stingy with what service people call 'fruit salad.' There were white cotton gloves, clutched rather than worn, and no headgear.

The mess kit resided most of the time in a thick plastic bag in my father's closet. The gloves, decorations, and a pair of white braces were kept in a separate plastic sarcophagus in my father's top dresser drawer, along with various cufflinks and tiepins, often of exotic aeronautical design: one in the shape of a French Mirage fighter, another fashioned after the distinctive double-delta silhouette of the Saab Viggen. This drawer was a source of continual fascination for me, explored extensively during periods of parental absence. Contrary to convention, I discovered nothing disturbing – no condoms or porn mags or letters from women not my mother. Just the detritus of masculine dress, the jangly hardware of maleness. The drawer smelled of aftershave and wood and leather.

Because my father wore a uniform or flight suit every day of his working life he didn't seem to possess any other clothes. The uniforms changed over the years, from the belted Royal Canadian Air Force tunics in grey-blue wool, indistinguishable from the ones to be seen in films like *633 Squadron*, *The Battle of Britain*, or *The Dam Busters*, to the mediocre garage-attendant green zipper jackets and trousers of the unified Canadian forces of the 1970s. When the RCAF was absorbed into this formless mass in the 1960s, in a misguided attempt at republicanism, it lost its royal prefix and my father's romantic rank of Flight Lieutenant (pronounced with the raf-and-jag *eff* sound) was modified to the unremarkable Captain. Whether from outspokenness, lack of ambition, or some other cause I was too naive to discern, he never advanced beyond it.

If the uniforms he wore were not always sartorially interesting, like the Italian Air Force designs supplied by Giorgio Armani in the 1980s or (more darkly) Hugo Boss's sharp silver-and-black outfits for the Gestapo in the 1930s, they nevertheless presented a stop-action essay in male attire. And when my father emerged, periodically, in the full glory of the mess kit, a peacock fanning to display, he was a brilliant reminder of the beauty masculine clothing can achieve when its vanities are unchecked. The military uniform is the ur-suit, the source of the norms that have for almost two centuries governed the presentation of the male form in everyday life. It spans both the range of ordinary working clothes, from the overalls of sappers to the T-shirts of naval gunnies, and the high-end, almost foppish finery of the dress uniform, an ensemble that, in its way, is the intrusion of dandyism into the serious male business of killing people. The spectacular military uniform is a kind of suited repression, an incongruous mixture of the lovely and the deadly. And so an encounter with the uniform is the first step on the road to the rich and edgy territory of male dress, perhaps the discovery of a personal sense of style, a long-overdue revival of dandyism at the dawn of this new century.

This is not simply a matter of the uniform enforcing a minimum level of presentable polish – though there is that, as the movement of the uniform into other areas of life amply demonstrates, from the chaos-prevention programs of boys' high schools to the casual-seeming but actually rigid dress codes of contemporary waitstaffs and chain-store employees. Likewise the common understanding of the business suit – sometimes, as on formal invitations, diplomatically dubbed the lounge suit – as a uniform of commercial life, the standard-issue duds for Wall Street or inside the Beltway. The uniform, whatever its details, is a bulwark against the uneven seas of individuality, and (let it be said) against unsettling variations in taste and income. The uniform is, paradoxically, both democracy and elitism in action.

But the relations between military uniform and suit are more proximate still, from the cuff buttons allegedly introduced to prevent nose wiping during the Napoleonic Wars, when Europe's armies first fully realized the heady combination of violence and regalia, to the silk flashes and cravats that once indicated regimental membership and now signal personal style in the necktie or choice between shawl and pointed collar, double-breasted or single-breasted jacket, vents or no vents.

In the shadow of this declension from function to decoration, my father confronts me as an image of himself reduced to his everyday uniform, complete with use-driven pockets and epaulettes, his name – my name – carved in white on a black plastic name tag pinned above the left front pocket. These name tags, which were secured with two spring-loaded tabs, were scattered around the house, including some in the seductive top drawer. Little chunks of identity, of uniformity, measuring three inches by three-quarters of an inch.

Also lying around the house was this sense of order in male clothing, the completeness of the uniform, even the beauty of it when got up in its formal version. I thought of my father's mess kit the first time I donned a black-tie dinner suit. I was an usher at the wedding of my college roommate, Tim Baker, and we rented outfits from a formal shop in Toronto. Twenty-one, a slightly built undergraduate at 5'10" and 150 pounds, I looked boyish and (I thought) rather devastating in the tux, snugly fastened in every imaginable place by cummerbund and braces and links. I felt like I was actually *wearing clothes* for the first time in my life, strapped in tight for whatever the world had to offer. Our ride to the church in Tim's beat-up blue Toyota, sun roof and windows wide open, Bruce Springsteen on the stereo, was for me one of those crystalline magic moments of late boyhood. We honked the horn and waved at people walking sloppily along Bloor Street, the lords of formal wear acknowledging these peasants of casualness.

In the end I didn't follow my father into military service, though I thought about it more or less constantly during the

final years of high school. I had a real twinge just once, at a
Christmas Day mass in 1979, a few months before I was to
graduate and go off (as I planned at the time) to study geology
at the University of Toronto. My decision to switch to philosophy and English came later in that up-and-down year, during
an early-summer vacation when, floating aimlessly in my
uncle's pool like Dustin Hoffman in *The Graduate*, the word
'metaphysics,' not 'plastics,' came swimming to mind. The
Christmas event was of another order. In jeans and an old football jersey, number 60 for my hero, Bubba Smith of the Detroit
Lions, I shuffled into church with my family. I had argued with
my father even as we were leaving the house, an old argument
that neither of us really cared for any longer. God doesn't care
what I wear, I had said. God deserves your respect, he'd
replied.

Now we were in the church, Pope John XXIII in the West-
wood section of Winnipeg, and there was a collective turning
of heads at something behind where I was sitting with my par-
ents and two brothers. I looked back. A young man in the
belted red tunic and black trousers of the Royal Military College, clearly back from Kingston, Ont., for the holidays, was
walking up the nave, his mother on his arm. He wore white
gloves and had his pillbox under his arm. He was upright and
tall and beautiful, and I suddenly felt like an idiot in my football sweater. My father said nothing but I could feel him radi-
ating I-told-you-so's down the pew. I thought: *I want to look like
that. I want to be the young warrior at home, earning admiration and
envy as I float through the crowd or congregation.*

The appeal of the uniform, like the violent conflict that created it, is atavistic and troubling. Wearing one establishes a
young man's relationship with a community, and with his own
masculinity. Putting on a uniform is also, therefore, taking
one's place in the larger order of things; it is a rite of passage
that asserts adulthood. The badges of rank and regimental
insignia, the orders of valour and corps identifiers, speak a
complicated semantics of hierarchy and accomplishment. As a
youth I could identify, by ribbon colours alone, most of the

major decorations of the Commonwealth armed forces, from the Distinguished Service Order and Military Cross to the Distinguished Flying Medal. In the film *Ryan's Daughter*, when the traumatized English army officer arrives in Ireland, a disabled hero of the trenches, the junior ranks of his obscure posting eye the plain maroon ribbon of his Victoria Cross with envy and awe. Like them, I recognized the tiny slash of ribbon for the sign it was, if not of valour then at least of mayhem ably survived.

The hint of violence is essential to the uniform's power. That is why there are so often hazing rituals associated with the privilege of wearing it, not merely formal qualifications like age or education. Hazing, often violent and humiliating, is a form of displacement ritual. We no longer think it appropriate to subject our young men to tests of pain and fortitude, to see if they belong in male society, but we do, in certain corners of that society – athletic teams, fraternities, the military – indulge in mild versions of such tests involving full-body shaves, canings, and beatings, or the forcible consumption of excrement. Even these second-order initiation ceremonies are too much for our sensitive times, though. When a pirated video of similar brutal practices in Canada's elite Airborne Regiment were brought to light in the mid-1990s, it led to a different, and far more public, form of humiliation: the commanding officer, a knife-like lieutenant-colonel in a beret, was forced to resign and the unit was disbanded.

The continued presence of shaving in hazing rituals would be fodder to a cultural anthropologist of the right inclination. Bobby Orr, the gifted Boston Bruins defenceman of the 1970s, related in his memoirs how he was welcomed to the team by being pinned to the locker-room floor, lathered up, and roughly shaved clean from top to toe. It was a favourite in my high school locker room, too, and continues to be the haze of choice in blue-collar minor-league hockey teams, daring fraternities, and elite squadrons the continent over. Just as interesting as the homoerotic sublimations of the act itself, with the helpless neophyte manhandled by his beefy new colleagues, is

the act of removing hair. Hair plays a large role in male entry
to adulthood, of course, from the first sproutings on groin
and chest to the first shave, an act of initiation so common
and apparently unremarkable as to have escaped sustained
theoretical attention. But that is too bad, because the test of
shaving, for many boys, marks their passage to a self-image of
manhood. It most often occurs before the loss of virginity, and
there might be years in between. Significantly, it is often done
in the presence of the father, who passes on the mundane
knowledge of razor and lather. Most very young boys are fas-
cinated and awed by the father's act of shaving, observing
technique in the service of transformation, a daily ritual of
maleness. My brother Steve and I used to take turns watching
our father shave when we were children.

Learning how to shave – to remove the very hair that marks
puberty – thus takes its place in the set of routine skills that
modern urban fathers routinely pass on to their sons. These
skills also include tying a necktie, polishing shoes, perhaps
wearing cologne. They are hardly the stuff of rugged male-
ness, at least as traditionally conceived, but they signal the creation of a presentable male figure in the non-lethal society of
business and everyday life. No one will ever make a movie
mythologizing these father-son bonding rituals, in the manner
of *Field of Dreams*, say, with its tear-jerking evocation of the
fabled Game of Catch between dad and junior, but for many of
us they loom just as large, if not larger.

It was my mother who taught me to tie my shoes and, later,
to bake and cook; but it was my father who taught me how to
tend to my body and its accoutrements, how to prepare myself
for presentation to the gaze of the world, how to dress. I laboriously copied his demonstration of how to create a chunky
full-Windsor knot, though I was not comfortable enough with
it to do it every day at my Catholic boys' school: like most of
us, I kept a knotted tie in my locker and simply pulled it over
my head each morning. When I did start tying ties regularly, I
was so fixed on my father's instruction that I stuck with the
full-Windsor well past the point of fashion, only shifting down

to the sleeker half-Windsor six or seven years ago. It was like learning how to throw left-handed.

Nowadays I shop for clothes by myself or in the company of one or two trusted female friends, who can be counted on for accurate flattery and good advice, but it was my father who took me to buy my first suit for school. And when I was in university, on a rare visit to take me out for lunch, he offered to take me shopping afterwards at Harry Rosen on Bloor Street in Toronto. It was 1984 and the fashions were all English and collegiate, long rows of striped ties in garish colours arrayed like confections in wood-and-glass cabinets. The shirts were fanned out in swathes of pastel broadcloth, multi-hued couches of cotton. Thinking of Tom Cruise in his underwear in *Risky Business*, and my then-girlfriend's recently communicated fantasy, I picked out a pale pink oxford-cloth button-down. My father smiled and got out his credit card. I kept that shirt for years, wearing it through at the collar and cuffs, fading it almost to white with many launderings, and finally left it in a closet during one of many moves in my late twenties. It no longer fit me at the neck or across the chest: I was no longer the boy my father treated that day in Toronto.

There is a depth of unrealized feeling in male attitudes to fashion and dress. My friend Russell, a novelist, for a couple of years wrote a weekly newspaper column about men's fashion. His sartorial advice was tart and peremptory but, to my mind, almost always accurate: no shirts with 'swanky' designs on the collar, no backpacks, no crummy shoes. He received a lot of mail, much of it intemperate to the point of derangement, from men who felt slighted by his pronouncements. He speculated that the reason for this lay in the fact that these men, like all men, acquired whatever basic understanding of fashion they possess from their fathers – or from role models to whom they stood in some kind of quasi-filial relationship. The phenomenon works in the other direction too. When Russell struck a chord with a man by recommending, say, a Burberry raincoat, he received letters suffused with longing and nostalgia, miniature and often halting paeans to lost fathers who wore that very symbol of male sophistication and, so attired, towered in the imagination of the boy now grown to manhood.

The complexity of this relationship overwhelms most of us, I think, but there is clearly a filial homage in play every time I put on one of my Italian suits, even though they are not the kind of thing my father would ever wear, even as a young man. Too expensive, too stylish, too dandyish. But my own dandyism, which proceeds more proximately from cinematic heroes like Cary Grant or Gary Cooper, is nevertheless implicated in those glimpses of the RCAF mess kit from my father's closet. My uniforms run to a Fendi silk-and-wool three-button in dove grey; a brown, two-vent, high-gorge, narrow-trouser number by Tombolini; a couple of classic-cut Armanis, one grey and one black. But every time I complete the ensemble of elegant male attire, I feel the sense of fulfilment that the French word for suit, *complet*, captures so much more economically, and truly, than the boring word 'suit.'

It is true that you can wear a suit like a uniform, the way bankers and downtown lawyers don their navy pinstripes and white-shirt/red-tie Identikit urban-hominid camouflage each morning; but the suit is also, and better, conceived as a stretched canvas, a blank slate. It does not allow *anything at all*, but within its limits lie nascent the possibilities of wit and dash, sex and seduction. The constrained freedom of assembling the elements in felicitous combination makes the suit a modern narrative *in potentia*, a story of downtown life waiting to be told. Beauty and utility emerge conjoined, in the pockets and buttons and padding that create the quintessential male silhouette – a silhouette whose minute variations from year to year (bigger shoulders, vents or no vents, and so on) are followed by the dandy not in the interests of fashion so much as those of connoisseurship. A truly good tailor can give back some of the elements that convenience and mass production have mostly taken away, the functional surgeon's cuffs that may be unbuttoned and folded back, the way Jean Cocteau wore his sports jackets; or the right-lapel button that will be received by the left-side buttonhole, whose usual flower, if present at all, just plays with an originally ordinary way to achieve more protection, as seen, say, in an old photo of a willowy Frank Sinatra.

The suit is an idea, a set of associations. It comes to us in images, stills and movies, that reflect its presence in twentieth-century male life. The received wisdom says that whereas most men like to imagine women naked, women like to imagine men in suits. The suit finishes them, puts them in proper context. It smoothes out their imperfections and pads their deficiencies. It is armour against the contingencies of a hostile, judgmental world. And yet, the last few decades have seen a steady decline in norms of dress in North American society, with the disappearance of evening wear, the nearly complete baseball-capping of the population, the tendency of grown men to dress like simulacra of Bart Simpson: T-shirt, sneakers, and shorts. In fact, most of them are worse than that, since Bart's invariable red T-shirt at least sports no corporate logo, no abusive or inane slogan.

Dandies, meanwhile, are almost universally disdained. Frasier Crane, the fussy television psychiatrist mocked successively in the prime-time comedy shows *Cheers* and *Frasier*, is the exemplar here. His fashion sense and aesthetic discrimination are at once displayed and undermined. He is frequently taken for gay. In a typical scene from the latter show, Frasier, off to meet an attractive policewoman at a cop-hangout bar, rushes off to his bedroom, saying, 'I've got to put in new collar stays, and – ooh, ooh – I have a fabulous new cashmere jacket I've been dying to premiere!' His long-suffering regular-guy father, a cop himself, sighs, 'Yeah, this is gonna work.' Here, a sense of style is equated with being educated beyond sense, a pointy-headed idiot. Given all this, which is hardly controversial, it is nevertheless dismaying how often the suit, when it is worn at all, is worn badly, or is simply a bad suit. It is impossible to have a suit that is *too nice*; the idea is a conceptual nonstarter. But it is easy, all too easy, to have a suit that creates deficiencies rather than hides them. Sometimes, as for the character Ben in Louis Begley's novel *The Man Who Was Late*, this is a tale of lifelong disappointments, miniature 'tragedies' of cuff width and sleeve buttons. Finally, late in life, Ben finds a Paris tailor who can solve these problems; but the man retires to the country soon after, leaving Ben disconsolate: another moment of arriving too late.

Surely part of the reason that so many suits one sees are bad suits is that they are resented by their wearers. This is self-defeating, and unnecessary. At its best, the suit is the outward sign of intelligence and attention. It takes its place in a lexicon of sophistication, an element in a grown-up world of travel and business in which bartenders know your usual drink, drivers bearing signs meet you at the airport, documents and telephones are brought to your table in restaurants, and every rental car in every visited city is a sexy convertible. This fantasy of male success, which surely cannot be unique to my daydreams, has little to do with the more robust pursuits of an Ernest Hemingway or Ted Williams, the fishing and hunting and horseback riding next to which this other ideal of male-ness may seem slightly effete, but its role models in literature and film are arguably more impressive: the *flâneurs* of the Symbolist moment, dandies like Wilde and Beardsley, the young Disraeli, Ronald Firbank and Diaghilev, slightly ambiguous figures like Grant. (Ellen Moers's work on the dandy as a staple literary figure, a central avatar of modernism, is the best assessment of these movements.)

One should also add the dandies of pop music. In the 1998 film *Velvet Goldmine*, a loosely fictional biopic about a David Bowie figure called Brian Slade, a voice-over describes the late-Sixties transition from Mods to Glam this way: 'Taking their cue from Little Richard, the swank London Mods, short for Modernists, were the first to wear mascara and lacquer their hair – the first true dandies of pop. And known to just about any indiscretion where a good suit was involved. Style always wins out in the end.' The last line is spoken over a scene of Brian, dressed in a purple French-cuffed shirt, black-and-white barred tie, taupe shoes, and a black pin-striped suit, having just sodomized a young boy in traditional British school uniform.

The film explicitly links the Mods and the glitter-rock crowd to Wilde's languid modernism – the film starts with him in Ireland, and a brooch allegedly belonging to him becomes a magic talisman through the narrative. But it also alludes more gently to interwar bird-of-paradise beauty junkies like Stephen Tennant, a man who used to go out with a handkerchief tied over his eyes so as not to expire from 'excessive sensibility.' Tennant's fictional counterpart appears as a lovely comic confection in Nancy Mitford's novels, as a Canadian-born (!) beauty who descends on the staid aristocratic household of *Love in a Cold Climate*, but he is also said to be the model, in darker form, for Anthony Blanche, the depraved stuttering dandy of Waugh's *Brideshead Revisited*. It is Blanche who, in two separate scenes of that novel, tries to poison the young Charles Ryder against winsome Sebastian Flyte, warning him of the Flyte family's 'fatal English charm' – a charm that, in the event, proves indeed to be Charles's undoing. In love in turn with alcoholic Sebastian and his self-hating sister Julia, it captures him in the sticky amber of Anglo-Catholic decline during the 1930s.

This may be the sombre side of the dandy-aesthete: the bitter outsider, given to outrages and cynical (if accurate) condemnations. Consider, for a different view, Cary Grant in a wide-lapel pinstrip in Hitchcock's *Notorious*, a dandified spy falling in love with Ingrid Bergman in Rio de Janeiro. Or, even better, as Roger Thornhill in *North By Northwest*, the suave Madison Avenue advertising executive thrown by mistake into Cold War intrigue. Thornhill is one of American cinema's great unlikely heroes, a modern paragon in slick hand-sewn dress. Habitually charming, even glib – 'In the world of advertising,' he says, 'there is no such thing as a lie; there is only expedient exaggeration' – Thornhill is Urban Man polished to a high gloss. Twice divorced, devoted to his mother, he favours cold martinis, French cuffs, and monogrammed matchbooks. In vivid Technicolor, his exquisitely tailored silver-blue suit, a three-button whose lapels nevertheless fall into a fashionable deeper gorge, precisely matches the distinguished greying hair at his temples. In the film's opening scenes, Thornhill emerges quickly as a fussy, narcissistic, apparently superficial mannequin.

But under pressure, he is also agile, wily, resourceful, and brave. When a typical Hitchcockian trope of misrecognition spins him into a world of espionage and betrayal, he manipulates all the apparatus of modern life – telephones, hotels, trains, taxis, bars, banter – with enviable, grown-up assurance. And in the vertiginous world ruled by the urbane menace of villains James Mason and Martin Landau, where Hitchcock's unexpected overhead shots and thrilling signature sequences (the strafing crop-duster, the scramble on Mount Rushmore) seem to reflect a sort of cognitive imbalance, it is Thornhill who finds his feet. The film's title evokes Hamlet's description of his feigned madness; it savours deception, mistaken identity, the yawning chasm between appearance and reality. It is also, in its off-kilter way, a romantic comedy. How ironic, but how fitting, that the professional deceiver should carry the day – and carry off Eva Marie Saint, the beautiful double-agent who entered the picture on a mission to deceive *him*. Under the suit lies a man, and a particularly appealing one, too. The suit doesn't disguise these properties so much as reflect them, allow them play.

In our society, dandyism comes haltingly when it comes at all. It is a function of early adulthood, I think, and that first blush of success that frees a man to close the frustrating gap, so typical of postgraduate life especially, between taste and means. The unspoken tragedy of urban life in our century is this constant struggle to afford the self-presentation we desire. I don't have to want the baggy convict-wear and brand-name jackets of the urban scene to appreciate the yearning evident in the startling statistic that in 1999 the average inner-city African American spent $2,440 on clothes, compared to the $1,508 considered sufficient by the average U.S. consumer. I would consider it rolling pretty high if I granted myself an annual clothes budget of $2,500, but apparently that's nothing to write home about in East Los Angeles or the Bronx. It's not about how much money you have; it's about what you choose to spend your money on.

I am struck by accounts of the entry into fashion consciousness, especially as granted by writers who might be thought above such things. David Mamet, in a long-ago article in the *New York Times Magazine*, described the way he would buy second-hand tweed jackets and then have them carefully tailored to his tastes: sleeves shortened, elbows patched, rear vent sewn shut to prevent 'rooster-tail' (this before the advent of the now-ubiquitous Italianate ventless jacket). In *The Facts*, Philip Roth mocks himself, post facto, for his clothes-horse tendencies as a youngish man, the way he ran out with his first big advance cheque and bought some tailored Savile Row suits: 'I proceeded to have clothes made by three distinguished tailoring establishments, half a dozen suits that I didn't need, that required endless, stupefying fittings, and that finally never fit me anyway.' This lack of fit is indicted as part of a 'restlessness,' mainly sexual, that afflicts Roth at age thirty-five. And yet, he cannot quite silence an enthusiasm for that reckless young man, nor can he entirely quell the affection aroused by an even younger, still more dashing version of himself, the hotshot freshman comp teacher he was in 1956, aged twenty-two, who bought a Brooks Brothers suit to look more impressive. Contrast with this the dourness of George Steiner's *Errata*, say, which is admirably forthright about professional jealousies and intellectual epiphanies but reads as if the author never wore anything in particular, indeed as if he were continually naked.

But the quintessential dandy of American letters is probably, for good or bad, Tom Wolfe, whose cream-coloured suits and high-collared dress shirts were adopted in the 1960s as a means of at once identifying the emerging social commentator and pissing off the people he was writing about and talking to. Wolfe is, in this sense, the early literary analogue of someone like Dennis Rodman, the Detroit Pistons and Chicago Bulls forward who took to extensive tattooing, cross-dressing, and polychrome hair-dyeing as a means of getting his share of available attention in the saturated late-century mediascape. Wolfe's latter-day attempts to pick fights with Norman Mailer and John Irving over his blowhard novel, *A Man In Full*, his tauntings of *The New Yorker*, are desperate versions of the same desire for notice. This is dandyism gone bad, its original impulse of disdain transformed into something far less defensible, and more dangerous: publicity seeking. When *Harper's Magazine* made the odd error of featuring Wolfe sitting opposite Mark Twain, another cream-suited dandy, on their hundred-and-fiftieth-anniversary cover (and, worse, including inside a ridiculous and shallow essay from the previously acute author of *The Painted Word* and *Radical Chic*), we knew that literary dandyism in America was in trouble.

Fictional accounts of young men at play are just as compelling as real-world examples, maybe more so, from John Barth's postmodern jape, *The Sot-Weed Factor*, which includes a description of the rituals and variables of eighteenth-century male dress so delicious it makes the mouth water, to Sebastian and Charles in Waugh's elegiac *Brideshead*. Charles's priggish cousin Jasper remonstrates with him about, among other things, his lunchtime drunkenness and flashy habits of dress: 'When you came up I remember advising to dress as you would in a country house. Your present get-up seems an unhappy compromise between the correct wear for a theatrical party at Maidenhead and a glee-singing competition in a garden suburb.' Charles, for his part, is undeterred by this precise insult. 'It seems to me that I grew younger daily with each adult habit that I acquired,' he says of this undergraduate flowering. 'Now, that summer term with Sebastian, it seemed as though I was being given a brief spell of what I had never known, a happy childhood, and though its toys were silk shirts and liqueurs and cigars and its naughtiness high in the catalogue of grave sins, there was something of nursery freshness about us that fell little short of the joy of innocence.'

Waugh's regard for style transferred itself easily into the

uniformed milieu of wartime England – though, as an officer with the extremely fashionable Household Cavalry, or Blues, he had only contempt for the Royal Air Force uniforms I grew up envying. Airmen come in for all kinds of superior joking in his *Sword of Honour* trilogy, finally depicted as cultureless near-morons in the concluding volume, *Unconditional Surrender*. Like all writers of his generation and class who served in the war and wrote about it – Anthony Powell in his roman-fleuve, *Dance to the Music of Time*; or Simon Raven in his second-rate version of the same, *Alms for Oblivion* – indeed like most soldiers of his time, Waugh was obsessed with the relative 'smartness' of English regiments. The Coldstream Guards or Corps of Rifles are honoured less for their prowess than for their fine red tunics or frogged green jackets. It is war to the tune of invidious social distinction, all passed for judgment in bright colours and badges.

Hans Castorp retails his partial seduction by the perfect turn-outs and slick style of the humanist Settembrini, and who can resist the pull of hard collars and spats, the cream-colored suits and high waistcoats of spa-life fashion? Even the cynical narrator of Graham Greene's *The Comedians* cannot conceal his admiration for a poverty-stricken dandy, who, despite living in near-squalor, is so fastidious about his suit that he covers himself with an expansive handkerchief when he urinates. Reading these accounts, you cannot help thinking: *I* want to wear silk all the time! *I* want to be festooned and beswagged!

They also have a young man's eagerness about them, the dandy in waiting. It is one thing to view Cary in all his grown-up perfection. His appeal is the appeal of the fashionable father you never had, a slightly foppish but unquestionably strong man who knew the ways of the world. This is surely his appeal for women too, whether realized with subtlety (Grace Kelly's sly banter in *To Catch a Thief*), or with crudeness (Audrey Hepburn repeatedly throwing herself at him in *Charade*). By contrast, watching Sebastian and Charles dress, or listening to the youthful ambition of Mamet and Roth, we hear something else, an echo from an earlier life-stage, the call of

possibility. Here the suit of clothes still has an air of playfulness, of a costume worn. It is a uniform not in the common
pejorative sense of the thing you don every day, without thinking, but in the antic sense of the uniforms worn by naval suit-
ors in Jane Austen's novels, the finery sported by subalterns
in the Raj, or the arrogant peacock strutting of young Floren-
tine carabinieri.

In my line of work, wearing suits is not normal, and so some of
this playfulness continues to be available. Universities are sites
of arrested development anyway, so a program of stylish ado-
lescent rebellion often seems called for, bucking the patched-
tweed-and-hairy-sweater norm in favour of something more
glamorous, more suggestive of the outside world's vast potential for beauty and pleasure. My students understand this very
well, in their own mass-produced way. They care about how
they look; like anyone alive today, they are past masters of the
nuances of brands and models, styles and options. This is
sometimes enervating, but among other things it issues in a
surprising and complimentary degree of interest in *my* clothes.
Style has become a running theme in the annual course evalu-
ations they fill out, sometimes even entering into otherwise
abstruse discussion of Aristotle or Spinoza in their papers.

Every professor realizes, sooner or later, the vast attention
that students give to every detail of his or her appearance. A
political science professor I had in college wore just two suits, a
blue and a grey, prompting the guy next to me to speculate that
he actually had a closet full of identical ones, like Superman
costumes. My colleague Allan receives on his course evalua-
tions long paeans to his impressive wardrobe and suggestions
he should go into acting. On mine I have been asked what
brand my watch is and where I bought a certain rather flam-
boyant tie. I have even been shyly consulted for fashion advice,
something to add to the already lengthy list of topics – illness,
relationships, car trouble, family conflicts – that make up the
unseen, pastoral element of university teaching.. The half-
formed dandyism of students, so depressingly conformist

compared to the fin de siècle wonders of the nineteenth century's turn, so apparently driven by consumerism and branded free advertising, nevertheless confesses itself. Their desires speak louder than the bright colours of their FUBU shirts, the need to individuate all the more insistent for being diverted into a back-turned Kangol cap. It is the least I can do to make myself an example.

All this concern with clothes strikes others as unseemly, of course, especially since it seems to sit oddly with the otherworldly ambitions of my subject, philosophy. How is it possible for someone to be engaged in lofty thoughts when he is checking the creases on his trousers? How can concern with the implications of the Habermasian ideal speech situation be reconciled with concern for a precise colour match between tie and socks? A simple answer to that is the one the former prime minister of Canada, Pierre Trudeau, himself a style maven of no mean gifts, once gave to reporters in an Ottawa press scrum. They wondered if he would have the nerve to call out the military to deal with separatist terrorists in 1970 Quebec. He said: 'Just watch me.' But sometimes, more seriously, I refresh the memories of my knit-brow colleagues with Machiavelli's account of his engagements with the ancient authors during his political exile, in a passage I happily underlined during an undergraduate political theory course in the long-ago year of 1981, when we all thought the end of the world was much closer than we do now.

'When evening comes, I return to my home, and I go into my study,' the disgraced diplomat wrote to his friend Francesco Vettori in December of 1513, describing his daily regimen. '[A]nd on the threshold, I take off my everyday clothes, which are covered with mud and mire, and I put on regal and curial robes; and dressed in a more appropriate manner I enter into the ancient courts of ancient men and am welcomed by them kindly. . . and there I am not ashamed to speak to them, to ask them the reasons for their actions; and they, in their humanity, answer me; and for four hours I feel no boredom, I dismiss every affliction, I no longer fear poverty nor do

I tremble at the thought of death ... I have noted down what I have learned from their conversation, and I composed a little work, *De principatibus*, where I delve as deeply as I can into thoughts on this subject.'

Would that we all possessed Machiavelli's jauntiness in the face of worldly adversity, and his sense of the finery's simultaneous mark of respect and bulwark against the misfortunes of this life. My buddy Mark Thompson used to own an expensive, cutting-edge tailored suit that he liked to wear to job interviews, not because it was suitable for them but precisely because it wasn't. It was tasty and beautiful beyond the expectations of the working world, a suit to wear while strolling in the Piazza San Marco, a suit to wear on a date with Elizabeth Hurley. Mark called it his 'fuck-you suit.'

Whenever possible, your suit should be a fuck-you suit. It should somehow, very slightly, irritate the mundane prejudices and routine pomposity of the Cousin Jaspers of the world. The socks should be a little too sky-blue (Astaire) or champagne-coloured (Grant). The tie should be a smidge too unusual for Wall Street, the shirt too lavender or citron, the silhouette a little too exaggerated. Your raincoat should be, as Allan's is, the result of a weeks-long quest in Parisian boutiques for the perfect white-cotton blouson with navy lining and dashing turned-back cuffs.

It also helps, of course, if, like me, you don't have to wear a suit every day, don't *have* to wear a suit at all. Then the suit as costume may have free rein, and every foray into the world can take its proper place as an urban adventure, a complex encounter of beauty with ugliness, of style with boredom, of youth with time. Thus arrayed, you may glide through your day in a Todd Oldham quasi-Edwardian frock coat in purple raw silk. You may skim the sidewalk in your chunky Comme des Garçons shoes. Your bright blue tie may billow and flap out behind you. Think of the dandies of another, allegedly more decadent age, and wonder why we do not set our bar so high most of the time, why we allow our own decadence to be one all of the mind and spirit, a decadence of mediocrity and acquisitiveness, rather than what it was meant to be, a challenge to received wisdom and bourgeois sluggishness. Think, finally, of your father and his own sense of style. Think of what you have borrowed, what you have invented, what you have painfully thrown off. Behind the careful tailoring and colourful silk, this stroll is a primal encounter with your culture and your upbringing. It is a personal story not yet told, a narrative of self-creation waiting to happen. You only get one chance to take this particular walk – don't waste it. You are the young and the restless. Don't seek approval; demand only respect. Be a man. Be a dandy.

Storage and Retrieval

The battle for the soul of the age, to use an antique expression, is happening not in our churches or universities but on television and via the Internet, in multiplexes and playdiums. This is not news.

Like all modern battles, it is one where victory goes to the swift. Speed is the essence of the times, and the relentlessness of cultural production and consumption has come to dominate our sense of ourselves. There is always more of everything, from television stations to web sites to video-game releases. Much of it is negligible, certainly, but none of it is ignorable, because ever-greater volume is the enforced order of the day.

Programs of planned obsolescence and continual technological advance loom large on the cultural landscape, they cannot be avoided. Being forced to buy a new computer because the old one cannot run the only available operating system calls forth our age's mundane version of the Rapture described in John's Book of Revelation, the restless combination of boredom and hunger I once called Upgrade Angst. We are all in danger of being *left behind*.[1]

The idea of continuous upgrade serves, furthermore, to heighten an idea of the future as *something that is happening to us*. We observe an increase in life's velocity – which increase is, in part, a function of our own expectations about how we interact with a world increasingly dominated by technology.[2]

Powerless in the face of gathering speed, we try to strap ourselves in tight and hang on, multitasking our way into a dim
future of ubiquitous cellphones and ever-present keyboards,
constant uplinks and ceaseless downloads. We don't know
where we're going, but wherever it is, it's going to be a fast
bumpy ride.

This sense of anticipation, complex in both aetiology and
symptoms, gives a particular resonance to the problems of
storage and retrieval – the problems, as I might put it, of information, technology, and information-technology. Storing and
retrieving are basic human activities, but our apparently limit-
less desire to consume information is something we need now
to rethink. For such a desire can never be fully satisfied, it can
only be fed; and that has negative effects on our sense of self,
for there is always more information than we can reasonably
act on.[3] Enervation steals over us, we want to flee.

How do we make sense of the unceasing barrage of information and imagery? Isaiah Berlin was said to read a few first few
pages of a book and then 'deduce' the rest; Paul Ricoeur allegedly offloaded the bulk of his reading to his wife. But not
everyone has such arrogance, or such biddable companions.
Given that we cannot read or see everything, how do we cope
with the burgeoning mass? What survival strategies exist
for the overstimulated? Here, as so often, wisdom involves
acknowledging not our appetites but our limits. The true ratio-
nale of consumption must be found within us, in our desires,
not in the heedless logic of production.

To see this, consider for a moment the library, that ancient
form of storage/retrieval device, so good at allowing us to
take a step back from the fast world. Some of my happiest
moments have been spent lost in libraries, oblivious to time's
passage and out of life's reach. I always found the volume of
the material around me comforting, not threatening. It is true
that, as a very young boy, I believed it was possible to read all
the books in the local library, every single one, which I naturally took to be all the books in the world. I imagined that this

was what education consisted in: reading literally everything there was to read. When one had read everything, therefore – but not before – one was qualified to speak with authority on something. It's possible that this particular delusion was responsible for my decision to enter graduate school in philosophy. Of course I discovered, as Stephen Leacock once said, that they give you a PhD not when you know everything but when you are incapable of learning anything further.

It's a good thing I'm happy in libraries, then, because I've spent a disproportionate amount of my life in them. All during my twenties, when the sun was shining and the sap should have been rising, I took myself off to the dusty neo-Gothic pile of Yale's Sterling Memorial Library, an edifice that might have been the inspiration for the labyrinthine killer library of Umberto Eco's *The Name of the Rose*; or to the hushed Haldane Philosophy Library in Edinburgh University's David Hume Tower, the sort of place where despairing doctoral candidates were known to die of ennui and then lie undiscovered for weeks. There I sat, away from any windows that might show happy undergraduates disporting themselves with frisbees or picnics on the sun-kissed lawns, and gathered my pile of books next to me, a paper-and-ink bulwark against the temptations of the outside world.

In this self-imposed exile from life, I learned a good deal – and not only about the history of early-modern liberalism or the necessary and sufficient conditions of a valid hermeneutics. Much of graduate school is spent preparing The Bibliography, and that means acquiring the books and articles germane to the subject. This particular form of paper chase is challenging to anyone's sanity, because it involves a bizarre, and in my experience unique, combination of the usually antithetical qualities of narrow-mindedness and imagination.

You have to survey the whole of your subject – in itself a task to drive one mad. Then you must find a suitable sub-field, preferably one relatively untilled. Then you have to chew the hell out of the field by reading, and if possible hoarding, everything that's ever been written on the subject. Trawling day after day through index catalogues and computer systems, you live in constant fear that there is something you're missing, possibly something in press, that will either illuminate the topic in one brilliant stroke or else lay waste to every small insight you have laboriously gathered. Or, worst of all, both.

We all took short cuts. Per convention, at Yale anyway, photocopying articles found in the stacks was considered tantamount to reading them. One could spend whole productive afternoons in the Sterling photocopy room, armed only with a plastic copy card and a stack of bound journal volumes, grinding out the hot pages with their distinctive smell of carbon-based fixer, flash by flash, under the cover. Imagine the sense of smug accomplishment, the feeling of well-deserved satisfaction, as one emerged, blinking, into the sunlight, a stack of stapled, double-sided copies under one arm! Twenty more entries for The Bibliography!

Reading books, by the same token, could be reduced to reading the first and last chapter, plus the first and last paragraph of every intervening chapter. You might then add an artfully chosen sample from page 317 or, better yet, page 568 that could be memorized, mentally labelled 'seminal,' and recited upon some appropriate occasion, like an oral examination or departmental cocktail party. Furthermore, by common consent, while in graduate school no book, no matter how obscure, is ever to be read for the first time. That is, if you are reading a book, you must always be sure to say that you are *rereading* it, thus casually indicating long familiarity with its ridiculously esoteric yet seminal contents, a familiarity in need of the merest superficial refreshment. 'Don't mind me! Just having a quick reread of John Scotus Erugina's Latin commentary on Anaximander's *Fragments*! You go play frisbee! No no no no no! Go on! I'll be there soon!'

The professorial equivalent of this, which must be mastered before one can attain tenure, is what the critic Gilbert Adair once called the *future procrastinate*, a language tense apparently reserved for the exclusive use of academics.[4] A sentence in future procrastinate goes, 'In this paper I am going to address ...' or 'My main focus in the following will be the following ...' and so on; such that, eventually, one reaches the end of an article or address without once having heard a plain declarative sentence declaring anything. Instead, a series of promissory notes have been issued, none of them destined for redemption; a train of thought is repeatedly announced but never arrives. The oral version of the future procrastinate, especially useful during conferences and question and answer periods, involves extensive use of the phrase 'Well, there's a whole body of literature on that.'

On the other hand, when we grad students did read things – when we did retrieve knowledge from that most beautiful of storage devices, the book – most of us felt compelled to take detailed notes, ostensibly for use later in the often-postponed 'writing up' phase of the dissertation. During long days in the Sterling periodical reading room I filled stacks of paper with summaries and quotations culled from the dozens of books I was responsible for. This led to a feeling that one was in the grip of some obsessive-compulsive disorder, like those mental patients who copy out whole books, sentence for sentence, as if assessing their merits. 'Ah, yes, that's a good thought, nicely phrased! Yes, and that's also good! Excellent, another one!' And so on, until a simulacrum of the original book rises in a pile from the mad scribblings.

These two extremes of storage and retrieval taught me, as probably nothing else could, the exquisite torture of the research project. It is in the nature of research that it can never be accomplished to the satisfaction of its own inner logic, because one never completes the task, only comes at best asymptotically closer to its beckoning edge. Every research project is, in this sense, a failure. But we keep on engaging in them because we cannot cease in our attempts, however limited, to make sense.

This likewise taught me that there is something beautiful

and human about the project of setting things down, or aside, so that they might be picked up, or taken up, later. Like taxonomy itself – the act of classification, whether in Linnaean biological categories or baseball box scores – storing and retrieving things is basic to our engagements of meaning with an otherwise undifferentiated world. It is part of what makes us who we are.

We have of course evolved numerous techniques of pursuing this human task. Language itself is one, and arguably the most basic one. We use language, among other things, so we don't have to do what those hapless foreigners in *Gulliver's Travels* do, namely, walk around all day with a backpack of objects to flourish in efforts at communication. When I say 'alarm clock,' I don't need to have one in my hand to show you. The phonemes of the phrase are themselves meaningless, at least in isolation, but taken together give us the ability to refer to the world to powerful effect. I will leave aside for now the issues of how language in turn affects the world, even in a sense creates it, and simply notice the remarkable fact that language allows us, in infinitely flexible ways, to represent – to make present again – what we like to call 'the world we find before us.' In fact, as Wittgenstein reminds us, we should be careful of this language of representation, which can lead us into confusion about our relation to the world. Using language is not so much a matter of placing accurate labels on an external world as it is a matter of playing games with other word-using creatures. Still, if language allows us to do things with words, it does so by, among other things, making (what we call) objects portable in (what we call) mind even when they are not portable in (what we call) space.

Writing is, in turn, a logical extension of the fact of spoken language, for with writing we, in a sense, overcome the time-based limitations of the medium of speech. Oral speech must float in the air. Like pre-notation music, it exists only in its action, suspended in the fourth dimension of duration. That is part of its appeal, even to those of us who love writing. Indeed, in Plato's *Phaedrus*, Socrates praises orality for just these timely reasons, noting that it can respond and revise in the face of external influence, and moreover choose its proper interlocutors, those who are ready to understand, whereas written language can only say the same thing, over and over again – somewhat like my father, I have always thought, who has a weakness for telling the same stories, without noticeable variation, day after day.

Written words, says Socrates to the young discourse lover, Phaedrus,

> seem to talk to you as though they were intelligent, but if you ask them anything about what they say, from a desire to be instructed, they go on telling you just the same thing forever. And once a thing is put in writing, the composition, whatever it may be, drifts all over the place, getting in the hands not only of those who understand it, but equally of those who have no business with it; it doesn't know how to address the right people, and not address the wrong. And when it is ill-treated and unfairly abused it always needs its parent to come to its help, being unable to defend or help itself.[5]

Plato's in some ways rather elitist view of things is not widely shared, however, despite the good arguments Socrates makes for dialectical or conversational philosophy. And Plato's own succumbing to the temptation of writing seems to destabilize the position somewhat – if it also, at the same time, gives us the very means by which we know, today, what Plato's unstable position was. Most people regarded, and continue to regard, writing as an advance on oral speech, or anyway a very good thing in its own right. Now we can master the limits of time by placing words in a kind of receptacle, drawing them out again at our leisure, and going back to check them if we are in danger of forgetting what they said.

This very likely means we will allow our capacity for memory to wane a bit, of course, and it is true that we no longer have people around who can recite Homeric epics over the course of three days, or hold a crowd spellbound for a weekend as they spin out a yarn from the troubadour stocks. We have probably even seen the last people like my friend Matthew Parfitt, who once kept a group of us awake all night, crowded in a tent in a Muskoka rainstorm, reciting from memory highlights of English poetry, 1750 to 1945. Writing, says Socrates, 'is a recipe not for memory, but for reminder.'

Now, written language is not actively hostile to the rhymes and rhythms that were so necessary, and so helpful, to oral language. And it is true, as any experienced writer will tell you, that the best test of good writing is to read it aloud. But writing does not demand language's best gifts in the same way that speech does, and sometimes those gifts are lost, or rendered dispensable, mere window dressing, in the relentless storage/retrieval imperatives of the written word. Writing seems forever to urge us onward, sometimes to the detriment of the very language it uses. Writing's success is also, as Plato seems to suggest, a kind of failure.

We often forget that for centuries after the invention of writing, even written words were meant to be read aloud. This was rooted in the communal goals of the monastery, for example, where the rule of silence is broken only for the ritual of prayer and the equally important ritual of words read to accompany meals. But it was also rooted in an implied distrust of what reading might do to us. Reading silently was until very recently thought bizarre, even subversive, an unseemly retreat from the public realm of language into a strange, self-imposed solitude of the mind. Here one might think all manner of thoughts, without any outward evidence!

There remains in some quarters an odd distrust of silent reading, this withdrawal into the self. The protagonist of A.S. Byatt's novel *Babel Tower*, appearing in a child custody trial, is repeatedly criticized for reading while her child is young and her mother-in-law sits nearby – as if reading itself constituted neglect of the gurgling baby. My father, bless his heart, cannot bear the proximity of someone reading silently, so that conversational gambits continue to issue from him even as one raises a book protectively to ward them off. From the other side, he cannot himself read in silence. This has parallel drawbacks.

So this dislike of the silent reader continues. At the same

time, somewhat contradictorily, nowadays we tend to disdain
people who can only read aloud, or by moving their lips. But
how much more love of language might be in them than in us?
Reading silently too often means reading quickly, not sound-
ing the words but merely seeing them. That is what is so
frightening about those horribly upbeat speed-reading info-
mercials that run on cable TV in the middle of the night, with
the squat 'reading expert' running his hands smoothly down
the pages, one a second, and then calmly – amazingly! –
answering questions about what he has just (I suppose we
must still call it) read.

I am not about to surrender my right to read in silence, but
every now and then an exercise in the roots of writing is worth
taking on. Last summer I sat in my back garden and spent a
couple of afternoons reading Shakespeare's sonnets out loud.
It was instructive. It probably goes without saying – to use that
lovely, ever-misused phrase – that poetry needs orality to
flourish. But we often forget it, sometimes especially those of
us who studied poetry so assiduously in academia. Reading
poetry aloud is hard, because we have mostly lost the rhythms
of poetic diction. Our eyes speed on ahead, eager for the next
word, the next stimulus. We stumble and stagger. And if there
is no loved one nearby to whom we are speaking, or even if
there is, we tend to feel embarrassed. Alas! Would that poetry
had better servants in these fast, last days!

When it comes to writing, success breeds volume. The more
writing there was and is, the more there seems to be. That is
not a good thing for the natural resources of the planet's
forests, I know, but it is what writing demands. Responding to
an oral argument or position costs nothing in the way of
resources, unless we count fresh air – as we perhaps ought to
do. But writing needs a material base, it needs some hardware
on which to run the software of thought. We have tried various
things, from the scraped and bleached skins of handy animals,
to the mashed, pressed, and dried leaves of various plants.
Pulped softwood, itself bleached and pressed, mixed with

some rag cotton or other softener, and then folded and sliced into useful sizes, is the best vehicle we have so far found for this peculiar undertaking of ours.

The important thing about the vehicle of writing is that it must last through time. One can write in the sand at the beach, or in the frost of a car window, melting messages into the whiteness as my brothers and I used to do on long prairie car trips. But that writing will soon disappear – almost as fast as speech itself. Writing on paper, using ink – itself a remarkable invention, that mixture of water and crushed pigment and fixative – is defined by its grapple with time. Writing works because the setting down of ideas also means the taking up of them again later, at some future date as yet undetermined.

No material base, no writing hardware, is perfect, however. Ink fades, paper crumbles to dust, and every day thoughts are lost, never to be recovered. And books make unfortunately good kindling, as fascists and philistines alike know. How dislocating to realize that the apparent preponderance of names beginning with 'A' in the world of ancient letters – Aristotle, our friend Anaximander – might be an adventitious result of the disastrous fire in the library at Alexandria. What wonders may have been lost there? Still, books, or more specifically the codex, the bound volume of pages printed on both sides, is the best vehicle for writing we have so far created.

To talk of books as storage/retrieval devices, hardware for the software of thought, might seem to be a way of giving in to the dominating technological imperatives of the day. I hope very much I'm not doing that. I am, rather, trying to see where the need for storage and retrieval comes from, and trying to expose, thereby, some of the limits of our current mania for more and more of it. That's why it is worth pausing for a moment to cherish the technology of the book, especially in the face of imminent challenges from other, allegedly superior forms of storage/retrieval device.

I like to tell my techno-happy, book-is-dead students that the book's main superiority is its power sources. Once extant, all books are costlessly solar-powered. They are also compact and portable, easy to hold and use, and relatively durable. Unlike almost any other storage/retrieval system one can think of, they are incapable of crashing or becoming virus-infected (except perhaps by bugs and mould). And unlike most of the 'dead media' archived by the science-fiction writer Bruce Sterling, the retrieval techniques of the book are embedded in the device: we will always be able to run this software – always assuming, that is, we are still able to run the human-based operating system called literacy.

In fact, one can go on in this vein. Book City, the small chain of independent bookstores in Toronto, now gives out bookmarks with a little essay on what they call 'the new Bio-Optic Organized Knowledge device – BOOK.' In it, mocking the breathless language of computer manuals, they note Opaque Paper Technology (OPT), which 'allows manufacturers to use both sides of the sheet, doubling the information density,' and cite the '"browse" function,' which 'allows instant movement to any sheet, forward or backward' with the flick of a hand. '[T]housands of content creators have committed to the platform,' they conclude, 'and investors are reportedly flocking to the medium.' They do acknowledge that, 'like other display devices it can become unusable if dropped in water.'

I don't really want to descend into a debate about the future of the book, though. Such debates are boring and, inevitably, inconclusive: no one can possibly know whether the book is going to survive the test of time, because the scope necessary to make the question interesting is denied us mortals. The book will probably outlast all of us, but beyond that we simply do not, and cannot, know. I simply want to note the lovely durability of this particular storage/retrieval technology, with its many aesthetic dimensions – the design of the cover, the smell of ink on paper – and its many workaday virtues.

To be sure, a book is only any good to its reader if he or she can find it, and a good deal of the storing and retrieving we do is of information about where information and knowledge themselves are stored. When I was in graduate school I had a part-time job that ranks high in my list of futile and/or pathetically low-paying attempts to make ends meet. I used to file index cards in the Yale library system for four dollars an hour. To do this I rose each morning at seven, walked to Sterling in the already humid heat, and then for eight hours sat on a kind of wheeled chair device – a go-kart going nowhere – sweating away in the nave of the library, which, like every other building at Yale, really wanted to be a church.

These cards arrived in packages from the Library of Congress and had to be interleafed with the existing catalogue. One took a drawer from the catalogue, which was a long row of cabinets, removed the screwed-in rod holding the cards in place, inserted the new one in the proper place, and then replaced the rod. Which sounds simple. Except that the subject index was, I discovered, a minefield of judgment calls and arcane triple-indented classification priorities. When did one index relative to first letter of last name of first author, and when by first letter of first name of primary title? My head used to spin in the cottony mid-afternoon heat of the nave.

My supervisor, a tiny hunched-over New Havenite called Miss Willoughby – in the manner of women of her generation, she had no first name – used to come by every few hours and *tsk-tsk* away as she looked over my work. 'Mark,' she told me one day when I was having a more than usually fierce desire to fling unrodded cards all over the stone floor, 'you are very fast. But you are a little inaccurate.' This made me sound, I thought, like a sort of rookie-league fireballer, the Nuke Laloosh of Sterling Memorial.

The really twisted thing about this job, apart from its role in my own version of the future procrastinate, keeping me from writing my dissertation, was that it was entirely pointless. This was the summer of 1989 and the card index was not long for the world. Already computer terminals had annexed one side of the Sterling nave, and I used to look over there from my perch on the stationary vehicle and see other grad students clacking away in front of their screens. Clearly they knew something that I didn't. They were actually finishing their degrees, while I was working on something already finished. The Sisyphean dimensions of the job eventually broke me. I quit before the end of the summer and went back to writing, by contrast a task full of glad confident mornings.

Disused index cards, meanwhile, are now employed in many libraries as the scrap paper on which due dates are stamped and inserted in those little pockets inside the back cover.[6] I always like to look at the information printed on the other side, sometimes helpfully corrected by a long-gone librarian's careful pencil, and think of those long rows of wooden drawers and the maps of meaning they held inside their little boxed universes. Like the books they pointed to, the card indexes were pretty good at what they did, and I miss them. Or rather, I miss the idea of them, just like I miss the old bound volumes of the Edinburgh University Library catalogue, which was a maze of typed and retyped slips of paper glued into large ledgers, a sort of profit and loss record of stored knowledge that was, truth be known, hell to use.

Indexing and classification systems are of course more important than ever, now that there is this huge volume of information to master. And there are many people out there who will tell you all about the virtues of different methods of classification. I am not one of them – even though I am clearly the beneficiary of numerous such systems, beginning with the alphabet and going through the Dewey Decimal System, which I used to know pretty much by heart, to the current Library of Congress system, with its alien-spaceship designations. I like the fact that my books have these alternative identities, these call signs from the outer universe: JC-578-K56; HM-101-K46; BJ-1481-K46. But classification systems are only as good as the people who use them, and none of them is perfect. There is a danger, I think, for us to try and meet the feelings of overload I mentioned earlier with the aspiration to create the perfect classification system. We feel that somehow, if only we possessed the right catalogue or search engine or index, we would be able to master the growing body of what is stored. Our retrieval missions would then be perfect, surgical strikes of the mind. But that is impossible, for information and knowledge, whether we think of the volume as good or bad, have a way of spilling out of our categories. And any complete classification system is, in its way, a metaphysical delusion, the often dangerous idea of the final explanation.

Jorge Luis Borges, himself a librarian of no mean gifts, was well aware of the futility of perfect classification, and of the simultaneous appeal and disappointment of the final explanation. The famous parody of classification offered by Borges, and a favourite of Michel Foucault and Umberto Eco, is allegedly from a Chinese encyclopedia called *The Celestial Emporium of Benevolent Recognitions*. It goes this way: '[I]t is written that the animals are divided into (a) those that belong to the Emperor, (b) embalmed ones, (c) those that are trained, (d) suckling pigs, (e) mermaids, (f) fabulous ones, (g) stray dogs, (h) those that are included in this classification, (i) those that tremble as if they were mad, (j) innumerable ones, (k) those drawn with a very fine camel's hair brush, (l) others, (m) those that have just broken a flower vase, (n) those that resemble flies from a distance.'

We might also think here of another piece of Borgesian trickery. In one of his stories, a man finds a quotation to the effect that one is born either Platonic or Aristotelian by nature: that is, either given to thinking there are supernatural essences, or given to taking the natural world on its own terms. The man checks the citation, and finds a reference to another book, source of the quotation. This book in turn cites another book, to which he goes in turn. The third book cites a fourth book as the source. The fourth cites a fifth. And so on, until the man finds, like some researcher caught in library hell, that all the books using this quotation point to some other book, a self-referential circle of citation without an original. Whatever else it does, the story exposes the throbbing fibres of what Harold Bloom called 'the anxiety of influence.' This is not a matter just for scholars; we are all shaped, in ways we hardly know, by unattributable quotations and borrowed bits of wisdom.

Borges's satires of classification are a good curb to meta-physical ambition. They are likewise warnings about the delicious futility of our engagement with words themselves. What is the ultimate wisdom of storage and retrieval? That, like a grad student in pursuit of a topic, there is always more to read, one more book or treatise – or, now, web site or newsgroup – to explore before one may play frisbee, go on that picnic? No. We have to remember that the logic of our tasks comes from the ends we set ourselves, not from the insatiable inner drive of information itself. Only when we see this, only when we see that the proper sovereign relationship is ours over information, not the other way around, will the world resolve itself into something approaching sense.

This is sense not because it perfectly reflects the nature of the universe, rather because it speaks to the needs that we, you and I, together determine as worthy of our attention. In this collective undertaking we are forever haunted by the distant, impossible prospect of final sense, of perfect retrieval. We are likewise haunted by the impermanence of our lives here. We wish that words might last longer than they do, that they might be stored and retrieved again after we are gone. And sometimes that is exactly what happens. But finally, no matter how efficient or durable the delivery system, not even words are proof against time. And wisdom, which is after all a different thing from both information and knowledge, lies in accepting that fact – even as we continue, ever hopeful, to make more words to store and retrieve.

I will leave the last word to someone who knew the value of words, and knew, too, the sad wonder of their combined power and limits when written down. This is Sonnet 65:

Since brass, nor stone, nor earth, nor boundless sea,
But sad mortality o'ersways their power,
How with this rage shall beauty hold a plea,
Whose action is no stronger than a flower?
O how shall summer's honey breath hold out
Against the wrackful siege of batt'ring days,

When rocks impregnable are not so stout,
Nor gates of steel so strong, but Time decays?
O fearful meditation! where, alack,
Shall Time's best jewel from Time's chest lie hid?
Or what strong hand can hold his swift foot back?
Or who his spoil of beauty can forbid?
  O none, unless this miracle have might,
  That in black ink my love may still shine bright.

It may. And sometimes – often enough – it does.

Notes

1 See Mark Kingwell, *Better Living: In Pursuit of Happiness from Plato to Prozac* (Toronto: Viking, 1998), ch. 8; cf. David Shenk, *Data Smog: Surviving the Information Glut* (New York: HarperCollins, 1997).
2 The classic analysis of the trope of speed in modernity is Paul Virilio, *Speed and Politics* (New York: Semiotext(e), 1995); orig. *Vitesse et Politique: Essai de Dromologie* (Paris: Galilée, 1977).
3 See, for example, Neil Postman, *Amusing Ourselves to Death: Public Discourse in the Age of Show Business* (New York: Viking, 1985), p. 67 ff., on the problem of the 'information-action ratio.'
4 Gilbert Adair, 'Derrida Didn't Come,' in *Myths and Memories* (London: Fontana, 1980).
5 Plato, *Phaedrus*, 275 e. Translated by R. Hackforth (Princeton, NJ: Princeton University Press, 1961).
6 Nicholson Baker's essay 'The Great Discard' is the best discussion I know on the implications of the change from card catalogues to on-line ones. On the whole, Baker is anxious about what is lost in the change: the curbed ability for true subject searches and the lowering of 'futility points' in routine searches – that is, people tend to give up sooner in on-line searches. See Baker, 'The Great Discard,' in *The Size of Thoughts* (New York: Vintage, 1997), pp. 125–81.

Fear and Self-Loathing in Couchland: Eight Myths about Television

Because I have some critical things to say about television in what follows, I want to make it clear from the outset that I write as someone who believes television is a medium *worth taking seriously*. Put that way, the point may sound a little condescending; but the reason I use that phrase is because it is part of my contention that people, both inside the television industry and outside it – makers and watchers alike, that is – don't take television seriously enough. When we *do* talk about the power of television, or the place of television within our cultural experience, we almost always do so in ways that leave all the important questions unasked. This in turn leads to a lack of precisely the critical discourse we need if we are to realize television's potential as a medium. Without such a discourse, television is all too likely to remain in its current dismal state: suffused with mediocrity, jangling with advertising, numbing in its pointless variety.

Despite this, I am not one of those intellectuals who despise television, who sometimes appear to think that moral worth is generated by removing all televisions from the home. This group of voluntary media-fasters, which includes some of my best friends, does possess a certain intellectual purity. And I think I understand something of the desire to excise television from their lives – even if I don't always share their sense of what such an excision proves or achieves. For instance, though the proposition is probably unfalsifiable, I don't believe television has made me more stupid or less productive. Of course, like most people who watch television, I am aware of its many shortcomings; naturally I have been tempted, at times, to throw my own set out the window, as in the famous opening sequence of the old *SCTV* comedy series. (The irony of illustrating the point with that particular cultural reference is obvious.) Television is annoying and pointless often enough to make it seem rational, now and then, to get rid of it altogether.

And yet, though I sometimes find television profoundly irritating and worthless – in particular because of its unbelievable accommodation of advertising – and occasionally loathe myself for not using better the time I spend watching it, I nevertheless think it necessary to explore our culture's ongoing engagement with it. Television is still, for better or worse, the dominant medium of information and entertainment of the age. That dominance may soon fade, may indeed already be fading, but I don't think we can be confident that it will do so in salutary ways unless and until we give television the critical attention it deserves. And that means, in the first instance, both watching it and thinking about it.

For some, these relatively brief arguments will be insufficiently wide in scope or insufficiently critical in tenor to be convincing: they will return to the self-approval of their television disdain with nothing much disturbed. For others, the arguments will be misplaced, since television is already a focus for their attention – but not for their critical engagements. They think structural criticism of the medium uninteresting, or out of proper focus. Both of these reactions need to be examined and overcome. Television has a way, in its very ubiquity, of evading critical engagement, and so the arguments presented here are for the rest of us, who want to find new ways, not necessarily always negative ones, of thinking about the medium.

I draw from my personal experience here. I have been involved in television in three separate but related ways: first and foremost, as a viewer – some would say a rapacious and insatiable viewer; second, as a television critic for a monthly general-interest magazine, *Saturday Night*; and finally, as a participant in programming, mostly in panel talk shows, news broadcasts, and documentaries. I am far from unique in this combination of experiences, I suppose, but not every philosophy professor has the opportunity, or the inclination, to engage with television in this way. Most of them – again, I speak from experience – consider it beneath their dignity. That, too, contributes to the lack of intelligent discourse about television, and it's one of the presumptions I want to challenge in what follows.

What I'm going to do is offer a list of *eight persistent myths* about television, things that have the status of received wisdom. These are myths not in the sense of being articulated stories, or even actively acknowledged falsehoods, but in being elements of what is considered 'common sense' or 'the way things are.' They are part of the assumed furniture of the world, and therefore somewhat difficult to see – and criticize – as propositions. Together they form a kind of force field of deflection around television, a buffer of protective nostrums that keeps us from penetrating to what really matters. At the same time, they leave our fear and self-loathing about television entirely intact.

Some of what I'm about to say may seem obvious, but we must be vigilant about that appearance of obviousness. We often think we know what's going on in television, and simply need practical advice: lists of maxims or workaday suggestions. That's too hasty. Accepting a point too blithely, or viewing it as already understood, is often not to understand it at all but, perversely, to dismiss it. It is the equivalent of smiling, nodding enthusiastically, and saying 'Yes, yes, of course,' when a friend tells you he finds your behaviour disturbing.

Myth #1: Television is a neutral medium.

In an age that is supposedly ruled by the legacy of Marshall

McLuhan, at least when it comes to understanding media, it is remarkable how many people, especially within television production, still cling to the idea that the medium itself is just an empty conduit, a pure vessel for content. At a recent conference on the future of culture, a veteran news anchor and the director of programming for a hugely successful cable channel – they shall go nameless – both claimed, with an air of finality, that television is a neutral medium.

The reasons for this insistence are worth exploring. Notice how the claim looks like an acceptance of responsibility: 'Television is a neutral medium. Therefore programming – or, as we now say, content production – is everything. Don't blame television as a medium; blame the people who make the shows. Since we are the ones generating that content and putting it on the air, the responsibility, both positive and negative, lies with us.' But as an acceptance of responsibility, this move is a bit like the NRA's repeated retreat to the position that guns don't kill people, people kill people. Television is a neutral medium the way a loaded gun could be used to hammer in nails or hold down stray pieces of paper. Indeed, calling any medium neutral is to ignore what McLuhan saw so clearly: media, in extending our senses in particular ways, restructure our experience and, ultimately, our world. They are never simple chutes moving data from one place to another; they are, instead, world-creating machines.

The first principle of the recent 'Technorealism Manifesto,' a statement of modest scepticism about our reigning technophilia, gets the matter right. 'A great misconception of our time is the idea that technologies are completely free of bias,' the principle runs,

> – that because they are inanimate artifacts, they don't promote certain kinds of behaviors over others. In truth, technologies come loaded with both intended and unintended social, political, and economic leanings. Every tool provides its users with a particular manner of seeing the world and specific ways of interacting with others. It is important for each of us to consider the

biases of various technologies and to seek out those that reflect our values and aspirations.[1]

Just so. To understand television, therefore, we have first to see how it makes its world – how it establishes its field of possibility, of what is thinkable. This in turn structures, before any show is ever produced, the powerful norms of what makes for 'good TV.' These norms, buried in the medium itself, are the more powerful for being unquestioned, even invisible.

Most significantly, we have to appreciate what seems transparent but is not: television is a *time-based* medium, and it is a medium dominated by the power of advertising. In its world, we buy, sell, and (of course) spend time. Here time is everything, from the seven- or eight-minute blocks a producer has between commercial breaks, to the seven or eight seconds that a talking head like myself might have to make a point. In some ways this is even more important to realize than the fact that television is a largely *visual* medium. When time is everything, and time is for sale to the highest bidder, then everything else is changed, including most significantly how control of the medium is distributed.

Myth #2: Television is controlled by individuals.

The most important single thing that is changed when a medium of information and entertainment is based on time is how particular decisions are made. Because television is the management of time, it requires constant attention to the business of allocation. Individuals – broadcast executives, executive producers, floor directors – appear to make these decisions, but in a sense the decisions are made before they leave for work each morning. The field of television is pre-structured, in large measure by the combination of the medium's biases with the influence of advertising money, and that structure is internalized by anyone who holds a high position in the television world. If it were not, the person would not hold that high position, but would be in some other walk of life – it's as simple, and as complicated, as that.

I am not suggesting that these individuals are mere automatons, marching robotically through their days. They are, rather, responding with what they see as rational choices within the field as it is already structured. What is important to see is that when they accept responsibility for a given decision, that gesture of localized integrity actually deflects attention from the structure. Focusing on the individual is another version of the television-is-neutral claim: it is a kind of evasion, because individual responsibility (usually made to someone higher up in the hierarchy, anyway) is meaningless without attention to what made a given decision rational.

Every field of human endeavour has its internal norms of rationality, the things that determine what 'makes sense' there. These are the rules of the game, and they are what run the field, not the individuals who put the rules into play. We must all acknowledge our participation in the norms of television, viewers and producers and broadcasters alike. By 'norms' I mean things like the assumed values of topicality, newness, or relevance – values that are rarely defined, and still more rarely argued about or defended explicitly. I mean, too, less visible things like the desire for pure spectacle, the assumed importance of speed in all things, the cults of personality and celebrity, and the need always to be entertaining or lively. Or, further, the unquestioned influence of money in the creation of value in the prior sets of norms. These norms condition our choices in television, making some things possible and others unthinkable, and yet we almost never pause to examine them, ask where they came from, or wonder what purpose they serve.

We are all players on this field. But the rules are set somewhere else, and every time we make a play ourselves, or single out an individual and hold him or her responsible for a good or bad play, we reinforce the invisible power of those rules. This looks like critical engagement with television, but it is really only a further surrender to television's overarching, and hence unchallenged, influence.

This is not to suggest that nothing can be done about the deep structure of the medium of television. One reason we often simply surrender to these norms is that we think that television is, at some basic level, beyond questioning – we say, that's just the way the world is. (This is another sense in which this myth parallels the previous one.) It's like the old joke about the weather: *everybody complains about it, but nobody seems to do anything about it*. This only shows the extent of a given medium's world-structuring power: it manages to put itself beyond question to a degree unmatched in any other medium of communication. Its very pervasiveness is part of this self-concealing genius, for television feels like it is greater than any single one of us. (Another old joke: a conference is a gathering of important people who singly can do nothing, but together can decide that nothing can be done. That's what television editorial meetings are like.) Holding this or that individual responsible for television won't help us here. But neither will taking refuge in the old claim that you have to give the people what they want.

Myth #3: Television is democratic.

When people say television is democratic, what they really mean is that it is crudely populist: ratings numbers rule, and that means the viewer is always right. This viewer is not a real person, but instead an undifferentiated mass or, at best, a demographic niche-market slice. If you believe the numbers, the viewer is mostly dumb, unsophisticated, apolitical, and inclined to violence. His favourite shows are *Cops, Jerry Springer, Judge Judy, Baywatch*, and *World Wrestling Federation*. He is suspicious of innovation and yet susceptible to the wiles of advertisers, who of course wield far more actual power in determining what makes it onto the screen than any viewer.

Programmers appear to have two choices in the face of the notional viewer's spectral existence: simply give him more of what he wants, or slip some quality past him when he's not looking. It is this feeling of confronting necessary evils that makes so many programmers dismissive, even despising, of the viewer. That in turn hollows out their own character, and, in television's version of a sick codependent relationship, they begin to despise themselves for making a career of satisfying someone they despise. Programmers are often highly intelligent people, and this takes a toll on them. Self-loathing becomes an occupational hazard.

Hence, I think, the prevalence of the claim that this is democracy in action. It is a respectable way to rationalize satisfying the base needs of a notional lowest-common-denominator viewer. People want it, you give it to them – end of story. My favourite version of this, the reductio ad absurdum of viewer populism, is the studio audience wired to record their minute changes in approval or disapproval as some performer or item is passed before them: instant judgment, democracy in action.

No. That is only a parody of democracy, and the people fingering their Nielsen indicators are no more genuinely responsible for the way television is than the world-weary programmers who go on giving it to them. Expectations and preferences are formed by prior experience. The idea that 'what people want' is a category pristine and beyond challenge, a pre-existing standard of judgment, is as dangerous as anything we have in this mass-produced, envy-driven, thoughtless world of ours.[2]

I have to be careful here, of course, because you might be about to accuse me of elitism. It has long been a vice of philosophers, I know. And frankly, a little elitism would probably go a long way on television, if by that we meant (as we used to) the application of high and defensible standards of aesthetic judgment to the products and activities of a medium. But these days it is difficult to make that kind of (valid) elitist point without incurring the wrath of someone who thinks one is making the (invalid) elitist point that everyone should like what I like, or lump it.[3] So, I am not saying that everyone should be forced to watch episodes of *Masterpiece Theatre*, or a succession of improving documentaries until they become better people – which is to say, presumably, people more like me. I am suggesting, rather, that ducking the question of how television gets made by waving in the direction of its allegedly democratic character is only another evasion of genuine responsibility – and an evasion of the influence critical judgment should have on what is done. As long as we do that, we will be unable to talk intelligently about the medium.

Myth #4: Television is all junk.

I turn a corner here, to show that I'm not merely indulging in an anti-TV rant. This proposition, though beloved of intellectuals, is indeed a myth, as anyone knows who actually watches television with care and discernment. Unhappily, television is not on the whole a medium that welcomes or rewards that discernment. And television permits junk, certainly; may even, in its current state, actively encourage it. But it also – now and then – permits brilliance, drama, brains, and emotion. That range of possibility doesn't make it a neutral medium, only a varied and relatively flexible one: the good and the bad are both still limited by what television allows as thinkable.

Mostly, television is good at being entertaining, on a relatively obvious and non-challenging level. But because of its ubiquity and power – also its relative cheapness, in reaching a mass audience – it rarely restricts itself to what it does well. Because television includes both entertainment and information, it has a tendency to let the norms of the former dominate the latter. Entertainment value becomes the only value of every piece of programming, and this has deleterious effects on what gets delivered to us as news or current affairs programming. This is Neil Postman's main complaint in *Amusing Ourselves to Death*. Television journalism, Postman says, becomes a series of disconnected and decontextualized images linked only by the feeble segue of 'And now ... this.' So that a report of a devastating airplane crash, causing the anchor to furrow her brow with emotion, is followed, seconds later, by a weather or sports report that she delivers with a happy grin.[4]

That problem is much remarked, but there is another one lurking behind it that is harder to make sense of when we want to talk about the quality of television programming. Most outside discourse about television, when it happens at all, is full of gloom and doom – amusing ourselves *to death*, after all – and like most apocalyptic bulletins, this has an enervating effect on us. We are left not knowing what to do about the situation, except perhaps hate ourselves for spending any time at all with a medium so obviously evil.

Among regular viewers of television, this enervation seems to afflict television critics particularly. I wrote my own television column for just over two years, but it was in a monthly magazine and I mostly wrote about shows that were, in some sense or other, successes of the medium: *Frasier, Homicide, Melrose Place, Buffy the Vampire Slayer*.[5] (I will not repeat the arguments here, but these may have been successes of form, of wit, of social consciousness, and sometimes of unintended social consciousness. Not all ironies, even in this age of aggressive self-awareness, are obvious to their creators.) I never suffered the world-weary burnout that seems to creep up on daily or weekly critics. Soon enough, their columns begin to smack of a multilayered disdain – for the medium, for the readers, for the viewers, for themselves.

What this means is that television critics are not performing their role, namely, articulating for viewers the critical standards those viewers wish they could articulate themselves, given world enough and time. There are exceptions. Anthony Lane in *The New Yorker* has written with wit and bite about television (though he has more lately moved on to the more 'serious' medium of film), and John Allemang, in *The Globe and Mail*, is Canada's best regular television critic. Perhaps not surprisingly, these writers have also written about many other things. They are writers first, and critics of television second. Which means they think about what goes on in couchland as part of a larger world. They cannot surrender to the blanket nature of the myth, approaching the entirety of their medium with a presumed negativity. At the very least, such an attitude can only lead, in the end, to cynical and bitter writing. Hard as it might sometimes be, for instance, after viewing a stack of cassettes previewing shows riveting only in their banality, critics have to believe in the medium, if not any single product of it, that they write about. That is an essential step in loosening the grip of television's internal norms.

Television critics have, on the whole, failed in the duty to assess television in ways that call out the best of the medium's possibilities. At the worst, they indulge in an unstable combination of cheap snootiness, taking aim at easy targets like Springer viewers, together with a bogus populism, dismissing anything too challenging as misguided. Unlike critics of almost any other medium, whether aesthetic or intellectual, they switch without warning from assessment of works to half-baked comments on the process of making those works. What we get, as a result, is the worst of both worlds: neither good work-based criticism, nor the kind of critical social analysis of the medium we really need. Hence, in part, the prevalence of this next myth.

Myth #5: Television is responsible for the world's evils.

It is not surprising that, in a world run by parcelling out time, the great value is *interest*: what is interesting, what will interest the viewer, what will hold his interest past the first commercial break?

Most often this so-called interest is actually a form of banality: what moves easily on television is what the sociologist Pierre Bourdieu calls 'the already-thought.'[6] Ideas and forms that work are the ones that are most familiar, and therefore most easily ingested. The conformity of broadcasting is not a conspiracy of mediocrity; it is a structural effect of the imperatives lodged within the system. These tend to favour the two poles of an unhelpful dichotomy. Something is either the all-new ('Children today are more violent than ever') or it is the ever-thus ('Children have always been violent'). Criticism of the medium is then likewise infected by this polarity, resulting in either ham-fisted disapproval or weary acceptance. Thus, for example, the depressing spectacle of the Littleton, Colorado, high-school massacre. I don't mean the events themselves, which were horrific, but the television response to them: the strangely familiar sights of ID banners across the bottom of the screen, pointless 'debates' between ill-informed yet vehement experts, and apparently endless photo ops with teary children, candlelit churches, and chain-link fences stacked with wreaths. It was a perfect example of the already-thought, a spectacle that was made-for-TV in the deep and apparently inescapable sense of being prestructured in both imagery and analysis. Everywhere you turned, someone was telling you, on screen, why this tragedy happened and how it could have been averted.

The breast-beating extended even to the predictable laying of blame for American school violence on 'the media.' President Clinton joined this chorus a week or two later, telling the producers of these media products, whoever they are, that he knew they could make themselves more responsible, just knew it, because they were not evil people. This is what passes for critical discourse about television today, as we all know. Notice the breathtaking simplicity of the world view, which wants to trace a clear and unbroken line between event and cause. Notice, too, the fear that underlies that wish for simplicity. The fact that these shootings, and others like them, are multifarious in cause, and beyond the explanatory abilities of any expert, especially on television, was not a factor. It may have been mentioned now and then as a blanket qualification – which was immediately followed by yet another inane 'analysis.'

For forgivable and often valid reasons, people fear complexity. They furthermore fear their own complicity in events or systems that are ugly or corrupt. The suggestion that somebody specific, usually somebody elsewhere – Hollywood,

New York, Madison Avenue, Wall Street, Washington – is responsible for the world's evils always finds a ready audience.[7] Once more, this *looks* like critical assessment of the power of television, but it is a sham, a cheap morality play that functions only as another ritual of avoidance. The power of television is real enough, but it lies in the way television structures social relations of power from top to bottom. Singling out individuals, or even classes, for blame when these relations generate bad outcomes is sloppy thinking. And it doesn't help, for it ends up by leaving everything as it is.

The crucial thing in a critical discourse about television, therefore, is (perhaps unexpectedly) learning not to judge too quickly. Television itself thrives on quick judgments, which is why it is so good at domesticating criticism. *We cannot look there for genuine critical discourse, especially about what is going on there.* Hence the central importance of confronting the next of my eight myths ...

Myth #6: You can talk about television on television.

I'm going to spend a little more time on this myth, because it is particularly close to my heart, and to the crux of the problem of intellectual engagement with television.

If you are at all familiar with Bourdieu's denunciation of talk television, the little book *Sur la télévision*, you know that I have agreed here with much of his analysis, even though I have taken issue with some other parts of it elsewhere.[8] In that book, which was a best-seller in France and started a fierce round of controversy about television, Bourdieu attacks what he calls *les fast-thinkers*, those made-for-TV intellectuals who are, as he says, always already booked. They lie at the ready on a producer's golden Rolodex. These days it's usually a greaseboard with names of people who, as they say, 'give good guest.' In any event, these are the people who get called again and again, and bounce from show to show to speak about whatever the occasion may demand.

Now I admit that I took this attack somewhat personally.

Bourdieu singles out the character he calls 'the journalist-philosopher,' and castigates the lowering of standards that allows this person to command a respect far beyond his or her genuine standing in intellectual circles. As I read the relentless dissection of this gruesome personage, with whom I unwillingly but inescapably identified, I was filled with my own kind of self-loathing. For I have, in the past few years, done more than my fair share of television punditry. I have opined and pronounced on many a cultural topic, from the Spice Girls to millennial cults to the films of David Cronenberg. While I continued to publish in academic journals, and while my first (scholarly) book won a prize in my field, I nevertheless seemed to be in precisely the position that Bourdieu describes, thinking in a hurry and reacting to this, that, or the other in what we frequent guests refer to as 'panelling.'

Of course, I have been flattered by the attention, and pleased to find, as most people secretly are – given the chance to find out – that I don't look hideous or crazy on television. Like most things, talk television is fun if you are good at it. I say that frankly, so you won't think I'm being disingenuous here. Anybody, especially any ambitious intellectual or writer with ideas to disseminate and a career to make, who claims they don't care at all about being on television is not being entirely straight with you. These days, the cultural marketplace being what it is, it is really not an option to have utterly no regard for television exposure. This is not, as most superficial critics claim, simply a matter of selling books. It is more deeply about getting ideas across to people who might otherwise know nothing at all about them. (It helps to have the books to back up the ideas, of course, because books remain the one form of communications technology that sell only themselves.) One may resent this fact, or rankle under it, or accept it calmly. What one may not do – and yet what so many attempt – is ignore it.

But there are dangers. For a while I governed my responses to television by saying yes to all the requests that interested me, and finding it hard to say no to the ones that didn't, and

therefore ending up doing some of them too. I regret this
somewhat, but I reasoned that I could do no worse than most
of the people on television already, and might just do better.
Lately I have tried to say no to these requests more effectively
and more often, and to some extent I succeeded. I'm happy to
say that I have, despite numerous phone calls from jittery producers, successfully resisted making any media pronouncements on the Clinton-Lewinsky scandal, the shootings in
Littleton, and the war in the Balkans. I hope this doesn't sound
self-congratulatory. Being in demand may seem like a nice
problem to have, but sometimes it feels a little like being
stalked.

Once you answer the telephone – once, that is, someone in a
production office has decided you are worthy of interest – the
only options are giving in to the request or making somebody
angry. Chase producers will deny this, but in their hearts they
know it is so. Being turned down is their greatest fear, and
sometimes it simply baffles them: they cannot imagine that
someone does not want to go on television. Now, I sympathize
with chase producers, I really do: it's an awful job to have,
especially under deadline pressure. But the situation can
become ridiculous, and the idea that *no means no* often simply
flies out the window. Saying no to producers is hard, if you
don't want to be rude. Often enough, they are rude to you first,
just because they think your politeness is some form of sly coy-
ness; or believe, as many have said to me time and again, that
they are giving you a terrific opportunity.

And it is indeed a good opportunity – if you are allowed a
minimum level of control. Too often you simply don't get it.
Media appearances, especially those on television, are more
time consuming than producers routinely acknowledge. They
involve, at a minimum, the time spent in pre-interviews, trans-
portation, make-up, and of course those many lost minutes,
so common in coordinated technological productions of any
kind, from football games to wars, where nothing much seems
to happen. Notice that this is not to mention any. time that
might be spent in actually preparing something to say – read-

ing a book, for example, or simply giving an issue some thought. Hence the relevance of Bourdieu's denunciation of the fast-thinker, and hence too the poor quality of most television punditry. To do even a three-minute segment of television *well* involves more time and work than many people, and many television producers, seem to believe.

There is, by the way, little or no money in talk television – something not widely known. The vast bulk of the media appearances I have done involved no money whatsoever. Sometimes a semi-regular engagement, as when I did a handful of shows as part of a culture panel, might result in a two-hundred-dollar cheque. Even here, you are never allowed the privilege of counting on it: the producer must decide you are the right person from the pool of panellists. In short, most of the time, television is not worth it unless you have a name to make or a particular idea to defend.

For reasons of this kind, then, plus a desire not to shoot my mouth off about anything and everything, I resolved towards the end of 1998 to do less television. I still accepted some invitations, and went about discussing a new book of essays, but I tried very hard to cut back the number of 'hits,' as television people call them.

The point is, it didn't really matter. Somewhere along the way I had crossed a conceptual line and become an item of television furniture – a 'TV guy,' in one of the more forgiving of the labels given to me by my colleagues. And naturally in a sense I really was a piece of panelling, if only in the limited world of Canadian news programming. As a result of this rather low-level form of ubiquity, certain predictable reactions set in. I was gently jeered by my colleagues in departmental meetings, and less gently insulted behind my back. My academic work, which might have been thought safe from guilt by association, was denigrated or (more often) simply ignored. I was mocked in gossip columns, and now and then, when some print journalist let their disdain and envy of the more powerful medium show, called everything from 'a usual suspect' to a 'dial-a-pundit.'

The disapproval eventually spread to television itself. Doing talk TV is a bit like dating somebody psychotic: nothing you do is ever taken at face value, all behaviour is entirely unpredictable, and you are always (apparently by definition) in the wrong. Early in 1999 I was dissected in a mean-spirited episode of the CBC show *Undercurrents*, which declared me winner of the title Pundit of the Year and then made fun of me for my range of interests. I was shown saying, over and over, 'I think ... I think ... I think ...' while a list of the things I had talked about scrolled quickly past. Partly as a result of this, I told one chase producer that I wanted to do his show less often, and he responded by posting an e-mail on his network's internal bulletin board reporting that I was declaring myself too good for television. One of his colleagues explained by saying, '*You* don't get to decide when you've had enough. *We* decide when you've had enough.' Another producer, after I had declined two invitations in a row to appear on her show, accused me of 'wasting everybody's time.' Wasting everybody's time by ... what? Being available by telephone?

In other words, these producers were giving me a hard time for trying to be more responsible about which, and how many, television appearances I agreed to do. This, more than any other single thing, convinced me of the danger of the situation as I had allowed it to develop. Notice that it is not really, as we usually say, the danger of overexposure. Overexposure is a condition that exists mainly in the minds of television producers, who don't like it when you appear on a show other than theirs; or of friends in the same line of work, who trace your progress the way journalists track their rivals' bylines. Certainly volume and range of appearances is a factor in such a backlash, but notice that it is often not under the person's individual control. Consider an important example.

Amazingly, television shows often rebroadcast even time-sensitive public affairs material in order to save money. This tactic, whose analogue in print journalism would be the unthinkable act of running a feature story a few times over the course of a year, means that one has no effective control of one's exposure: turn on the television on a summer's day and you might just see yourself on a call-in show from two seasons past. And naturally producers never mention this possibility when they ask you to be on a show, never ask you how many times you are willing to be shown saying the same thing, however badly. (Sometimes, but not always, one is asked to sign a general release – usually hurriedly, in the make-up room.) In other words, 'live TV' simply means live the first time, not the last. This, more than any single practice, contributes to the irritation people begin to feel with a given talking head.

Even having said all this, though, I still maintain that if you have something to say, there is no reason not to say it on television. In fact, there may be every reason to do it there, if you can get it said without distortion. The risk, as always, is subjecting yourself to the self-hatred that rules far too much of the television world. That may sound harsh; I think it is accurate. Producers, especially of current affairs shows, are usually smart, educated people. But they are often frustrated by the limits of the medium in which they work. So they dress up their work as something other than it is, claiming an inflated importance for it. Their envy for people who do intellectual work often manifests as hostility, sometimes as outright anti-intellectualism. If they think someone is getting away with being smart on television, or doing it too often – whatever that might mean – they will eventually attempt to bring him or her down a peg or two. It is an apparently ironclad law of television: success breeds success, until (of course) it breeds failure.

Importantly, this resentment is passed off as critical assessment of television itself, as in the *Undercurrents* example, which prides itself on being a 'hard-hitting' show about the media. That's why I say the myth in question is that you can talk about television on television. Who should be blamed if a given talking head talks more than another? The head? The producers who booked him? The programmers who scheduled the show? The programmers who reran the show the next summer, and the one after that? All of the above? The difficulty here is not individual, it belongs to the field of television itself. Each of us has to think carefully about our responsibility within the field, but none of us is personally responsible for the entire situation. To suggest otherwise is once more mere scapegoating, the worst kind of bad faith. We pass around the blame like a hot potato.

For a while, like these purportedly critical shows about media that run on television, I flattered myself that I could do genuine media criticism within the medium I was criticizing. But this is not really so, not least because no critic has the real control necessary to make a medium good, namely, choosing when, how, and where an opinion will be expressed. One can make distinctions between programs and choose opportunities to speak, but very few of us can do what Bourdieu himself did in the original broadcasts of *Sur la télévision*, namely, select a time and venue and control it completely. One's criticism is therefore always in the precarious position of being overcome by the circumstances of its own communication – circumstances that are, after some initial decisions, beyond one's reach. It is just more television, television by other means.

And therefore, as with the good-natured jabs at TV addiction in clever satirical shows like *The Simpsons* or *The Family Guy*, or any other allegedly satirical television program, most attempts at media criticism within the medium are ultimately self-defeating. They are taken up and swallowed by the all-enveloping world of television. Or they are made the subject of further interior criticism, pushing the situation to new levels of self-reference but not of insight. The thinking possible here is limited and most often superficial, and it soon collapses down under the weight of its own reflexivity. To have intelligent discourse about television, in other words, you must, at some point, turn the television off. You must go somewhere else.

Myth #7: Intellectuals are right to disdain television.

The problem now, as I've already indicated, is that most intellectuals working in other media – usually print media, naturally – do not consider television worth their attention. The reasons I have just detailed for my complicated engagement with television would seem to give sanction to that position, and there is no shortage of more pointed rejections too. Bourdieu's book, for example, has become a bible of sorts for disgruntled academics looking for intellectual sanction to bolster their ivory-tower retreats. In what is in fact a sly act of self-justification, one part of his argument is excised from the whole and made the sum of the book's message, contrary to its author's intention – and, ironically, not unlike the kind of television distortion he is trying to combat. But you can hardly blame academics for this one-sidedness. They love the fact that Bourdieu celebrates the 'internal standards' of their scholarly worlds, and shows an unshakeable faith in the power of peer review. They are cheered by his claim that non-academic ideas are 'highly perishable cultural product' that ought to be ridiculed in favour of the supposedly built-for-the-ages publications of their small priesthood.

Such an attitude simply reinforces the old hostility between academic and mainstream culture, however, creating a situation of duelling disdain in the process. In fact, of course, peer review is a suspect practice, full of personal vendettas and hidden prejudices; and there is nothing more highly perishable, when it comes to cultural product, than an academic article that will be read by exactly twelve people before being indexed and forgotten forever. But these countercharges are not my main complaint here. What really worries me is that the important ideas of my colleagues should be locked away within a forbidding and impregnable specialist language, lost to view because of the fear associated with venturing out of the fortress. Scorn of popular media leaves the teaching mission of academics in a sorry state, a failure which is then passed off as maintaining intellectual standards.

There is a quotation, variously attributed, that goes, 'If Socrates were alive today, he'd be the host of a TV talk show.' I don't think that is true, actually, but I do think he would consider it important to understand the power and pathologies of television. He would, I like to think, make some appearances now and then to ask demanding, unsettling questions of his audience. He would be, in short, very much the same presence as he was in ancient Athens. He would have to engage in the act of communication as we understand it, even though it entails many dangers. If, as people sometimes claim, television is the modern-day equivalent of that city's famous *agora*, the open marketplace in which Socrates prowled and practised his method of probing questions, he would certainly make his presence felt there. Or so I like to think.

'Academic' and 'intellectual' are distinct terms, and I do not confuse them here. There is every reason for many academics to fold themselves into a safe space where they never have to explain or justify an idea to the uninitiated. And their fear of the world of television is partially justified, as I said earlier. They may simply prefer to avoid the engagement, and there's not much anyone can do then to convince them otherwise. My contention is that this is a failure of intellectual duty, an evasion of responsibility which harms the potential of television as much as anything done inside TV production. The other side of my previous claim, then, is this: if it's true that to think intelligently about television, you have to turn it off sometimes, it's also true that sometimes you have to turn it back on – and sometimes you have to be on it.

Myth #8: Television is beyond saving.

We won't get better intellectual discourse about – or on – television until we begin to understand the situation we have created in the current marketplace of ideas. The first thing we can do about the lack of intelligent discourse about television, therefore, is to try and understand why. That is what I have been trying to do here.

But understanding is only the beginning, and further hand-wringing about the state of the medium is unhelpful. This is an appropriate time for us to take stock and try to imagine a world of television that is more what we want, more dramatically accomplished and more socially responsible. But then we have to start acting on that new clarity of perception and demanding (or, if it is our business, producing) a responsible product. Individual choices do matter in this world, even if, as I have argued, that world is larger than the sum of its individuals. Change will come, however slowly, only if we individuals all think hard and work to make the medium better.

There are no instant solutions here, and, as I said at the beginning, no easily digestible roster of practical advice for me, or anyone, to give you – the sort of bullet-by-bullet wisdom that media consultants might hand out on slickly reproduced pages to some momentarily self-critical TV executives looking to salve their consciences. I will, however, offer the following general imperatives for viewers and makers alike who want to see a better television world: Go more slowly. Judge less quickly. Reserve your blame. Challenge what seems to make sense. Question your instincts. Never underestimate yourself or your audience. Embrace complexity. Consider the structure, not simply what the structure supports. Think more.

And thank god every day for print. Because I couldn't have said any of this on television. It took more than eight minutes.

Notes

1 From David Shenk, *The End of Patience: Cautionary Notes on the Information Revolution* (Bloomington: Indiana University Press, 1999), p. 142. Shenk, an author and critic, is one of the guiding intelligences behind the loose technorealist movement, an attempt to find middle ground in a cultural field increasingly split by the false dichotomy between technophiles and technophobes. His book contains the whole of the Technorealist Manifesto, together with discussion and other, related articles.

2 For more on this argument, see Mark Kingwell, *Dreams of Millennium* (Toronto: Viking, 1996), ch. 5.

3 For a full (and acerbic) discussion of this debate, see William Henry III, *In Defense of Elitism* (New York: Basic Books, 1994).

4 Neil Postman, *Amusing Ourselves to Death: Public Discourse in the*

Age of Show Business (New York: Viking, 1985). Postman's polemic is the classic statement of the position that entertainment values now infect (and distort) the practice of public debate, especially about politics, religion, and culture.

5 These columns are reprinted, together with some other writing on culture and media, in Mark Kingwell, *Marginalia: A Cultural Reader* (Toronto: Penguin, 1999).

6 Pierre Bourdieu, *Sur la télévision* (Paris: Liber, 1996); as *On Television*, Priscilla Parkhurst Ferguson, trans. (New York: The New Press, 1999). This is the finest example I know of a serious intellectual engagement with the problems of talk television, even though I do not share all of its conclusions. The present essay is really just a halting response to some of the points Bourdieu raises.

7 For an extreme example of this kind of blame-laying, see Michael Medved, *Hollywood vs. America: Popular Culture and the War on Traditional Values* (New York: HarperCollins, 1992).

8 See, for example, the essay 'The Intellectual Possibilities of Television,' in Kingwell, *Marginalia*.

What Does It All Mean?

'Human reason has this peculiar fate that in one species of its knowledge it is burdened by questions which, as prescribed by the very nature of reason itself, it is not able to ignore, but which, as transcending all its powers, it is also not able to answer.'
– Immanuel Kant, Preface to *Critique of Pure Reason*

I take as my title a question that outlines the modest theme I will pursue: the nature of meaning itself. Like many philosophers, I am fond of titles that are questions – or, at least, of titles that end with question marks, which is not always the same thing. A colleague of mine was once advised that everything in his book called *The End of Metaphysics* could be rendered true, or anyway less false, if he added a question mark to the end of it. The end of metaphysics? Could be, could be. In fact, why not? But we have to be careful with those face-saving question marks, because they can look like a failure of nerve – the functional equivalent of a scholarly book's subtitle, which, broken over the crisis of faith symbolized by the two-story full stop of a colon, tempers the enthusiasm of a bold, snappy title with some dull, informative, back-pedalling phrase. You know the kind of thing I mean. Title: *A Civil Tongue*. Subtitle: *Justice, Dialogue, and the Politics of Pluralism*. (That one is mine.)

The question at hand, you'll notice, has not been weakened

with a soapy subtitle. It is, to all appearances, a genuine request for information, a question it is possible to hear actual people actually asking. True, those people are very likely to be, variously, children, the mad, the anguished, the ironic, and the damned. Moreover, the question is an uneasy question, shot through with anxiety. But one of the duties of a philosopher is to ask questions that, for good reasons and bad, are pushed to the margins of everyday life by the pressures of time and routine sanity. I say that as if I had a firm grasp on what it means to be a philosopher, and as if I were confident that I have a good answer to the question I'm asking. But like so many members of my odd profession, I am only ever half-convinced – if that – that I know what I'm up to.

The professional philosopher is a walking paradox, because he is doing most acutely whatever it is he does precisely when he is most plagued with doubt, covered in confusion, mired in ramifying banks of questions. The philosophical task is not so much self-defeating as baffling, a sort of Moebius strip of the mind. In fact, philosophy is an *impossible profession* because the idea of a profession of philosophy is a contradiction in terms. As the philosopher Jonathan Lear notes, '[W]e want to pass on fundamental truths, and in our attempts to do so truth becomes rigid and dies.' Philosophy, as a project of critical openness, is fundamentally opposed to the defensive, closed structure of a profession.

In the popular imagination, philosophers are the masters of meaning. They know what they're doing, and can tell others how to do it too. But in my experience, that's really not true, though there are often good reasons for pretending it is. Professional philosophers are not, as a group, wiser or deeper than other people. The tools we possess are, like all tools, limited in their application by goodwill and insight. Logic, for example, is effective and worthwhile only if wielded with compassion and a sense of proportion. And much of what makes philosophy interesting is not tool-like at all, which is one reason the profession, unlike those of, say, medicine or actuarial science, is impossible in the deeper sense.

So there's reason to be anxious about the question we've chosen to ask if the people we habitually consider its guardians are really not up to it. Meaning cannot be professed. We may go out on a limb now and then and say what this or that means, though even that probably constitutes a certain kind of hubris and folly. And yet, even impossible pursuits have their pleasures. So let us pursue the question of what it all means by considering, as a first step, what it means to ask a question, any question at all.

Questions have many rhetorical uses, and requesting information is only one of them. Even what look like straightforward questions are, in many contexts, bearers of hidden agendas, as lawyers' and politicians' questions often are. The same is true of questions that might be called philosophical, especially when they are asked in a certain kind of way. There are also questions that fall into the category of what might be called 'drive-by objections' – questions that are meant not to elicit information or establish agreement but to demand an answer so that the answer may be found wanting. If, realizing this, one resists the demand for an answer, one is labelled evasive. If one provides a paradoxical answer ('The good life is the life spent seeking the good life,' 'Virtue is its own reward,' 'The essence of being is the being of essence,' etc.), one is labelled obfuscatory as well as evasive. In all cases, the questioner and his audience go away feeling better because none of their deep-seated convictions have been challenged. In fact, they have been reinforced. Philosophy: every bit as useless as we always suspected!

There is a profound difference between the questioner who cares about an answer and the one who cares only to dismiss the answer. The drive-by objector lacks the quality the ancient Greek philosophers associated with the beginning of wisdom. I mean *wonder* – bare astonishment before the world. The close-minded are not moved by the fact of the world; they do not find it amazing. They have lost their capacity for bafflement, and hence lost their ability to imagine the world as other than it is. They are reluctant to slow down in their relentless ingestion of the passing scene for fear, ironically, that something will pass them by. Meanwhile, of course, everything is passing them by. That is what everything does – if you let it.

Perhaps I'm being a little unfair. Perhaps such people do not know what to make of the vestigial wonder they do feel, and the feelings of unease that come with it. There is no wisdom without that unease, and no chance to do anything but leave the world of meaning exactly as we find it. The world without wonder is not a world entirely without meaning. On the contrary, everything means exactly what we already thought it did. But this is meaning that never goes beyond the glib certainty of a newspaper column, the depressing sameness of a situation comedy. By contrast, it takes a certain kind of courage – or just a certain kind of perversity – not to 'understand' everything, but instead to welcome unease and put it at the centre of one's life.

One feature of this unease is the realization that, as Kant reminds us, we are equipped to ask questions we may not be equipped to answer. That is to say, we can give answers of a kind, but they may not do the sorts of things we have come to expect of answers. They may lead to more questions, or throw us back upon ourselves, or reveal that we are bound up by linguistic and conceptual confusions – or all of the foregoing. And that is not a condition to which most people readily submit.

At this point, you may well be wondering why I'm taking up your time in this manner and tying the issue in knots. But before you pass a death sentence on philosophy (or this philosopher), let's return to the initial question: 'What does it all mean?' Well, first of all, what does it mean to ask such a question? I said earlier that it was a real question, in the sense that we might actually find people asking it. But I was being a little disingenuous. In fact, it is a decidedly odd question – one we rarely hear articulated in anything like an ordinary context. One might ask it in a dramatically exasperated manner – say, after viewing yet another round of senseless action-movie trailers or breathless fashion pointers. More seriously, one might ask it in a dejected way, after viewing yet another round of anonymous human suffering on the nightly news. But curiously enough, when asked with true seriousness, the question is most often asked silently, as are others like it ('Am I happy?' 'Is that all there is?'). We speak them to ourselves, not to someone else.

We have to be on our guard for these silent questions, asked outside the usual contexts of meaning. We are alone with them, wrestling with them in our nakedness, the way the ancient Greeks practised the sport. No wonder we feel so uneasy when they arise. No wonder we seek an array of distractions to keep them at bay most of the time. No wonder that for some people they are simply too big to admit of meaningful answers. That latter group includes some philosophers. Ordinary-language philosophers, who ruled the roost of meaning during most of the twentieth century, would tell us that the oddness of the questions reveals the basic problem with them. Meaning, these philosophers say, is an engagement of mind with world via the necessarily shared medium of language. A question that has no ordinary context of usage is not a real question, for, as the eccentric Cambridge philosopher Ludwig Wittgenstein put it, *meaning is use*. If you want to know what something means, look at the way it actually arises in language.

A key reason meaning is use is that language is necessarily shared. Words mean nothing – they are literally nonsense – if they are not stable enough to be understood by at least one other person. That is the sense in which language is normative: we can't just decide that a sound will mean anything at all. In his book *Philosophical Investigations* (1953), Wittgenstein asks: 'Can I say "bububu" and mean "If it doesn't rain, I shall go for a walk"?' Well, no, because 'bububu' doesn't mean anything. You might conceivably intend for it to mean 'If it doesn't rain, I shall go for a walk,' but it doesn't mean that unless and until at least one other person, and normally a whole lot of people – all the competent users of the natural language you normally speak, in this case English – can parse that intention.

The point cannot be emphasized too much: meaning resides in the shared practices of what Wittgenstein called a language-game. And a game is not a game if everyone is playing by different rules. The rules needn't be explicit, or specify every possible move within the game. But they must enable us to make sense of any move at all. Otherwise, there is no such thing as meaning. Meaning has to be shared to be real.

The bluff good sense of this view is appealing. Ordinary-language philosophy is, in its way, a response to the impossible nature of philosophical inquiry. It purchases conceptual success at the cost of drastically lowered expectations. We can say what things mean, one at a time and with close attention to the details of context; but we cannot say what it all means, because the question does not really arise meaningfully. It arises only in odd contexts – call them philosophical in a pejorative sense – where it lurks and glowers like a mythical beast, impossible to slay.

I call this view appealing, and of course it is. It allows us to get on with the business of shaping and exchanging meaning in the shared medium of language and does so, moreover, by wanting to cure us of the lingering ills we suffer in the form of unanswerable (metaphysical) questions. But it is also mistaken in thinking that these questions can so easily be laid to rest, or that we would give them up even if we could. Wittgenstein, to his credit, did not believe any such thing. There is a point to asking what it all means – even if we have not yet seen the point.

But don't worry; this essay will keep its promise. Promises, after all, are themselves acts of meaning, forged in the medium of a shared language. They are what J.L. Austin, one of the early masters of ordinary-language philosophy, called *performative utterances* – that is, not just words but actions. To say 'I promise' is to do something as well as to say something, and promises don't mean anything unless they're kept most of the time.

Still, let's not be too hasty in our pursuit of the answer to the big question. At the opposite extreme from ordinary-language *minimalism* about meaning is a form of *maximalism* that is, in its own way, just as appealing. I mean the desire, with us since at least Biblical times, to find not an ordinary language of meaning but a perfect or universal one. That is the dream of the post-Babel world, the world of multiple and messy meanings, and it comes down to us in various forms, from the medieval Scholastic attempt to translate all teachings into the terms of the one true faith, to the twentieth-century project of deriving all meaning from first principles of logic and mathematics.

The cyber-feminist Donna Haraway has given contemporary expression to the desire for a perfect language (and signalled its danger): 'Communications sciences and modern biologies are constructed by a common move, the translation of the world into a problem of coding, a search for a common language in which all resistance to instrumental control disappears and all heterogeneity can be submitted to disassembly, reassembly, investment, and exchange.'

Haraway is right to see the far-reaching ambitions of universal coding in those terms. If everything were translatable into, say, digital code – including the idiosyncratic clusters of genetic information we call persons – then everything would be made disposable, not in the sense of being destined to be thrown away, but in the sense of being available for any kind of redeployment. Binary code is not fussy. From the point of view of the code, there is no difference between a text document, a film, a sequence of events, or an entity. The more our lives and experiences are fused into the play of this code, becoming chunks or nodes of code in an ever-fluid sea of information transfer, the more likely it is that the transition from a partially coded to a completely coded world will begin to make sense to us.

Notice that Haraway uses the word 'translation' to describe this transition. Before there is universal translatability, there must be a meta-level translation of all systems of meaning into a single, all-encompassing one. It is this meta-level translation we have to keep an eye on. Universal languages are reductive, obviously. But what is reductive about reductionism is not that it reduces the number of entities or substances in the world. What is reductive about reductionism is that it reduces the number of meaningful ways we have to talk about the world. And that makes the world a poorer place.

Meaning lodges in the community-based structure of our engagements with the world. It resides neither entirely in language nor entirely in the world, but in the complex codependent relationship that exists between them and in the complex web of speech-acts to which we commit ourselves every day. Seekers after a perfect or universal language see this codependent relationship as dysfunctional (which, of course, it often is), but then meet that condition with a strategy of maximalist translation – all dialects rendered into one supertongue. They think this move will solve everything, but it solves everything the way any totalitarian regime does – by ruthlessly eliminating diversity and possibility.

Binary code is not the only maximalist solution we are being peddled these days. Sociobiology, the bastard child of evolutionary theory, sometimes appears in the guise of a final explanation, as does physics in its less nuanced forms – a blithe explanation of everything based on the unified field theory. Meme theory, which explains human culture entirely in terms of inherited replicator units, and other forms of reductive cultural determinism are currently fashionable examples of the same way of thinking. We are here, these theories say, as part of a grand design to transmit genetic information, or increase complexity, or build more intricate machines. Religious fundamentalism is another kind of maximalist final explanation: we are here to be judged by God. All these explanations of final purpose are suffused by the closed-mindedness that comes when one believes (a) that there is a master key to meaning, and (b) that one has it. Most dangerous of all, of course, is the person who also believes (c) that nobody else can have it.

Most of the time these forms of maximalism function on a timescale, or a level of abstraction, that renders them pointless. They have no pull with us, down here on the ground. Even so, they often exert a malign influence and encourage a certain kind of passivity, a listlessness that is easily mistaken for 'philosophical' wisdom. The biggest problem with all of them is that, in explaining what it all means, they somehow still fail to explain why meaning moves us in the first place. Thus, their weirdly self-contradictory quality: in its effort to explain everything – to dispel all mysteries in one fell swoop of meaning – maximalism misses the deepest mystery, which is that things mean anything at all.

Consciousness, as materialist biologists know, is functionally redundant. That's the bad news, for you conscious beings out there. There is simply no reason that our genetic transfers, even our cultural constructions, should be accompanied by subjective experiences like love, triumph, dejection, or happiness. But they are – and that's the compelling mystery at the heart of meaning. There is no need for meaning, and yet here it is. Indeed, we might begin to suspect that the answer to our big question is not genetic persistence, or cultural complexity, or biological diversity, but what all those forces seem to serve: meaning itself.

The world of meaning is, in that sense, not unlike a work of art. We can speak of how it came to be, what it's made of, even how it functions. We can talk about its place in our lives and about the things we try to express when we say it matters to us. What we cannot do is reduce it to propositional content. And that suggests a different kind of answer altogether to the question we've been pursuing. At the risk of descending into what a drive-by objector would view as evasive paradox, it's this: The meaning of meaning is meaning itself.

What am I getting at by saying something so strange? Let me begin to explain in terms of a familiar example. The combination of empty success and hidden failure in maximalism is not unlike the peculiar conjunction of stimulation and boredom that is endemic to the modern age, when most people have finally had enough free time to escape from the drudgery of work – only to face the drudgery of leisure. The condition is too common to need a detailed description here. Who among us has not felt the creeping ennui of overstimulation, the dull paralysis of having too much time and too many options? Entertainment, like so many things, contains its own negation: an excess of it, paradoxically, is boring.

But we should not try to dispel the boredom with further rounds of frantic distraction, for our boredom has something to tell us. In precisely such a condition we may be most inclined to ask, desperately but usefully, 'What does it all mean?' This feeling of too-muchness is not, in fact, a recent phenomenon, or one restricted to the modern era of democratized leisure. It is more basic than that, linked intimately to our relations of meaning with the world. It is a function of mind itself, of our vast plastic capacity to find things significant. We have evolved as creatures with brains both decentralized and task-generic. That is, while certain actions can clearly be associated with certain parts of the brain, the human brain itself has a generalist architecture. It is not built to do one thing, or even a few, but to do a vast number of different, often complex things, which is why so many things strike us as interesting – from puns to madrigals, from cave paintings to the internal combustion engine, from folk songs to the Doppler effect, from baseball to chess.

A generalist brain is both a blessing and a curse. For creatures like us, there is always too much meaning to make sense of – not simply because we have evolved tools of reminder, like books and techniques and institutions, but because each of us is every day creating more meaning than we can ourselves comprehend. Wishes and fantasies, dreams and visions – here and elsewhere, surplus meanings escape the bounds of the daily routine of trying to make sense.

Which means that to ask the question 'What does it all

mean?' is to set oneself up for constant disappointment. For there is no adequate general answer, no maximalist translation, equal to its scope. We may fool ourselves with the translations, or use them to overpower others, but at heart they are all corrosive of meaning. That is not to grant the field to the minimalists, however, because the question is still a real question, even if a rather odd one. And its real import is this: It sounds a cry of frustration, not with too little meaning but with too much. That is what makes us uneasy, because so little of the meaning in the world seems to mean anything in particular. It does not matter, and that lack of mattering troubles us. And so, paradoxically, a surfeit of meaning (in the world, in ourselves) seems to be matched by a dearth of meaning, or of the right kind of meaning (in the world, in ourselves).

Our anxiety about meaning is really an anxiety about ourselves, therefore, or, more precisely, about ourselves as we engage with the world. When we ask, 'What does it all mean?' we are raising another question: 'How should I shape my life?' Socrates knew this, and laboured under no professional delusions that, in the end, the projects of metaphysics or epistemology, which concern the nature of reality and knowledge, respectively, could be separated from those of ethics. All inquiry, whatever its subject, has as its final object the matter of how to go about living. Philosophers have lost sight of this idea often enough over the centuries that it sounds, unsurprisingly, a trifle bizarre today, when most people, perhaps, would be incredulous if you were to suggest that all questions ultimately point to the one question: How ought I to live?

Before expanding on this crucial point, let me enter certain caveats. First, we're still addressing a question, not an answer. That is very important. Plato's mistake was to think that Socrates' questions as to how we should live could be worked up into a system, a web of ultimate meaning, a superanswer. Ingenious and beautiful though his answer was, Plato could not finally escape the looming reductionism of his project. In the final analysis, Platonism is not in the Socratic spirit.

Second, I'm by no means entirely confident that I myself am

pursuing the question well (though I hope I am). This point is worth emphasizing, because the drive-by objectors among you will perhaps be inclined to dig for dirt. But anything you might find to discredit me, however amusing, is beside the point. If Plato's mistake was trying to systematize a deep insight, ours too often is failing to distinguish an insight from the person who reports it.

Third, though my emphasis is on the individual, because I want to throw the question back onto each one of us, I do not mean to defend meaning as individual or idiosyncratic. It is not the case that 'each of us has his own meaning.' The ordinary-language philosophers are right that meaning, to be meaningful, has to be shared by a group of language users.

The whole point, and the problem, of meaning is that it reveals the complex isomorphic relationship between us (as readers, or perhaps slaves, of meaning) and the rest of the sociocultural world (as the site, or reflection, of meaning). We are always both creating and being created by the world around us – which includes, crucially, other creatures in the same fix. It is the condition of being so stranded, of being both trapped inside our heads and able (sometimes) to fashion meanings that other meaning creators can parse, that makes the whole question of meaning so unsettling. If we arrive at different answers to the question of what this or that means – and we will – that does not mean meaning is whatever each one of us thinks it is. It means merely (merely!) that we have ahead of us an even harder task than we thought.

There remains, then, one issue for us to consider: What practical import, if any, does the question 'What does it all mean?' have for our lives? It is one thing to say that asking how we ought to live is central to human life, and quite another to explain how this cashes out in day-to-day terms. I want to track the application of insight that arises from confrontation with our unanswerable question. If the cry of frustration elicited by the question remained at the level of frustration, if it did not change anything at all, we would be in very desperate straits indeed. The question is not a request for information.

All right. And it cannot actually be answered in full without doing violence to itself. Fine. But if it had no purchase at all on the world of our actions and experiences, it would not be worth our attention. I want here to speak of orientations rather than policies. Immersed in meaning, awash in content, how best can we cope?

There are at least five principal responses. First, we have to recognize the enduring temptation of what were above called maximalist solutions, the attempts to find a universal code, to command and control our engagements of meaning with the world. The temptation does not go away, and its dangers are manifold. In its worst and most obvious form it issues in *knowingness*, a sense that we know exactly what's going on. Knowingness is murderous of wonder and of insight, and ultimately it does a violent disservice to that which it sought to serve, the vast array of meaning itself. It sucks the meaning out of meaning.

That might lead to a second kind of temptation, which is really minimalism taken to an extreme (if logical) conclusion. I mean the tendency to *avoid* engagements of meaning with the world – often by diminishing one's world by stages to a tiny ordered corner where meaning is rigid, a corner safe from the myriad complications and ramifications that lie just outside the sacred space.

In the right circumstances, of course, that orientation can be productive, as, for example, when the protected space is a specialist discourse – say, quantum physics or baseball. But anyone who begins to think that quantum theory or baseball exhausts the meaning in the world is on the fast track to madness. Eventually, avoidance collapses into a form of command and control; its responses and anxieties are the same. Minimalism becomes a form of mad maximalism. Its triumph is not to expand a particular language to encompass the world, but to shrink the world to fit a particular language.

The third response tries to *accept and ingest* the endless variety of meaning-engagements. It's popular in our day, partly because we have so many shiny new toys that make it possible, and partly because we are training successive generations in a greater facility for it. But as a response to the vastness of meaning, this option, too, is self-defeating. There is no velocity that can take us beyond the limits of mortal life, and the speed merchants of the current mediascape are no better off in knowing the meaning of meaning than any of us. Arguably, they are much worse off, for their hasty engagements soon begin to lack texture and depth. Expanding intake does not satisfy the need for meaning because there is always more volume to accept and ingest, and a great deal of that volume is trash. The mind becomes an Augean stable, with too much manure to move about. Great art and great philosophy are rare, and always have been. Beware the simple growth of volume in meaning; it makes what is precious harder to find.

A fourth response to the array of meanings is *defeatist or nihilist* (or maybe simply bored). It follows hard on the heels of the speed merchants' restlessness. This response says of every meaning, large or small, rich or paltry, 'Whatever.' The indifference is a natural, or at least widespread, response to the great array of meanings on offer in our cultural experience. It's a perfect illustration of the isomorphism that exists between self and world. If the world is a five-hundred-channel universe of offerings to which one is equally indifferent – a crowded catalogue of been-there, done-that web sites – what more appropriate response than to become a person who has no interest in anything at all? The limit-case of the Socratic interlocutor's art is to engage people who have no interest at all in having meaning matter to them. One can only hope that they will grow out of this attitude and begin to realize that meaning ought to matter, at least sometimes. Until then, it will be difficult to persuade them, for from their point of view, that effort of persuasion is just another boring message directed at them from some point on the mediascape, another doomed bid for their already-gone attention.

Which brings me to a fifth response, and the only truly good one. It's what we might call *critical immersion* in the world of our meaning-engagements. This option may seem obvious after everything that's been said so far, but obvious things are often true, and the obvious, after all, is a philosopher's stock-in-trade. More to the point, its being obvious doesn't make it any less difficult. In fact, if we understand the question of meaning as really being about shaping a life so that it's a worthwhile life, one can hardly imagine a task more severe. It must encompass the ridiculous and the sublime, the banal and the stunning, because every moment of waking life is a form of engagement with the world of meaning – another line or two in the story we tell about ourselves.

At that story's centre is the enduring ineffability of human consciousness, the peculiar ability in humans (and maybe in other entities; we ought to be open-minded on the issue) for existence *to be like something*: to have a mood and particularity and texture that's experienced directly only by the subject and that's irreducible to anything else. What it's like for me to be me, or for you to be you, is a condition that repels reduction or translation. It cannot be rendered into anything other than itself. This quality of individual consciousness makes everything else possible, for, without it, there is nothing we could call meaningful, and therefore no things or thoughts we could call questions, and therefore no subclass of questions we could call philosophical.

Questions such as these: Have I taken pleasure in beauty? Have I fashioned humour or wit? Have I forged genuine friendships? Have I established a beachhead of civility and justice in my political interactions? Have I taken up roles and professions with integrity and joy? Have I left the world a better, more interesting place than I found it? Have I done one simple thing – change a tire, write a letter, cook a dinner, perform a heart bypass – as well as it could be done?

In such moments we are asked to make many choices and judgments. We can make them well or badly. But whatever we do, our actions will add up to a mortal span, to the story that is my life or yours. Our most basic choice, the one that grounds all the others, is this: Do we attend closely to the business of our choices, or do we flee from them, in arrogance, or fear, or boredom – or some combination of all three? That's the only ultimate purpose, or meaning, that we can make sense of. But it's enough.

An old saw suggests that any decent thesis can be stated while standing on one leg. That works only if you and I are already talking about the same thing (not in agreement, necessarily), as I hope by now we are. So let me return, one last time, to the question at the head of this essay, and do so on one metaphorical leg.

What does it all mean? That life is full of meaning, too much meaning to make sense of in any simple fashion. That wonder in the face of meaning's richness is appropriate and necessary – is, in fact, indispensable. That only open-mindedness, and the humility that comes with it, will allow us, finally, to sort good meanings from bad, the worthwhile from the mere distraction. That in the fullness of our allotted time and after our fashion, we may perhaps put together enough meanings-that-matter to judge of ourselves that we have told a good story, lived a life that was worth living.

That it all begins with a question mark ...

Index

Odysseus, 123
Oedipus, 15
opera, 12
ordinary-language philosophy,
311–13; common sense, 50; language, 318; scepticism, 52,
59n22, 60n24
Orr, Bobby, 253–4
Oxford English Dictionaries, 200

Paine, Thomas: *Plain Truth and
Common Sense*, 35, 57n1
Palladian norms, 218
paper, 277
Pappas, George, 42
Parmenides, 91
parole, 201, 210
Paxton, Bill, 9
Perera, N.M., 117–18
Peripatetic School, 231
personal and political, 121
Phaidon Books, 214
phenomenology: *episteme* and
doxa, 84; non-relative knowledge, 74–5; radical self-reflection, 83–6; as vocation, 85–9; of
wonder, 64, 75, 79, 92–3
Philby, Kim, 146n1
philistines, 277
philosopher, profession of, 3,
229–30; amateurs, 230; anti-
intellectualism, 29n2; architects as, 217; business, 30n8;
clothing, 265; contradictions,
26–7, 308; duties of, 308, 320–1;
elitism, 291–2; how to go on
living, 317, 322; need *phronesis*,

112n1; Sartre, 230; television,
286; titles that ask questions,
307–8; walking, 231
philosopher-kings, 225
philosophic conversation:
modernity, 156; questions,
309–10, 317–18; writing, 274
philosophic reflection: attention
to everyday life, 6, 321–2; furniture as site of, 231–4; oddball
practitioners of, 6–7; as philosophic method, 82–6
philosophy: acknowledging limits, 210, 269; common sense,
56–7; Greek origins, 71–5;
materialist, 196; modernity,
156; origins in wonder, 63–70,
93, 309–10; *phronesis*, 112n1;
pluralism, 156–7; reason, 173;
theory of knowledge, 54;
unembodied thoughts of, 232;
usefulness, 12, 17–18
photocopying, 271
phronesis, 6, 28; community-specific, 110; definition of, 97–9;
ethical reflection, 109–10;
ethico-political application,
95–112; moral knowledge, 101;
practical forms of, 111–12
Piaget, Jean, 175
Piazza San Marco, 266
plain-dwellers, 56
planned obsolescence, 268
Plato, 229, 281, 317; certainty, 54,
60–1n30; defence of true philosopher, 10; Ideal Forms, 208;
theory of Forms, 230; wonder,